EXPLORING THE OLD TESTAMENT

Volume 3

The Psalms and Wisdom Literature

After working in biochemical research for a few years, Ernest Lucas studied theology at Oxford University and was ordained as a Baptist minister. He has been the minister of churches in Durham and Liverpool. While at Liverpool, he was awarded a Ph.D. by the university there for his research on the book of Daniel. For several years he worked as Education Director and the Associate Director at the London Institute for Contemporary Christianity. In 1994 he moved to Bristol Baptist College, an Affiliated College of Bristol University, where he is Vice-Principal and Tutor in Biblical Studies. *Can We Believe Genesis Today?* (IVP, 2001) and a commentary on Daniel (Apollos, 2002) are two of his recent publications. He is married and has two grown-up sons.

Exploring the Old Testament

The Pentateuch by Gordon Wenham

The Psalms and Wisdom Literature by Ernest Lucas

The Prophets by Gordon McConville

Exploring the New Testament

The Gospels and Acts by David Wenham and Steve Walton

The Letters and Revelation by Howard Marshall, Stephen Travis and Ian Paul

OLD
TESTAMENT

Exploring the Old Testament

A Guide to the Psalms & Wisdom Literature

ERNEST C. LUCAS

Volume
Three

IVP

InterVarsity Press
Downers Grove, Illinois

InterVarsity Press
P.O. Box 1400, Downers Grove, IL 60515-1426
World Wide Web: www.ivpress.com
E-mail: mail@ivpress.com

InterVarsity Press® is the book-publishing division of InterVarsity Christian Fellowship/USA®, a student movement active on campus at hundreds of universities, colleges and schools of nursing in the United States of America, and a member movement of the International Fellowship of Evangelical Students. For information about local and regional activities, write Public Relations Dept., InterVarsity Christian Fellowship/USA, 6400 Schroeder Rd., P.O. Box 7895, Madison, WI 53707-7895, or visit the IVCF website at <www.ivcf.org>.

Cover photograph: National Gallery Budapest/SuperStock

ISBN 0-8308-2553-3

Printed in Great Britain ∞

Library of Congress Cataloging-in-Publication Data has been requested.

P	25	24	23	22	21	20	19	18	17	16	15	14	13	12	11	10	9	8	7	6	5	4	3	2	1
Y	25	24	23	22	21	20	19	18	17	16	15	14	13	12	11	10	09	08	07	06	05	04	03		

Contents

THE PSALMS AND WISDOM LITERATURE

KEY TO PANELS

This key to the panels helps locate the special and suggested exercises that occur throughout the volume. It should be noted that the panels are not exhaustive treatments of topics, and are meant to be read and used in their contexts. Panels sometimes cross-refer to other parts of the book.

OTHER PANELS

PREFACE

Exploring the Old Testament is designed to help the beginning student understand the writings of the Old Testament. It serves the purpose of an introduction, but its unique format is devised to make the volumes accessible to the modern reader. *EOT* engages with the reader, by interspersing interactive panels with the main text. These panels ask for responses, suggest lines of thought, give further information, or indicate ways in which particular topics might be followed up in more depth. This design aims to make the volumes useful either for independent study or as a class text.

EOT aims to show the relevance of Old Testament study both to theology and to modern life. Its four authors, each writing in areas in which they have previously published extensively, believe that the Old Testament has foundational significance for theology and Christian belief and practice.

For that reason *EOT* expressly aims to incorporate modern approaches to interpreting the text. While the traditional historical questions are given their due place, newer approaches such as canonical and rhetorical criticism are represented. It is hoped that this will enable the student to see the potential applications of the books of the Old Testament to modern life.

EOT is a companion series to *Exploring the New Testament*.

Gordon McConville
Series editor

INTRODUCTION

This book aims to help students study the Psalms and Wisdom Literature of the Old Testament. Like other volumes in the *Exploring the Old Testament* and *Exploring the New Testament* series, it is intended to give students a primary resource to enable them to study the texts independently. It provides an introduction to each book, which includes a survey of the main trends in recent study of the book. There is a basic textual study. For Job, Ecclesiastes (or Qoheleth) and the Song of Songs, this amounts to a basic commentary on the book. In the case of Proverbs 10—31, the nature of the material makes such a commentary problematic, since it would require discussion of many individual, unrelated proverbs. Instead of the basic commentary the discussion of the compilation of the book provides a general overview of each section, with Proverbs 1—9 discussed in more detail. In the case of the book of Psalms, a representative selection of psalms is discussed in some detail. The discussion of each book includes a survey of the main theological issues it raises and of various theological approaches to interpreting it. Quotations from the Bible in English are

taken from the New Revised Standard Version, unless otherwise indicated.

The book is interactive. Interspersed through it are a number of panels. Some (Think about) encourage the student to think further about what has been learnt. Others (Digging deeper:) encourage further study of some issue dealt with in the main text. There are also some panels that simply provide background material to supplement the main text.

The book is intended to introduce students to a range of critical and interpretative literature on the Psalms and Wisdom Literature. Each chapter has an annotated list of further reading, covering commentaries and other works. Most of these are referred to in the chapter in question. Items marked with * are considered suitable as first ports of call. Others are more complex, or related to specific issues.

It might be asked whether the Psalms and Wisdom Literature have been put together for anything more than pragmatic reasons. One justification for putting them in one volume is the preponderance of Hebrew poetry in these books. Psalms and the Song of Songs consist purely of poetry. Job has a prose prologue and epilogue, but most of the book is in poetry. The Hebrew proverb is poetic in its form. Ecclesiastes contains some proverbs. Some scholars conclude that it also contains a few poems, but there is debate about just how much of the book is poetic in form. The Wisdom Literature 'proper' of the Old Testament is usually limited to Job, Proverbs and Ecclesiastes. However, as we shall see, it can be argued that there are grounds for regarding the Song of Songs as at least a close relative to the Wisdom Literature. Also, the book of Psalms contains some 'wisdom psalms', though scholars debate just how many of them there are and some question the existence of this category.

Above all, this book is written in the belief that the Psalms and Wisdom Literature have important things to say to people today. Probably few would question this with regard to the Psalms, which have always had an important place in Jewish and Christian spirituality, both in corporate worship and personal devotional life. Although the book of Job has excited philosophers, artists and, more recently psychologists, from time to time, it is generally only the prose story that is known by most people – and sometimes misunderstood. The other books are less well known, and their content is sometimes misunderstood. Proverbs get mistaken for 'laws' and the Song of Songs has been routinely allegorized, so that its actual message is ignored. One or two passages of Ecclesiastes are fairly well known, but the book as a whole is neglected. It is hoped that this book will contribute to a better understanding of these biblical books and appropriation of their message.

ABBREVIATIONS

AB — Anchor Bible

BZAW — Beihefte zur Zeitschrift für die alttestamentliche Wissenschaft

CBQ — *Catholic Biblical Quarterly*

DSB — Daily Study Bible

EC — Epworth Commentaries

FOTL — Forms of Old Testament Literature

HSM — Harvard Semitic Monographs

ICC — International Critical Commentary

JBL — *Journal of Biblical Literature*

JQR — *Jewish Quarterly Review*

JSOT — *Journal for the Study of the Old Testament*

JTS — *Journal of Theological Studies*

LXX — Septuagint

MT — Massoretic Text

NCB — New Century Bible

NEB — New English Bible

NICOT — New International Commentary on the Old Testament

NIDOTTE — *New International Dictionary of Old Testament Theology and Exegesis*

NIVAC — New International Version Application Commentary

NRSV — New Revised Standard Version

OTL — Old Testament Library

PEQ — *Palestine Exploration Quarterly*

SBLDS — Society of Biblical Literature Dissertation Series

SR — *Studies in Religion*

TOTC — Tyndale Old Testament Commentary

VT — *Vetus Testamentum*

VTSup — Vetus Testamentum Supplements

WBC — Word Biblical Commentary

WMANT — Wissenschaftliche Monographien zum Alten und Neuen Testament

The Ancient Near East

Chapter 1

PSALMS

The book of Psalms has always had an important place in the spiritual life of both Jews and Christians. The fourth-century Christian leader, Athanasius, summed up one important reason for this when he said that while most of Scripture speaks *to* us, the Psalms speak *for* us. Down the centuries the people of God have found in the Psalms the language of praise and complaint, trust and doubt, petition and thanks, which has nourished their relationship with God. Perhaps because individuals found that the psalms often spoke for them, there was a general assumption that the book of Psalms is a collection of religious poems written by individuals, especially King David, essentially for their personal use.

DIFFERENT TYPES OF PSALMS

The study of the book of Psalms entered an important new phase in the 1920s with the work of Hermann Gunkel and some of his students. The predominant impression that a casual reader of the book of Psalms gets is probably the great variety of material that it contains. The insight that Gunkel had was that within this variety there are some common patterns in the form and content of the individual psalms. He set out to categorize all the psalms according to their respective literary types (*Gattungen* in German). Behind this was the belief that these distinct types had their roots in the use of psalms in the worship of the temple in Jerusalem. Gunkel recognized two major categories: the *hymns* and the *laments*. Within each he found subcategories. He also recognized some additional less common types.

Gunkel's work has been subject to criticism and discussion, and subsequent scholars have disagreed over the details of his classifications. This is not surprising since poets are always free to vary or break away from set forms. He has been criticized for the fact that in practice his analysis took into account not only the literary form of a psalm but also its content. In fact some of his categories are based primarily on content. However, this is probably the price one has to pay for a useful system of classification. It can be justified to some extent if the nature of the content helps to explain why a group of psalms does not fit into one of the common types.

Although there is not universal agreement, the following classification scheme is one that would be widely accepted.

1. Hymns
   a. General Praises of God
   b. Psalms celebrating Yahweh's kingship
   c. Songs of Zion
2. Laments
   a. Individual Laments
   b. Communal Laments
3. Songs of Thanksgiving
   a. Individual Thanksgivings
   b. Communal Thanksgivings
4. Royal Psalms
5. Minor Types: Psalms of Confidence, Wisdom Psalms, etc.

Think about HYMN BOOKS

Look at some modern hymn books. On what basis are the hymns arranged – alphabetically, according to the Christian year, according to the different parts of a church service? Looking at the hymns themselves, can you see any general 'types'?

HYMNS

Characteristically, the General Praises of God have a simple, threefold structure.

- They open with a call to praise God.
- The main section gives the grounds for praise, often introduced by the word *ki* ('for').
- The psalm closes with a renewed call to praise, which often echoes the introduction.

Psalm 117, the shortest in the Psalter, illustrates this structure.

v. 1 Praise the LORD, all you nations!
      Extol him, all you peoples!

v. 2 For great is his steadfast love
         towards us,
      and the faithfulness of the LORD
         endures for ever.

Praise the LORD!

Another good example is Psalm 113, in which vv. 1–3 are the introductory call to praise, vv. 4–9b give the grounds for praise and v. 9c is the conclusion. This basic structure can be modified in various ways. In Psalm 150 the reason for praise is quite brief (v. 2) and the concluding exhortation to praise greatly expanded (vv. 3–6). Psalm 33 has the introduction (vv. 1–3) and main section (vv. 4–19) expected of a hymn of praise, but it concludes with an expression of trust in the Lord (vv. 20–22). Some of the General Praises centre on the theme of Yahweh's lordship over creation (Pss 8; 29; 104). Others celebrate his acts in history (Ps. 104).

Although there are a number of references to the temple and Zion in the psalms, there is a group of six hymns which centre on Zion as their main theme. They praise Yahweh by praising the city that he has chosen to be the centre of his worship, and his protection of it. These Songs of Zion are: Psalms 46, 48, 76, 84, 87 and 122. They do not have the characteristic structure of the General Praises.

Another subgroup of the Hymns consists of the psalms that celebrate Yahweh's kingship (Pss 47; 93; 96—99; some scholars include Ps. 95). Apart from Psalm 98 they all contain the phrase 'The LORD/God is king' or similar. Psalms 97 and 99 share the threefold structure of the General

Praises. We will discuss later the place these psalms may have had in the worship in the Jerusalem temple.

LAMENTS

The Laments are the commonest type of psalm. They form about one-third of the Psalter. They express the psalmist's response to God when in a situation of need or affliction. Their structure is flexible, being made up of a number of elements, not all of which will occur in any one psalm, and the order of which varies. Below is a list of the more common elements.

- Invocation of God. Most of them begin with this.
- Complaint. This is a description of the distress or misfortune that the psalmist is suffering. It might be regarded as the heart of the lament.
- Petition. The psalmist appeals to God to intervene and deliver. Sometimes grounds are advanced to support this appeal – the nature of God, God's honour, the depth of the psalmist's need.
- A call for vengeance on the evil-doers who are the cause of the psalmist's distress. This may be part of the petition.
- Confession of sin.

- Protestation of innocence is an alternative to the confession of sin.
- A vow to praise and thank God following deliverance.
- Expression of confidence and trust in God.
- Exclamation of praise and thanksgiving.

Psalm 54 provides an example of an Individual Lament.

v. 1 Invocation of God
> Save me, O God, by your name,
> and vindicate me by your might.

v. 2 Petition
> Hear my prayer, O God;
> give ear to the words of my mouth.

v. 3 Complaint
> For the insolent have risen against me,
> the ruthless seek my life;
> they do not set God before them.

v. 4 Expression of trust
> But surely, God is my helper;
> the Lord is the upholder of my life.

v. 5 Call for vengeance
> He will repay my enemies for their evil.
> In your faithfulness, put an end to them.

v. 6 Vow
> With a freewill-offering I will sacrifice to you;
> I will give thanks to your name,
> O Lord, for it is good.

v. 7 Exclamation of praise
> For he has delivered me from every trouble,
> and my eye has looked in triumph on my enemies.

In the Individual Laments, the psalmist's situation of distress is described in very general terms. However, three motifs recur and have caused considerable debate. Some psalms (e.g. Pss 7; 26; 27) seem to be the pleas of someone who feels falsely accused of some crime. Both H. Schmidt and W. Beyerlin have, in different ways, made this the starting point from which to argue for some formal procedure of sacred trial in the temple. There may be an element of truth in this since 1 Kings 8:31–32 refers to an accused person coming to swear an oath before God in the temple. However, the evidence is lacking for the kind of detailed procedures that Schmidt and Beyerlin have proposed.

Other psalms seem to refer to illness of some kind (e.g. Pss 6; 31; 35; 38; 88). Most of these psalms also refer to enemies. Occasionally they are called 'workers of evil' (e.g. Ps. 6:8). S. Mowinckel argued that these people were sorcerers who had cast spells on the psalmist. The psalms would then be a form of counter-spell. His view has gained little acceptance. The fact is that there is nothing in the psalms to suggest that the enemies are the cause of the illness. Indeed, sometimes Yahweh himself is thought of as its source (e.g. Ps. 38:1f.). Also, Hebrew has a specific term for 'sorcery' and this word is not used in the phrase 'workers of evil', which uses a general term for 'evil'.

In a few laments the enemies appear to be foreigners (e.g. Pss 10:15–16; 56:7; 59:5, 8). This suggests that the individual reciting this psalm may be a representative of the nation. Many scholars have assumed that this would be the king, but it could be some other senior military commander, or even the high priest. This issue will be

raised again later when discussing the Royal Psalms.

Where the 'I' of a lament is a representative figure, the lament is really a Communal Lament. Those laments that are clearly communal, because they are cast in terms of 'we/us', are less numerous than the Individual Laments. They reflect disasters such as defeat in war (Pss 44; 60; 74; 79; 83) or drought and famine (Pss 126; 144).

A considerable number of Individual Laments contain an expression of confidence that Yahweh has heard the psalmist's prayer, often at the end of the lament (e.g. Pss 6:8f.; 28:6f.; 56:9f.; 140:12f.). A widely held explanation of this is the suggestion that a priest or cult prophet delivered a salvation oracle, to which the closing words of the lament are a response. In support of this it has been pointed out that there are a number of salvation oracles in Isaiah 40—55 (characteristically containing the words,

---

Digging deeper:
LAMENTS

Analyse the structure of the following Laments: Psalms 3, 6, 51, 60.

Note that Psalm 51:18–19 presupposes the destruction of the walls of Jerusalem and seems somewhat out of place in this individual lament. These verses are probably a post-exilic addition to an already existing psalm, picking up on the theme of sacrifice in vv. 15–17.

Psalm 60 is unusual in including a prophetic oracle in vv. 6–8.

'Fear not . . .') and some of them contain language also found in the laments of the Psalter. Also, there are prophetic oracles in some psalms (e.g. Pss 32:8–9; 50:5–23; 60:6–8; 89:19–37). Against this explanation it is objected that it is strange that few salvation oracles have been preserved in the laments themselves (Pss 12:6 and 60:6–8 are the only examples). However, this might be because the psalms were a fixed liturgy to which a spontaneous response was expected.

SONGS OF THANKSGIVING

The Songs of Thanksgiving express thanks and praise to God for some specific act of deliverance that the psalmist has experienced. However, their aim is not only to praise God. They are also a form of witness to the saving work of God, declared before the whole congregation. Because they express praise by speaking *about* God, whereas the General Praises express praise *to* God, Claus Westermann regards these two forms of psalm as related to one another, and calls the Thanksgivings 'Declarative Psalms of Praise' and the General Praises 'Descriptive Psalms of Praise'. He also argues that there is no distinctive word for 'thanks' in Hebrew and that the verb *hodah*, which is often translated as 'to thank', is better taken to mean 'praise'. Although some scholars have adopted Westermann's terminology, most have not. The fact is that, unlike the General Praises, the Thanksgivings stand in a close relationship to the Laments. In the Laments the psalmist often promises to express thanks for God's deliverance publicly (e.g. Pss 7:17; 35:28), sometimes vowing to offer a sacrifice of thanks (e.g. Pss 27:6; 54:6f.).

The Songs of Thanksgiving can therefore be seen as the psalmist's response to God answering the prayer uttered in a Lament and as accompanying a sacrificial thank-offering. This gives them a setting that is quite distinct from that of the Hymns of General Praise. Moreover, Westermann probably over-presses the point about *hodah*. A word that has quite a wide range of meaning has to be understood within the specific context in which it is used. When *hodah* denotes a response to a particular act of deliverance by God, 'thanks' seems an appropriate meaning for it.

The Individual Thanksgivings have a threefold structure.

- The introduction, which invokes Yahweh's name. It may include a declaration of intent to thank Yahweh, and can be expanded by various hymnic additions.
- The main section is essentially an account of the psalmist's experience. This may include:
  1. a description of his previous state of distress.
  2. the prayer for deliverance which he uttered in that state.
  3. an account of Yahweh's act of deliverance.
  4. a reference to the fulfilment of his vow.
- The conclusion, which often includes an exhortation to praise Yahweh addressed either to the congregation or to himself.

Psalm 116 is an example of an Individual Thanksgiving.

vv. 1–2   Introduction: invocation of Yahweh's name and expression of the intention to 'call on him'

I love the LORD, because
 he has heard my voice
 and my supplications.
Because he inclined his ear
 to me,
 therefore I will call on him
 for as long as I live.

vv. 3–11   Description of the psalmist's
 state of distress, including the
 prayer he uttered (v. 4) and a
 reference to Yahweh's act of
 deliverance (vv. 6b,
 8–9)

The snares of death
 encompassed me;
the pangs of Sheol laid hold
 on me;
I suffered distress and
 anguish.
Then I called on the name
 of the LORD:
'O LORD, I pray, save my
 life!'
Gracious is the LORD, and
 righteous;
our God is merciful.
The LORD protects the
 simple;
when I was brought low, he
 saved me.
Return, O my soul, to your
 rest,
for the LORD has dealt
 bountifully with you.
For you have delivered my
 soul from death,
my eyes from tears, my feet
 from stumbling;
I walk before the LORD in
 the land of the living.
I kept my faith, even when
 I said, 'I am greatly
 afflicted';

I said in my consternation,
 'Everyone is a liar.'

vv. 12–19a   Expression of intention to fulfil
 his vow

What shall I return to the
 LORD for all his bounty to
 me?
I will lift up the cup of
 salvation and call on the
 name of the LORD.
I will pay my vows to the
 LORD in the presence of
 all his people.
Precious in the sight of the
 LORD is the death of his
 faithful ones.
O LORD, I am your servant;
I am your servant, the child
 of your serving-maid.
You have loosed my bonds.
I will offer to you a
 thanksgiving sacrifice
and call on the name of the
 LORD.
I will pay my vows to the
 LORD in the presence of
 all his people,
in the courts of the house of
 the LORD,
in your midst, O Jerusalem.

v. 19b   Exhortation to praise Yahweh

Praise the LORD!

As with the Individual Laments, there are
some Individual Thanksgivings where the
speaker could be a representative figure.
This is the case with Psalms 18 and 118,
which clearly relate to a conflict with
foreign nations. There are very few psalms
that scholars have regarded as Communal
Thanksgivings. Most would put Psalm 124
in this category. Even though it does not

use the word 'thanks', its theme is clearly thankfulness to God for some act of deliverance. Psalm 129 has some points in common with Psalm 124 (including the exhortation, 'let Israel now say' in the opening verse). However, the theme seems to be more one of confidence in Yahweh because of what he has done rather than thanks. Psalm 67 has a dual theme. There is praise to God for the harvest, which can be seen as a form of thanksgiving. However, there is also a prayer for his blessing in the future, which may reflect an element of lament, the desire that they may not experience famine again.

> **Digging deeper:**
> **SONGS OF THANKSGIVING**
>
> Analyse the structure of the following Songs of Thanksgiving: Psalms 32, 34, 118.
>
> Note that Psalm 32 is unusual in containing a prophetic oracle (vv. 8–9).
>
> Although most of Psalm 118 is written in the first person singular it is about deliverance in battle. The 'I' who speaks may be an army commander, or the king, speaking on behalf of the nation. This would make sense of the change to the plural in vv. 25–27, which could be the people's response to the victory.

ROYAL PSALMS

Although Gunkel included Royal Psalms in his list of the main types of psalms, they do not form a distinctive literary type. They are psalms of various types whose distinguishing feature is their content, which concerns the relationship between God and the king. Gunkel considered the following to be Royal Psalms: Psalms 2, 18, 20, 21, 45, 72, 89, 101, 110, 132, 144. These all make clear reference to the king. Some scholars have argued for the addition of other psalms to the list. As we have seen, there are both some Individual Laments and Thanksgivings in which the speaker seems to be a representative of the community. Those who think that the representative was probably the king would add these to the list of Royal Psalms. Some would extend the list to include other Individual Laments and Thanksgivings where there is no clear representative role for the speaker but in which they discern other 'royal' features. These are subjective judgements that have not found wide acceptance. A few have argued that the mention of David in the heading of a psalm should be taken seriously as an indication of its royal character. The problem here, as we shall discuss later, is the uncertainty about the date and nature of these headings.

The psalms in Gunkel's list cover a range of royal occasions and situations. There is general agreement that Psalms 2 and 110 are both coronation psalms. They both contain divine oracles addressed to the king. The opening of the oracle in Psalm 2:7, 'You are my son; today I have begotten you' echoes the word of God through Nathan the prophet concerning David's successor recorded in 2 Samuel 7:14, 'I will be a father to him, and he shall be a son to me.' This, no doubt, would be a promise passed on to each successive ruler of the Davidic dynasty. In the account of Joash's coronation there is reference to the high priest giving the king 'the covenant' (2 Kgs 11:12). It is not clear what this was, but it could have been a document containing something like the 'decree' of Psalm 2:7–9. In the cases of both Joash and Solomon (1 Kgs 1:33f.) the coronation ceremony had two parts: anointing of the king in a sacred place and his enthronement in the palace. Psalm 110 would relate naturally to the enthronement of the king. In Psalm 101 the king (v. 8 strongly implies he is the speaker) commits himself to high moral ideals. This would be a fitting 'coronation oath', but might have been used on other occasions also. Psalm 72 is a prayer for the king, and sets out an idealized picture of his rule. It, too, could have its setting in a coronation.

The king was the commander-in-chief of the nation's forces and so it is not surprising that some of the royal psalms have a battle context. There is general agreement that Psalms 20 and 144 are prayers appealing for Yahweh's aid prior to engagement in battle. Psalm 18 (a variant of which occurs in 2 Sam. 22) seems to be a king's thanksgiving for victory in battle. The setting of Psalm 21 is unclear. In vv. 8–13 victory over enemies is envisaged in the future, and so some see it as a psalm to be recited before battle. On the other hand the element of thanksgiving in vv. 1–7 suggests to some that it is celebrating a recent victory. Its ambiguity, and the mention of the crowning of the king in v. 3, suggests to others that it may have been sung at the anniversary of the king's coronation. Psalm 89 begins by extolling Yahweh, and particularly his covenant promise to David (vv. 1–18). There is an extensive divine oracle in vv. 19–37, which seems to have its roots in the oracle of Nathan in 2 Samuel 7. The psalm closes with painful words of lament, accusing Yahweh of failing to keep his promise to David (vv. 38–51; v. 52 is the doxology closing Book 3 of the Psalms). This implies that the king has been defeated in battle, and probably killed. Yahweh is urged to step in and deliver his people. This could refer to the death in battle of Josiah in 609 BC (2 Kgs 23:29f.). However, the depth of despair expressed in it may indicate that it comes from after the destruction of Jerusalem by the Babylonians in 587/6 BC.

Psalm 45 was written for a royal marriage. The bridegroom is described in vv. 2–9 and the bride in vv. 10–15. The mention of Tyre in v. 12 has led some to link it with King Ahab of Israel, who married a Tyrian princess, Jezebel. However, v. 6 seems to allude to the promise to David and so suggest a Judean king. The Tyrians in v. 12 may be mentioned simply as the epitome of wealthy foreigners who send envoys to the wedding.

Psalm 132 is clearly closely related to the narrative in 2 Samuel 6–7, which records David's search for the Ark of the Covenant, his bringing of it to Jerusalem and Yahweh's promise to him delivered through Nathan the prophet. Part of this psalm is quoted in 2 Chronicles 6:41f., in the chronicler's account of Solomon bringing the Ark up into the temple during the Feast of Tabernacles. Psalm 132:6–10 seems to reflect a cultic re-enactment of the bringing of the Ark to Jerusalem. This may have taken place annually as part of the Feast of Tabernacles.

We will postpone until later a discussion of what these psalms reveal about the ideology of kingship in Judah, and the messianic interpretation of them.

PSALMS OF CONFIDENCE

This is another group of psalms that does not form a distinct literary type. What unites them is their 'mood'. They are sometimes called Songs of Trust. Although there is general acceptance of them as a distinct group, there is disagreement over how big the group is. Psalms 11, 23 and 62 are widely accepted as Individual Psalms of Confidence, and share the feature of referring to God entirely in the third person. Many would add at least Psalms 4, 16 and 131 to the list. Psalms 115, 125 and 129 may be classed as Communal Psalms of Confidence, but in each case the classification has been disputed.

Gunkel regarded these psalms as a development of the expression of confidence found in the Laments. Others have seen a closer connection with the Thanksgivings.

WISDOM PSALMS

There is widespread agreement that there is a category of psalms that have some kinship with the wisdom literature of the Hebrew Bible. This is another group that is not defined by literary form. The criteria used to define which psalms should be included are such things as the presence of ideas, and of linguistic and stylistic features, that are characteristic of the wisdom literature. However, disagreement arises because of the difficulty of deciding how many wisdom characteristics a psalm must have in order to be classified as a Wisdom Psalm. This has led a few to question the value of this category. The following appear in most lists of Wisdom Psalms: Psalms 1, 34, 37, 49, 73, 111 and 112. What these have in common is that the poet is addressing the question of the meaning of life, and in particular the problem of the prosperity of the wicked and the suffering of the righteous. They also make use of words and phrases found in the wisdom literature.

Some scholars, including Mowinckel, have argued that these psalms were never used in worship. They regard them as reflective and didactic poems that were used in a teaching setting separated from worship. However, it is then not clear why they were included in the Psalter. Nor is it clear why the material in these psalms should not have sometimes found a place in worship.

OTHER MINOR TYPES

There are two psalms that are linked by their content, praise of God's Torah (Law). These are Psalms 19 and 119. Psalm 19 falls into two halves. The first (vv. 1–6) speaks of creation, especially the sun, as a witness to God's glory. The second (vv. 7–14) extols the Torah. Although some scholars regard it as two originally separate poems that have been combined, this ignores an internal unity of thought. In the ancient Near East, the sun was not only regarded as the source of light and life, but as the source and upholder of justice. There is evidence for this from Egypt, the Mesopotamian civilizations and the Hittites. It may be that behind this is the idea of the sun as an 'all-seeing eye' in the heavens (cf. Ps. 19:6c). So, mention of the sun in the first half of the poem is a preparation for the theme of the second half. Moreover, if we ask in what way the creation witnesses to God, the answer that is given is the reference to the regularity of the sun's movements. God's giving of 'law' to the physical world is the counterpart to the giving of the moral Law. Psalm 119 is an anthology of meditations on the Torah.

PSALM 119

It seems to be a coincidence that the two psalms which have the Torah (Law) as their theme are Psalms 19 and 119. Psalm 119 is both the longest and the most carefully structured psalm in the Psalter.

The psalm is an acrostic in form. Each of the first eight verses begins with the first letter of the Hebrew alphabet, each of the next eight with the second letter, and so on through the 22 letters of the Hebrew alphabet, making 176 verses in all.

Eight major terms are used for the Torah throughout the psalm.

1. Torah/instruction (25 times)
2. Testimony (23 times)
3. Judgement (23 times)
4. Commandment (22 times)
5. Statute (22 times)
6. Word (22 times)
7. Precept (19 times)
8. Way (3 times)

Every verse in the psalm, apart from vv. 90 and 122, has one of these terms.

There is no clear progression of thought in the psalm. It is basically an anthology of meditative sayings about the Torah.

Although the overall theme of Psalm 1 is usually described as 'the two ways' – the ways of the righteous and the wicked – central to the 'way' of the righteous is delight in the Torah and meditation on it (v. 3). For this reason Psalm 1 is also classified as a Torah Psalm.

Psalms 15 and 24 are both 'gate liturgies', which seem to have been used when worshippers arrived at the gate of the temple. The worshippers ask who may enter the temple (Pss 15:1; 24:3), the gate keeper responds (Pss 15:2–5b; 24:4–5), and the worshippers then affirm their acceptance of the conditions (Pss 15:5c; 24:6). A similar liturgy is found in Isaiah 33:14–16.

The headings of Psalms 120—134 link them together as 'Songs of Ascent', although this group includes a variety of types of psalm (hymns, laments, songs of thanksgiving, psalms of confidence). There is a widespread view that these are psalms which came to be used by pilgrims going up to Jerusalem for the great festivals (cf. Ps. 122:4). A variant view points out that the word translated 'ascents' nearly always means 'step' or 'stair' elsewhere in the Hebrew Bible. It is therefore suggested that these psalms were recited either on a set of steps that went up to one of the gates of Jerusalem, or a set of steps within the temple precinct itself. A few scholars have argued that the 'ascent' referred to is the return of the exiles from Babylon. Against this is the implication in some of the psalms that Jerusalem and the temple have been rebuilt (e.g. Pss 122; 126; 134). Goulder points out that the 'return' took place in several phases over a lengthy period and tries to link these psalms with the book of Nehemiah. He suggests that these psalms were part of the liturgy of the Feast of Tabernacles held after the completion of the rebuilding of the walls of Jerusalem by Nehemiah. He tries to link them with the

TYPES OF PSALMS

It is not surprising that no two scholars agree exactly in their classification of the psalms into specific types. We would expect poets sometimes to modify the traditional forms that they use as their basic models. The result is that some psalms seem to fall between the main types and it is debatable as to which one they fit into best. Others do not seem to fit into any of the accepted types. Below is a classification of most of the psalms that would be fairly widely accepted.

Hymns
General Praises 8, 29, 33, 65, 95, 100, 103, 104, 113, 114, 117, 134—136, 145—150
Celebrations of Yahweh's kingship 47, 93, 96—99
Songs of Zion 46, 48, 76, 84, 87, 122

Laments
Individual Laments 3, 5—7, 13, 17, 22, 25—28, 35, 39, 41—43, 51, 54—57, 61, 64, 69, 71, 86, 88, 102, 109, 130, 140—143
Communal Laments 12, 44, 60, 74, 79, 80, 83, 85, 90, 126, 137

Songs of Thanksgiving
Individual Thanksgivings 9, 10, 32, 34, 92, 116, 118, 138
Communal Thanksgivings 67, 107, 124

Royal Psalms
2, 18, 20, 21, 45, 72, 89, 101, 110, 132, 144

Psalms of Confidence
Individual Psalms of Confidence 4, 11, 16, 23, 62, 91, 121, 131
Communal Psalms of Confidence 115, 125, 129

Wisdom Psalms
1, 34, 37, 49, 73, 111, 112

Torah Psalms
1, 19, 119

'I' passages in the book of Nehemiah, suggesting that the psalms were written as a response to these passages which, he proposes, were Nehemiah's 'testimonies' delivered at the festival. Some of Goulder's suggested links between the psalms and the 'testimonies' are plausible, others seem tenuous.

Psalms 146—150 each begin and end with the exclamation, 'Hallelujah' ('Praise the LORD'). In Judaism they came to be called the Hallel Hymns and form part of the daily morning prayer in the synagogue.

A Christian liturgical tradition going back to the Middle Ages has grouped seven psalms together as 'penitential psalms': Psalms 6, 32, 38, 51, 102, 130, 139 and 143. Most of these are individual laments, but the classification is based more on content than literary form. In the Late Middle Ages in particular, paraphrases were made of these psalms and commentaries written on them as aids to personal piety. Some commentators linked them to the 'seven deadly sins', with each psalm acting as a deterrent to one of the sins.

THE PSALMS AND ISRAEL'S WORSHIP

According to their headings, about half the psalms are linked with King David. As we shall see, the exact meaning of these headings is unclear, as is the date at which they were added to the psalms. However, they do make the point that from an early time the psalms tended to be regarded as arising out of the experiences of an individual poet, and in that sense to be primarily autobiographical. Even when a psalm is clearly about the concerns of the whole community it was assumed that these were presented through the personal insights of the psalmist. This continued to be the dominant approach to the psalms up until the early twentieth century, even though during the nineteenth century most scholars moved away from the assumption that David was the principal poet of the book of Psalms.

Gunkel's form-critical approach provoked a fresh look at the origin of the psalms. He recognized that the different psalm-types that he identified originated in Israel's cultic worship. They reflected different activities that took place in the cult. However, he still considered that the psalms preserved in the Psalter are the free compositions of individuals who used the traditional forms to express their own feelings and thoughts. In his view they were a 'spiritualized' development of the psalms that were actually used in the cult. The references that they contain to cultic matters are to be taken metaphorically.

It was Mowinckel who took Gunkel's approach to its logical conclusion. He believed that most of the psalms had their original setting in the worship of Israel, and that therefore if we are to understand them properly we have to discern and understand the cultic settings of the various poems. This is not to deny that the authors of the psalms put something of their own personal piety into their compositions, but it is to stress that they were professional poets working with the conventions of Israel's liturgical worship and in the service of the communal cult.

There are numerous allusions to the cult and cultic activities in the psalms. These make more sense if the psalms were used in public worship in the temple in Jerusalem than they do if taken as 'spiritualized' metaphors. There are several references to the temple (e.g. Pss 27:4; 63:2; 96:6; 122:1). As we have seen, Psalms 15 and 24 contain 'gate liturgies' to be performed at the entrance to the temple. In Psalm 24 this appears to be part of a procession in which God, in some sense, enters the temple. There is no doubt that God would have been represented by the Ark of the Covenant. The language of v. 8 implies this, since in the early period of Israel's history the Ark symbolized God's presence with the people in battle (cf. Num. 10:35f.).

> Who is the King of glory?
> The LORD, strong and mighty,
> The LORD, mighty in battle. (Ps. 24:8)

> Whenever the ark set out, Moses would say,
> 'Arise, O LORD, and let your enemies be scattered,
> and your foes flee before you.'
> And whenever it came to rest, he would say,
> 'Return, O LORD, of the ten thousand thousands of Israel.' (Num. 10:35–36)

Psalm 132 is possibly related to the procession of Psalm 24 and looks like the accompaniment to a re-enactment of the bringing of the Ark to Jerusalem by King David (cf. 2 Sam. 6). Psalm 68:24–27 gives a quite detailed description of a procession.

> Your solemn processions are seen, O God,
> the processions of my God, my King, into the sanctuary –
> the singers in front, the musicians last, between them girls playing tambourines:

'Bless God in the great congregation,
the LORD, O you who are of Israel's
fountain!'
There is Benjamin, the least of them, in
the lead,
the princes of Judah in a body,
the princes of Zebulun, the princes of
Naphtali.

This psalm begins with words which echo
Numbers 10:35, and so it too may refer to a
procession accompanying the Ark of the
Covenant. Psalms 48:12f. and 118:19f. also
refer to cultic processions of various kinds.

Other cultic activities are mentioned, such
as singing (e.g. Pss 9:11; 30:4; 33:2) and
dancing (Pss 87:7; 149:3; 150:4). There are
references to various kinds of musical
instruments (e.g. Pss 33:2; 47:5; 81:2; 98:6;
150:5).

If we accept Mowinckel's approach, we
can conclude that the Songs of
Thanksgiving were intended for use when
offering a thanksgiving offering, such as is
described in Leviticus 7:11–15. At least
some of the hymns might have been used
to accompany the burnt offering (Lev.
1:3f.), which seems to have been primarily
an act of praise and homage to God. As
well as general references to sacrifices (Pss
4:5; 27:6; 50:8), specific kinds of sacrifices
are mentioned: burnt offerings (Pss 20:3;
50:8; 51:16, 19), thanksgiving offerings (Pss
50:14; 107:22; 116:17), a covenant-making
sacrifice (Ps. 50:5), the freewill offering
(Ps. 54:6).

As we have seen, some of the Royal Psalms
are related to specific occasions such as
coronations, weddings and prayers before
and after battle. These, no doubt, took
place, at least in part, in the temple.

The Psalter has often been called 'the hymn
book of the second temple', referring to the
temple that was rebuilt after the return
from exile in Babylon (Ezra 5—6). As we
shall see, it is certainly true that the book of
Psalms took the form that we know now in
the post-exilic period. So, on this ground it
can be called 'the hymn book of the second
temple'. However, as our discussion of the
dating of the psalms will show, there is
good reason to believe that some of the
psalms are from the pre-exilic period and
so were used in the first temple, built by
Solomon. This is most obviously the case
for those that mention royal occasions or
the Ark of the Covenant. With the fall of
Jerusalem in 587/6 BC the monarchy came
to an end and the Ark was lost.

E. S. Gerstenberger, like a few other
scholars, has argued that most of the
psalms originated outside the temple in the
context of local communities meeting for
worship. He saw the primary setting for
this to be the synagogue worship of the
post-exilic period. The major weakness of
his case is that nothing is known about
synagogue worship in the Persian period,
and it is not even clear that synagogues
existed then. Given this lack of evidence,
there is little to commend his argument in
the face of the evidence that many of the
psalms reflect the worship of the temple,
and in some cases worship in the pre-exilic
temple.

THE AUTUMN FESTIVAL: YAHWEH'S ENTHRONEMENT?

According to the earliest Israelite cultic
calendars (Exod. 23:14–17; 34:22f.) in pre-
exilic times all male Israelites were
expected to appear at the sanctuary three
times a year for major festivals. These were
the Feast of Unleavened Bread, which was

Think about
THE ORIGINS OF HYMNS

You might find it interesting to discover the origins of some of your favourite hymns. There are a number of hymn book 'companions' which give this kind of information. Here are some brief notes on a few fairly well-known hymns.

'*Amazing grace*' This expresses the personal testimony of its author, John Newton (1725–1807). He described himself as 'once an infidel and libertine' who was 'by the rich mercy of our Lord and Saviour, Jesus Christ, preserved, restored, pardoned and appointed to preach the faith he had long laboured to destroy'.

'*Beauty for brokenness (God of the poor)*' This modern hymn was written by Graham Kendrick (1950–) for the twenty-fifth anniversary of the Christian international aid agency Tear Fund.

'*Eternal Father, strong to save*' Having been written by William Whiting (1825–1878), Master of Winchester Choristers' School, for a pupil who was about to sail to America, it has become 'the sailors' hymn'.

'*God of grace and God of glory*' Harry Emerson Fosdick (1878–1969) wrote this hymn for the dedicatory service at the formal opening of the new Riverside Church in New York in 1931. He described it as 'a very urgent personal prayer' for the ministry of the new church.

'*Onward, Christian soldiers*' Sabine Baring-Gould (1834–1924) wrote this for a Sunday school procession headed by a cross and banner. Lord Curzon, Viceroy of India, is said to have forbidden the use of it in services at the time of the Great Durbar of 1902 because he objected to the lines, 'Crowns and thrones may perish, Kingdoms rise and wane'.

Some source books are Colquhoun, 1980, and Routley, 1979.

associated with the barley harvest in the spring; the Feast of Weeks, which celebrated the wheat harvest in the early summer, and the Feast of Tabernacles in the autumn, when the grapes and other fruit were harvested.

Digging deeper:
THE PILGRIMAGE FEASTS

Using Bible dictionaries, find out what you can about the three 'pilgrimage feasts' of Unleavened Bread, Weeks and Tabernacles/Booths.

Mowinckel suggested that the Feast of Tabernacles was a new year festival and had features in common with the New Year (Akitu) Festival celebrated in Babylon (though that was in the spring). In this the so-called Babylonian creation epic (*Enuma Elish*) was recited. It tells of the god Marduk's victory over the forces of chaos, symbolized by the monster Tiamat and a host of other sea monsters, and the creation of the world. Marduk's enthronement as king of the gods was associated with this. Mowinckel argued that there are hints within the Hebrew Bible and later rabbinic material that suggest that the Feast of Tabernacles had a similar theme. He read Exodus 23:16 as meaning that the feast took place at new year. Zechariah 14:16f. specifically links the Feast of Tabernacles with the worship of Yahweh as king.

> Then all who survive of the nations that have come against Jerusalem shall go up year by year to worship the King, the LORD of hosts, and to keep the festival of booths. If any of the families of the earth do not go up to Jerusalem to worship the King, the LORD of hosts, there will be no rain upon them.

In post-biblical times one of the important themes of the Jewish New Year Festival was, and is, Yahweh's kingship. The heading of Psalm 29 in the LXX connects it with the Feast of Tabernacles. It concludes with reference to Yahweh's enthronement as king and a call for him to bless his people. The psalms that Mowinckel identified as 'enthronement psalms' (Pss 47; 93; 96—99) contain the phrase *Yahweh malak* (*malak 'elohim* in Ps. 47:8). He proposed that this should be taken to mean 'Yahweh (God) has become king' rather than as 'Yahweh (God) is king', as had been generally supposed. These psalms, he argued, were used in a re-enactment of Yahweh's enthronement over the forces of chaos in primeval times. By re-enacting it, his control over the forces of chaos was sacramentally experienced afresh to ensure Israel's well-being in the year ahead. In this re-enactment the Ark would represent the presence of God. Mowinckel therefore linked those psalms that imply that it was carried in procession with the autumn festival. He also assumed that the king would be involved, representing Yahweh,

and so regarded the Royal Psalms as closely linked with it too.

Much of Mowinckel's evidence for linking the Feast of Tabernacles with both the new year and the theme of Yahweh's kingship is post-exilic, even post-biblical, and therefore its relevance to what happened in pre-exilic times has been questioned. The earliest evidence is Zechariah 14:15f., which probably dates from the fifth century BC. Mowinckel's defence for use of this evidence rested on the assumed conservative nature of the religious cult. There is some validity in this, but there must always be a question mark against very late evidence.

Mowinckel's understanding of the phrase 'at the going out of the year' in Exodus 23:16 as referring to the new year is now generally discounted. When the Hebrew root (*ys'*) that is used for 'going out' in this phrase is used with time periods in the Hebrew Bible it always refers to the end of that period. Hence here it means 'at the end of the year'. This fits with the fact that in both Exodus 23 and 34 the Feast of Tabernacles is the last in the list. However, the ending of one year means the imminent beginning of another, and Exodus 34:22 puts the Feast of Tabernacles at 'the turn of the year', so some link with the new year is possible. David Clines has made the point that Exodus 23 and 34 refer to the agricultural year, and has argued that in pre-exilic times the civil calendar new year began in the spring, as it did in Babylon. However, this makes it difficult to explain why in later Judaism the new year has been celebrated in the autumn. It is perhaps more likely that references such as Leviticus 23:34, which put the Feast of Tabernacles in the 'seventh month', are a result of Judean adoption of the Babylonian calendar either in the late sixth century BC when under Babylonian hegemony, or while in exile. Overall, on balance, the evidence for linking the Feast of Tabernacles with the new year is not strong.

In the late nineteenth century and early twentieth century it was often argued that the Royal Psalms related to the Maccabean or Hasmonean rulers of Judah in the second or first centuries BC. This would clearly rule out Mowinckel's linkage of these psalms with a pre-exilic festival. Very few scholars today hold such a position. To begin with, there is general agreement that the Psalter was finalized before the Maccabean era. One piece of evidence for this is that 1 Chronicles 16:36 quotes Psalm 106 including the editorial doxology that was added to it when the Psalter was compiled. The books of Chronicles are usually dated to the fourth century BC. Second, by Hasmonean times there was a reluctance to use the divine name Yahweh, yet it is used freely in the Royal Psalms. Finally, there are features in some of these psalms that reflect pre-exilic times, such as reference to the Ark (Ps. 132:8) and to the king as a priest 'according to the order of Melchizedek' (Ps. 110:4).

There are some striking similarities in themes, and even phraseology, between the poetry used in Isaiah 40—55 and that of the so-called Enthronement Psalms. This includes the phrase 'your God reigns' in Isaiah 52:7. In the light of this it has been argued that the psalmists are drawing on the poetry of the prophet, with the implication that the psalms are therefore post-exilic. However, against this

is the fact that the prophet was clearly monotheistic in outlook, denying the existence of other gods (e.g. Isa. 44:6; 45:5, 14, 21; 46:9), an attitude that shaped later post-exilic Jewish faith. In some of the psalms, on the other hand, Yahweh is spoken of as pre-eminent among the gods (Pss 96:4f.; 97:7).

Mowinckel's translation of *Yahweh malak* has been hotly debated. The perfect tense verb form *malak* is used frequently to mean both 'he was king' and 'he became king'. In the context of coronations it is used in the sense 'he has become king' (2 Sam. 15:10; 2 Kgs 9:13 cf. 1 Sam. 12:14; 1 Kgs 1:11, 13, 18). Therefore Mowinckel's translation of the phrase in the psalms is clearly permissible. In fact it seems natural in Psalm 47:8 after the reference in v. 5 to God having 'gone up with a shout', which could well refer to an enthronement. The main resistance to Mowinckel's translation is now not grammatical but theological and conceptual. Who could enthrone Yahweh? In Marduk's case it is the other gods who proclaim him king. Does the annual enthronement of Yahweh imply that there ever was, or is, a time when he was, or is, not king? In response it is argued that here we face the inevitable problems associated with cultic and sacramental language, which refers to realities outside our space-time frame. Maybe what was done in the festival was thought of, not in terms of 'remaking' Yahweh's kingship, but as celebrating it and making it real afresh in Israel's experience. For this reason most scholars now favour the translation 'Yahweh reigns' or 'Yahweh is king'. For more on this, see the discussion of Psalm 96 on p. 47–49.

THE AUTUMN FESTIVAL: COVENANT RENEWAL?

Other scholars have also linked many of the psalms with the Autumn Festival, but have suggested that its main theme was different from that proposed by Mowinckel. In his commentary on the Psalms, A. Weiser suggested that the theme of the festival was the renewal of the Sinai covenant.

Two psalms can very plausibly be linked with covenant renewal. Psalm 50:5 refers to the making of a covenant between God and his people. The psalm goes on to take to task those who pay lip-service to the covenant but do not keep its laws (v. 16) and calls them to repentance. The apparent allusion to v. 2 of this psalm in Lamentations 2:15 ('Is this the city that was called the perfection of beauty?') suggests that it is a pre-exilic psalm. Psalm 81 is clearly intended for a feast day (v. 3).

> Blow the trumpet at the new moon,
> at the full moon, on our festal day.

This combination of trumpet blowing at the new moon (the first day of a month) and a feast at the full moon (the middle of the month) fits with what is said of the seventh month and the Feast of Tabernacles in Leviticus 23:23f. The psalm then refers to the exodus from Egypt and other events which took place before the Israelites reached Sinai (Ps. 81:5–7). A call to listen to God (v. 8) is followed by verses that echo the beginning of the Ten Commandments (vv. 9–10). Then God expresses the desire to bless the people, if only they would listen to and obey him. Later Jewish tradition links this psalm with the Feast of Tabernacles and new year. If, as several scholars have argued,

the Sinai covenant was modelled on the form of a 'vassal treaty' between a 'great king' and a vassal, with Yahweh as the 'great king' and Israel as his 'vassal', then the theme of Yahweh's kingship would fit naturally within this proposed festival theme. Indeed, Psalm 95:8 (an enthronement psalm) refers to the Israelites' rebellion against God at Meribah, an incident also mentioned in Psalm 81:7. Since Moses is said to have put the tablets with the Ten Commandments written on them in the Ark of the Covenant (Exod. 40:20; Deut. 10:5), one would expect the Ark to play a role in any covenant renewal ceremony, and therefore Psalms 24 and 132 could have a place in the festival. In fact Weiser suggested a setting for most of the psalms within this proposed covenant renewal festival. Sometimes the links he suggests are rather tenuous.

The main evidence that there was a covenant renewal festival in pre-exilic times, and that it was linked with the Feast of Tabernacles, is Deuteronomy 31:9–13. However, this states that the covenant is to be renewed every seventh year, not annually. Some scholars have argued that covenant theology itself is something that was introduced only in the seventh century BC, which is the period to which most date the book of Deuteronomy in the form in which we have it. However, the concept of the covenant seems to be part of the theology of the eighth-century prophets, even if it is only Hosea who explicitly uses the term (Hos. 6:7; 8:1). It is possible that the reference in Deuteronomy 31 reflects what was done in the later pre-exilic period. According to Nehemiah 8, Ezra read the book of the Law during the feast of the seventh month, the Feast of Tabernacles. This reading led to a renewal of the covenant. However, at some point in the post-exilic period covenant renewal came to be associated with the Feast of Weeks. The careful dating of the feast in Leviticus 23:15f. places it in the third month, at the time the Israelites are said to have arrived at Sinai (Exod. 19:1). A covenant renewal festival was held at this time by the community at Qumran. In wider Judaism the Feast of Weeks has come to be associated with the making of the covenant and the lawgiving at Sinai.

THE AUTUMN FESTIVAL: A ROYAL ZION FESTIVAL?

H.-J. Kraus argued that the main purpose of the Autumn Festival was to celebrate Yahweh's choice of Jerusalem/Zion, the founding of the temple, and the consequent protection and security of God's chosen people. He thought that this celebration owed something to the pre-Israelite, Canaanite royal cult of Jerusalem.

The Songs of Zion would have an obvious place in this proposed festival. Two of these have possible Canaanite connections. According to Psalm 46:4:

> There is a river whose streams make
> glad the city of God,
> the holy habitation of the Most High.

Jerusalem does not have any such river. At best this would be a very hyperbolic way of referring to the spring of Gihon. However, in Ugaritic poetry the dwelling place of the Canaanite high god, El, is said to be at the source of the rivers. Moreover, here God is called *El Elyon* (Most High). This is the

title given to the God whom Melchizedek, the Canaanite priest-king of Jerusalem, served according to the story about his meeting with Abraham (Gen. 15:18). It seems as though Canaanite language about *El Elyon* is being transferred to the God of Israel in this psalm. In Psalm 48:1b–2, Zion is described as:

> His holy mountain, beautiful in elevation,
> is the joy of all the earth,
> Mount Zion, in the far north,
> the city of the great King.

Neither the reference to its height nor to its position 'in the far north' fits well with the geographic reality of Mt Zion. However, these do echo what is said of the mountain that is the dwelling place of the god Baal in Ugaritic poetry. It seems that traditional Canaanite language about the dwelling place of God is being applied to Mt Zion. Both of these psalms speak of the security of Zion as a result of God's presence there (Pss 46:5; 48:3). Since God's presence was symbolized by the Ark, the psalms that are connected with it would have a place in Kraus's proposed festival. Historically the choice of Zion as Yahweh's dwelling place was inextricably linked with Yahweh's choice of David and his successors. It was David who captured Jerusalem from the Jebusites and made it the capital of his kingdom. He made it the centre of the worship of Yahweh by finding the Ark and taking it there. It was his son and successor, Solomon, who built the temple. Therefore one can see why Kraus proposed a royal Zion festival. The Royal Psalms would have their place in it, and so might the Psalms of Yahweh's Enthronement, since the Davidic king represented Yahweh's rule on earth.

Kraus's proposal is rather more speculative than those of Mowinckel and Weiser since it lacks even the minimal evidential basis outside the psalms that their proposals have.

THE AUTUMN FESTIVAL: CONCLUSION

Mowinckel, Weiser and Kraus cannot all be right in their claims about the Autumn Festival. It is possible that they have each hit upon evidence of different major festivals. However, there is a problem with the methodology on which they rely. To see this one has only to think of the Book of Common Prayer (or some similar liturgical compendium) being dismembered and the various prayers, canticles, creeds and so on being reassembled in a more or less random order. Without clear evidence of the structure of, say, Morning Prayer, it would be very difficult to recreate its liturgy. Perhaps the most we can conclude from the proposals made by Mowinckel, Weiser and Kraus is that they point to different major themes of the worship that took place in the Jerusalem temple.

Think about
YAHWEH'S KINGSHIP

One group of psalms that figures prominently in all three different reconstructions of the Autumn Festival by Mowinckel, Weiser and Kraus are those that celebrate Yahweh's kingship. That this is possible suggests the centrality of this theme in Israel's worship. With the replacement of absolute monarchies by democracies, this 'model' of God has become problematic for many people. What problems do you see in it? Can you think of a suitable alternative 'model'?

THE PSALM HEADINGS

In the Hebrew Bible all but 34 of the psalms have a heading of some sort. Although they are often referred to as 'titles' this is a misleading term. They are better regarded as 'ascriptions' that indicate such things as: the collection to which the psalm belongs, what type of psalm it is, how it was to be performed, the situation in which it was written, and occasionally other details. The Greek translation of the Psalter adds a heading to all those without one, except Psalms 1 and 2. It also makes some changes to several of the other headings. The fact that the Greek translators made these additions and changes shows that the headings were not considered fixed by the second century BC. The fact that two versions of the same psalm (Pss 14 and 53) have somewhat different headings indicates that the headings were not originally part of the psalm but were added later. In this case they were presumably added after the two versions of this psalm had become part of two different collections.

The material in the headings can be classified according to the kind of information it seems to give. Some headings contain information of more than one sort.

INDICATION OF AUTHORSHIP OR COLLECTION
'Of David'

This is found in the heading of 73 psalms in the Hebrew Bible. Its meaning is debatable because both the Hebrew preposition l^e and the word 'David' can be interpreted in more than one way. The preposition may indicate authorship ('by'), ownership ('belonging to'), the person for whom it was written ('for'). In some Ugaritic texts the preposition *l-* seems to indicate the person who is the main character of a poem ('about'). The word 'David' could denote King David or any king of the house of David (as in Hos. 3:5; Ezek. 34:23f.; 37:24f.). These possibilities have led to a number of suggested interpretations.

In both Jewish and Christian tradition this heading came to be understood as indicating Davidic authorship of these psalms. There is certainly an ancient tradition linking David with music and psalms. In the eighth century BC the prophet Amos refers to David's skill with musical intruments (Amos 6:5). According to the story in 1 Samuel 16:14–23, it was this which brought him into the court of King Saul. He influenced the development of Israel's worship by bringing the Ark of the Covenant to Jerusalem (2 Sam. 6) and by planning to build the temple (1 Sam. 7). In later tradition he is remembered as encouraging the composition of psalms and organizing the music and liturgy of the temple (1 Chr. 13—29). It is therefore likely that in the Psalter there are psalms, or parts of psalms, which were composed by David. However, a few psalms that have the heading 'of David' seem, at least in their present form, to come from a time later than David (e.g. 51:18f.; 69:35f.). In the LXX, 14 psalms have the heading 'of David' in addition to those that have it in the Hebrew Bible, indicating a growing tendency to link psalms of unknown origin with David.

It is possible that in some cases 'of David' means that it was written for use by the king (e.g. Ps. 18, a thanksgiving for deliverance in battle) or to be prayed on behalf of the king (e.g. Ps. 20, a prayer for a king to be given victory in battle).

Perhaps the most likely origin of the heading 'of David' is that it denotes psalms derived from a royal collection of psalms, possibly including some originally composed by David and others composed for the use of later kings.

Thirteen of the psalms in the Hebrew Bible that have the heading 'of David' make reference to some historical circumstance in his life as the supposed setting for the composition of the psalm. Most of these refer to events known from the books of Samuel. Michael Goulder has argued that the historical headings in Psalms 51—72 were actually written for David, by a close attendant, reflecting specific events during his life. The order of these psalms follows the order of events. However, there are some discrepancies between the headings and the account in the book of Samuel. For example, the heading of Psalm 34 refers to David feigning madness before Abimelech, while in 1 Samuel 21:10 the king concerned is Achish. The heading of Psalm 60 attributes to Joab a slaughter that 2 Samuel 8:13 attributes to David, and the number killed differs. The fact that in the LXX several more 'historical' headings are added suggests that they represent a growing tradition of linking psalms with known incidents in David's life that were suggested in some way by the psalm. For example, the mention of God as a 'refuge' for the psalmist who is beset by enemies (Pss 57:1; 142:5) may have prompted the linking of these psalms with the time when David was hiding in caves while being hunted by Saul. Peter Ackroyd points out that some ancient Hebrew manuscripts of 2 Samuel leave spaces at certain points in the story of David, and suggests that these were the points at which relevant psalms were intended to be read. This would encourage the attribution of the origin of such psalms to these historical episodes.

Digging deeper:
THE HISTORICAL HEADINGS IN THE PSALMS

Read some of the following psalms together with the related passage from the books of 1 and 2 Samuel. What connections can you see between the psalm and the story? Do you think it more likely that the psalm was written in the context of the events recounted in the story, or that it was written independently and only subsequently linked with the story?

Psalm 3   David's flight from Absalom (2 Sam. 15—16)
Psalm 7   Concerning Cush the Benjaminite (original event unknown)
Psalm 18   David's deliverance from Saul (1 Sam. 24; 27)
Psalm 34   David feigns madness (1 Sam. 21)
Psalm 51   Nathan's condemnation of David's adultery (2 Sam. 12)
Psalm 52   Doeg's betrayal of David (1 Sam. 22)
Psalm 54   The Ziphites' betrayal of David to Saul (1 Sam. 23)
Psalm 56   The Philistines seize David in Gath (1 Sam. 21)
Psalm 57   David's flight from Saul (1 Sam. 22)
Psalm 59   Saul sends men to kill David in his house (1 Sam. 19)
Psalm 60   David's wars against the Arameans and Edom (2 Sam. 8; 10)
Psalm 63   David in the wilderness of Judea (1 Sam. 23—24)
Psalm 142 David's flight from Saul (1 Sam. 22)

'Of Asaph'

This is found in the heading of 12 psalms which, apart from Psalm 50, form a distinct group, Psalms 73—83. In Chronicles, Asaph appears as a leading musician and singer in the time of David (1 Chr. 15:19; 16:4f.). The 'sons of Asaph' have this role in later times (1 Chr. 25:1; 2 Chr. 5:12; Ezra 2:41; 3:10; Neh. 7:44; 11:22). It seems reasonable to assume that the Asaphite psalms originate from this continuing guild of temple musicians. The fact that the headings ascribe these psalms to Asaph himself when some clearly come from a time much later than that of David (e.g. Pss 74 and 79 attest the destruction of the temple in 586 BC) indicates that 'of Asaph' refers to an ongoing collection of psalms in the same way that it is suggested that 'of David' does.

- There are a number of distinctive features about the Asaphite psalms that support the view that they come from a specific collection.
- The theme of divine judgement runs through them all, though it is present in varying ways. Thus the object of judgement may be Israel (Pss 50; 77; 78; 80; 81), Jerusalem (Pss 74; 79), other nations (Pss 75; 76; 83), wicked people (Ps. 73) or the gods (Ps. 82).
- Several of them refer to Yahweh's mighty deeds in the past: creation (Ps. 74), the exodus (Pss 77; 78; 80; 81), the conquest of Canaan (Ps. 78); the period of the judges (Pss 78; 83).
- Within this group there are more allusions to Israel as the flock of which Yahweh is the shepherd than there are in the whole of the rest of the Psalter.
- There are a number of references to the northern Israelite tribes, especially under the name Joseph. There is only

one other reference to Joseph in the Psalter (Ps. 105:17).

- There are divine oracles in Psalms 50, 72, 81, 82.
- Apart from Psalms 73 and 77 these are communal psalms.

Some see a prophetic background to these psalms in view of their emphasis on divine judgement, appeals to Yahweh's past acts and the presence of divine oracles, and point out that 2 Chronicles 29:30 speaks of Asaph as a seer, and 1 Chronicles 25:1–6 of the sons of Asaph and other temple singers as prophesying. Because of the references to the northern tribes some have suggested a northern origin for the Asaphites before they came to Jerusalem. However, Psalm 78 is distinctly anti-northern in tone, and the references to Joseph are largely the result of the interest in the events surrounding the exodus.

Goulder has argued that the Asaphite psalms are part of the liturgy of the New Year Festival held at Bethel in the latter part of the eighth century BC, and that they contain the earliest form of the traditions that now exist in a more developed form in the books of Exodus to Numbers. He specifically links these psalms with the 'Elohistic' material in these books. This is the material which refers to God as 'Elohim' rather than 'Yahweh'. 'Elohim' is the dominant way of referring to God in these psalms. Goulder argues that, after the fall of the northern kingdom of Israel, these psalms were taken to Jerusalem. The strongest part of Goulder's case is the affinity between the Asaphite psalms and the 'Elohistic' material in Exodus to Numbers. His identification of the time and place of their origin and their later history involves a

good deal of surmise and speculation. It does not help his case that he has to explain away the anti-northern tone of Psalm 78, and the references to the destruction of Jerusalem in Psalm 79, as later editorial additions.

'Of the Sons of Korah'

This appears in the heading of 11 psalms (counting Pss 42—43 as one psalm), which occur in three groups (Pss 42—49; 84—85; 87—88). Oddly, Psalm 88 is also attributed to Heman the Ezrahite (see p. 23). Several of these psalms are concerned with Mt Zion (Pss 42—43; 46; 48; 84; 87), and their stress on its inviolability suggests a pre-exilic origin in the worship of Solomon's temple.

Michael Goulder argues that the Korahite psalms originated in the northerly sanctuary of Dan, before they came to be used in the worship in Jerusalem from the seventh century BC onwards. In support of this he cites the phrase 'the heights of the north' (as he translates it) in Psalm 48:2 and identifies the river of Psalm 46:4 as the Jordan. However, most scholars see in these verses the application of mythical Canaanite imagery about the abode of the gods to Jerusalem. Also, whereas Goulder sees support for his view in the reference to the land of the Jordan and Mt Hermon in Psalm 42:6 because they are near Dan, others point out that the emphasis of this verse is that these places are far from Yahweh's sanctuary.

J. Maxwell Miller has argued for a southern origin of the Korahite psalms. He bases this on the reference made to 'the sons of Korah' on an ostracon found near the sanctuary at Arad in southern Judea. It is not clear whether this refers to the levitical sons of Korah of the Bible. Miller supports his case by appeal to the statement in Psalm 48:2 that Mt Zion is 'in the far north'. However, as we have already noted, most scholars see this as a mythical description, not a literal geographical one.

The concentration of many of these psalms on Mt Zion indicates an origin in Jerusalem. In 1 Chronicles 26:1 the sons of Korah appear as gatekeepers of the temple, but in 2 Chronicles 20:19 they appear as temple singers in the reign of Jehoshaphat.

'(According) to Jeduthun'

Jeduthun is a name that occurs several times in Chronicles (e.g. 1 Chr. 9:16; 2 Chr. 5:12) and once in Nehemiah (11:17) as a temple musician and singer of the time of David and Solomon, whose sons followed in his footsteps. Therefore the reference in the psalm headings could be to a guild of singers like the Asaphites and Korahites. However, Psalms 39 and 62 have a double attribution to Jeduthun and David, and Psalm 77 is attributed to both Jeduthun and Asaph. Moreover, in Psalms 62 and 77 the preposition used is *'al* ('according to'). This has led to the suggestion that 'jeduthun' is the name of a musical instrument or style of playing. Less likely is Mowinckel's suggestion that the word is a noun meaning 'confession' and so indicating a psalm intended for some penitential ritual.

'Of Solomon'

Two psalms have this heading: Psalms 72 and 127. Psalm 127 is probably post-exilic, and it is likely that the linking of both these psalms with Solomon is a late tradition based on the contents of the psalms. The reference to 'building the house' in Psalm 127 could be linked with Solomon's construction projects, especially the building of the temple. References to the king's judgement (Ps. 72:1) and to tribute from Sheba (vv. 10, 15) might be reasons for linking Psalm 72 with Solomon.

'Of Ethan the Ezrahite'

In 1 Kings 4:31 Ethan the Ezrahite is named as a famous sage of Solomon's time. The heading of Psalm 89 is presumably equating him with the temple musician of David's time named Ethan son of Kushiah, mentioned in 1 Chronicles 15:17, 19. To add to the confusion 2 Chronicles 2:6 makes Ethan and the other sages mentioned in 1 Kings 4:31 all sons of Zerah (is 'Ezrahite' a corruption of this?).

'Of Heman the Ezrahite'

In 1 Kings 4:31 Heman son of Mahol is one of the famous sages of Solomon's time mentioned along with Ethan the Ezrahite. The heading of Psalm 88 may be identifying him with the temple musician of David's time named Heman the son of Joel who is mentioned in 1 Chronicles 15:17, 19. In 1 Chronicles 25:5 he is also called 'the king's seer'. As we have noted already, 2 Chronicles 2:6 makes Ethan and Heman and the other sages mentioned in 1 Kings 4:31 all sons of Zerah.

'A Prayer of Moses, the Man of God'

This is the heading of Psalm 90. There is nothing in the psalm to link it specifically with Moses, or indeed to suggest that it is a particularly early poem.

INDICATION OF THE TYPE OF PSALM
mizmor

This occurs 57 times and is found only in the Psalter. It probably denotes a cultic song to be sung to the accompaniment of stringed instruments, and is usually translated 'psalm'.

shir

In 13 of its 29 uses, this term occurs alongside *mizmor*. It is a common term for 'song', but in the psalm titles it presumably has a specialized meaning that is now lost.

maskil

This is in the heading of 17 psalms. Its use in Psalm 32:8 suggests that it refers to a psalm that has a teaching purpose.

mikhtam

This term is used in six psalms. Since in Akkadian the root *ktm* is used to mean 'atone', Mowinckel takes it to mean 'a psalm of atonement'.

t^efillah

This word for 'prayer' is found in the heading of five psalms. Here it may have the narrower sense of a psalm of lamentation because that is what these psalms are (Pss 17; 86; 90; 102; 142).

t^ehillah

Although this is the term used of the whole Psalter, it occurs in only one psalm heading (Ps. 145). It means a song of praise.

shiggayon

Found only in Psalm 7, this word could be from a root meaning 'wail'. If so, it could indicate a psalm of mourning or lament.

shir y^edidhot

This means 'a song of loves', i.e. 'a love song', and is an appropriate term for Psalm 45.

shir hamma^{ʿe}lot

This term, usually translated 'song of ascent', is used in the headings of Psalms 120—134. We have discussed its meaning when discussing the minor psalm types.

INDICATION OF LITURGICAL USE

A few psalms have headings suggesting their liturgical use. Psalm 30 is said to be for 'the dedication of the temple'. This is often taken to refer to the purification of the temple by Judas Maccabeus in 164 BC, the origin of the Jewish Feast of Dedication or *Hanukkah*. The headings of Psalms 38 and 70 link them with the memorial offering, and the heading of Psalm 100 links it with the thank-offering. Psalm 92 is designated as a psalm for the Sabbath.

TECHNICAL MUSICAL TERMS

The most common of these, *lam^enasseah*, occurs in 55 headings. Its meaning is not clear. The translators of the LXX did not know what it meant, as indicated by their translation of it as 'for the end/eternity'. The most widely held view is that it means 'to the chief musician/choirmaster'.

There are references to the musical instruments to be used to accompany some psalms. Psalms 4, 6, 54, 55, 61, 67 and 76 are to be accompanied by stringed instruments. Presumably this is meant to exclude the use of wind and percussion instruments. Psalm 5 is to be accompanied by flutes. It is a lament and the Babylonians had a special flute accompaniment for laments. The term *sh^eminit* 'the eighth' (Pss 6 and 12) may mean an eight-stringed instrument, or possibly eight voices.

A number of phrases are thought to be references to particular tunes: 'The

Digging deeper:
THE PSALMS AND MUSIC

There is evidence in the book of Psalms of a close link between the psalms and music.

- In Hebrew the book is called t*e*hillim ('songs of praise'), although in the book the noun is used only in the heading of Psalm 145.
- The verb zamar ('to accompany the singing') is used more than 40 times in the psalms and the corresponding noun, mizmor ('a song sung to musical accompaniment'), occurs about 57 times. The noun shir ('song') is used about 40 times.
- The term 'to the choirmaster' is prefixed to 55 psalms. The headings concerning Asaph (Pss 50; 73—83) and Korah (Pss 42—49; 84; 85; 87; 88) probably indicate the origin and/or use of these psalms within guilds of temple musicians. The chronicler makes Asaph one of the chief temple musicians (1 Chr. 15:17, 16:5f.; 2 Chr. 5:12).
- Some terms in the headings may refer to specific tunes, e.g. 'according to the lilies' (Pss 45; 69; 80), 'according to do not destroy' (Pss 57—59; 75).
- Several musical instruments are mentioned both in the headings and in the psalms themselves. The stringed instruments include the lyre (Ps. 33:2) and harp (Pss 33:2; 43:4; 57:8; 150:3). Among the wind instruments mentioned are the horn and trumpet (Ps. 98:6), the pipe (Ps. 150:4) and flutes (the heading of Ps. 5). Percussion instruments mentioned include cymbals (Ps. 150:5) and tambourines (Pss 81:2; 149:3; 150:4).

Look up what Bible dictionaries have to say about the various musical instruments mentioned in the psalms.

Gittith' (Pss 8; 81; 84); 'Do Not Destroy' (Pss 57; 58; 59; 75); 'The Lilies' (Pss 45; 69; 80; Ps. 60 has 'The Lily of the Covenant'); 'The Deer of Dawn' (Ps. 22); 'The Dove on Far-Off Terebinths' (Ps. 56). The meanings of 'Muth-labben' (Ps. 9), 'Alamoth' (Ps. 46) and 'Mahalath (Leannoth)' (Pss 53, 88) are unclear.

THE STRUCTURE AND GROWTH OF THE BOOK OF PSALMS

STRUCTURE

In the form in which we have it, the book of Psalms is divided into five 'books' by four doxologies, which stand out as being separate from the psalms at the end of which they come.

STRUCTURE OF THE BOOK OF PSALMS

Book 1 **Psalms 1—41**
Blessed be the LORD, the God of Israel, from everlasting to everlasting.
Amen and Amen. (Ps. 41:13).

Book 2 **Psalms 42—72**
Blessed be the LORD, the God of Israel, who alone does wondrous things.
Blessed be his glorious name for ever; may his glory fill the whole earth.
Amen and Amen.
The prayers of David son of Jesse are ended. (Ps. 72:18–20)

Book 3 **Psalms 73—89**
Blessed be the LORD for ever.
Amen and Amen. (Ps. 89:52)

Book 4 **Psalms 90—106**
Blessed be the LORD, the God of Israel, from everlasting to everlasting.
And let all the people say, 'Amen.'
Praise the LORD!' (Ps. 106:48)

Book 5 **Psalms 107—150**

The similarities in the four doxologies are clear. Psalm 150 lacks a similar doxology, but the whole psalm is, in fact, a doxology on the theme of 'Praise the LORD!' It is probably placed where it is for this very reason. Most scholars now believe that Psalm 1 was added at the start of the Psalter at a late stage as an appropriate introduction to it. It is one of the very few psalms in Book 1 not headed 'of David' and its theme of the two ways, the way of the righteous and the way of the wicked, suits its introductory position. A mark of the righteous is that 'their delight is in the law of the LORD, and on his law they meditate day and night' (Ps. 1:2). It is very probable that the fivefold division of the Psalter was based on an analogy with the five books of the Torah. The *Midrash Tehillim* on Psalm 1:1 says, 'Moses gave Israel the Five Books, and David gave Israel the five books of Psalms.' As has been mentioned already, it is interesting that the quotation from Psalm 106 in 1 Chronicles 16:35–36 includes the doxology (Ps. 106:48). This suggests that the division of the Psalter into books had taken place by the time Chronicles was written, sometime in the fourth century BC.

It has been suggested that the fivefold division of the book of Psalms is related to its use in the synagogue lectionary alongside the readings from the Torah. This suggestion has not found much favour because the attempts to find parallels between the lectionary passages in the Torah and particular psalms seem forced, and the numbers of psalms in each 'book' and lectionary passages in the corresponding book of the Torah do not correspond to each other. In addition, the practice of having lectionary readings in the synagogue probably developed too late

to have influenced the final editing of the Psalter.

A COLLECTION OF COLLECTIONS

There are clear indications that the existing book of Psalms contains within it earlier smaller collections and is the end result of a process of gradual growth. One such indication is the statement in Psalm 72:20 that 'The prayers of David son of Jesse are ended'. Since several of the following psalms have the heading 'of David' this makes sense only if it marks the end of a collection of 'Davidic' psalms that once stood as a separate entity from Books 3—5. There is also the fact that there are some 'duplicates' in the book as we have it: Psalm 14 = Psalm 53; Psalm 40:13–17 = Psalm 70; Psalm 108 = Psalms 57:7–11 + 60:5–12. This is most readily explained if the duplicates originally belonged to different collections, which have been amalgamated in the process of forming the current Psalter. A number of possible earlier collections can be discerned on various grounds.

Psalms 3—41

With two exceptions, these psalms are all headed 'of David'. Psalm 10, which lacks this heading, is really the second half of Psalm 9. This is suggested by the (somewhat imperfect) acrostic pattern that embraces both of them. In the LXX and some Hebrew manuscripts the two psalms are combined. Psalm 33, the other psalm without a heading, may be a later addition to this collection, perhaps prompted by some similarity between Psalm 32:11 and Psalm 33:1. Most of the psalms in this collection are individual laments. The group of psalms is sometimes referred to as 'the first Davidic collection'.

The Elohistic Psalter

In Psalms 3—41 God is referred to as 'Yahweh' ('the LORD' in English translations) over 278 times and as 'Elohim' ('God' in English translations) 15 times. This is reversed in Psalms 42—83, with 'Yahweh' occurring 44 times and 'Elohim' 201 times. The predominance of 'Yahweh' returns in Psalms 84—150, and is even greater than in Psalms 3—41. The fact that the predominance of 'Elohim' in Psalms 42—83 is the result of deliberate editing is indicated by comparing two pairs of duplicate psalms: Psalm 14 = Psalm 53 and Psalm 40:13–17 = Psalm 70. Also, when passages from psalms in the Elohistic Psalter have parallels outside the book of Psalms it is 'Yahweh' that occurs in these parallels (Ps. 50:7//Exod. 20:2; Ps. 68: 1, 7, 8//Num. 10:35 and Judg. 5:4–5).

The Elohistic Psalter itself contains at least three smaller collections. Most of the psalms in Psalms 51—72 have 'of David' in their heading, and the conclusion 'the prayers of David son of Jesse are ended' at the end of Psalm 72 may originally have referred just to this 'second Davidic collection'. Psalms 42—49 all have headings attributing them to 'the sons of Korah'. Psalms 50 and 73—83 are all attributed to Asaph. Although 'Yahwistic', Psalms 84—89 seem to be a deliberate 'appendix' modelled on the Elohistic Psalter. It is made up of a Davidic psalm (Ps. 86) embedded in Asaphite psalms (Pss 84—85; 87—88) plus another psalm attributed to a temple musician, Ethan (Ps. 89). The evidence suggests that Psalms 42—89 was the result of a somewhat complex process of growth from smaller collections with additional psalms added, before it was added to Psalms 3—41, at which point Psalm 2

may have been added as a suitable introduction to a predominantly 'Davidic' collection. This probably illustrates what happened with regard to the Psalter as a whole.

Psalms 90—150

Psalms 90—150 is less clearly structured than the preceding part of the Psalter. Some smaller collections are discernible within it. Psalms 120—134 are all headed 'Songs of Ascents' (discussed earlier among the 'Minor Types' of psalms). There are small Davidic collections in Psalms 108—110 and 138—145. Psalms 93 and 95—99 are united by the theme of Yahweh's kingship, and Psalms 146—150 all begin with the word 'Hallelujah' (Praise the LORD).

THE GROWTH OF THE PSALTER

It is impossible to reconstruct the process of growth of the Psalter with any degree of certainty. Some scholars have, nonetheless, put forward fairly detailed proposed reconstructions (e.g. A. A. Anderson, S. Gillingham, K. Seybold). Although these differ in detail, there are some points over which there seems to be a fair degree of consensus.

- At an early stage several small collections came into being. These may have been united by such things as their subject matter, cultic usage or their origin within a particular group.
- The first Davidic collection coalesced and became the foundation of our present Psalter.
- The Elohistic Psalter came into being and was eventually joined to the first Davidic collection. At this point Psalm 2 may have been added, as suggested above. It is debatable whether the

'appendix' of Psalms 84—89 was also added at this point or had already been added to the Elohistic Psalter.

- How this 'combined psalter' grew to what we have now is unclear. It may be that at some point the collection ended with Psalm 119. It might have been then that Psalm 1 was added, to give a wisdom/Torah introduction and conclusion.
- Finally, the collection was divided into five books. The books vary considerably in length. The reasons for the points of division are not clear. The divisions after Psalm 41 and Psalm 72 may have retained the 'end of collection' mark from when they came at the end of earlier, smaller collections.

Given the uncertainty about the process of growth, there is little definite that can be said about the dating of the stages of it. This is made even more difficult by the fact that most of the psalms cannot be dated with certainty. The most that can be said is that the most natural setting for the origin of the Royal Psalms and the Songs of Zion is the pre-exilic, monarchic period. The psalms that meditate on the importance of the Torah (Pss 1; 19; 119) probably reflect post-exilic thinking. More debatable is whether psalms that stress the importance of inner attitudes rather than outward cultic actions (e.g. Ps. 69:30–31) must be post-exilic. What they say is very similar to what is expressed by the eighth-century prophets (e.g. Hos. 6:6). As we noted above, the quotation from Psalm 106 in 1 Chronicles 16:35–36 may indicate that the Psalter had taken basically the form we know before the end of the fourth century BC. This is supported by the absence of evidence of Greek influence in any of the psalms.

THE NATURE OF THE BOOK OF PSALMS

Following the work of Gunkel and Mowinckel, study of the Psalms concentrated on the form and content of individual psalms and their probable original life-setting in the context of the temple cult. One result of this was to encourage the view that the book of Psalms is a loose collection of diverse poems or more accurately, as we have seen, in its final form a 'collection of collections'. There was therefore little interest in reading it in a holistic way as a single literary entity.

During the 1980s there was a marked shift in focus of the study of the Psalms as a number of scholars began to ask questions about the overall composition, editorial unity and message of the book of Psalms. Could the Psalter be read as a 'book' in the sense of a literary entity with a coherent structure and message? This changed the focus of study from individual psalms seen more or less in isolation to how both the individual psalms and the collections into which they are grouped fit together. Does this indicate that the book has a specific theme or message? Two developments in biblical scholarship in general contributed to this change. One was the rise of 'canonical criticism', advocated by Brevard Childs and James Sanders among others. This encouraged the understanding of biblical books in the final 'canonical' form in which they have become Scripture for Jews and Christians. The second development was the rise of various forms of 'literary criticism', which encouraged holistic readings of texts (e.g. 'rhetorical criticism', 'narrative criticism', 'structural analysis').

KINGSHIP AND WISDOM

Seminal work on this new approach to the Psalms was done by G. H. Wilson. He studied other ancient Near Eastern hymn collections (the Sumerian 'temple Hymn Collection' and 'Catalogue of Hymn Incipits' and the Qumran Psalms manuscripts). In these he discerned various editorial techniques. With this basis he looked for the presence of similar editorial techniques in the book of Psalms. He divided the evidence he found of editorial activity into 'explicit' and 'tacit' evidence. The psalm headings and the postscript to Books 1–2 at Psalm 72:20 ('The prayers of David son of Jesse are ended') provide explicit evidence. Examples of tacit evidence are the doxologies at the end of Books 1–4, or the groupings of the 'hallelujah psalms' (Pss 104—106; 111—117; 135; 146—150).

Earlier scholars (e.g. C. Westermann, B. S. Childs) had suggested that Psalm 1 was deliberately placed where it is to provide an introduction to the whole book of Psalms. Wilson describes it as providing 'hermeneutical spectacles' through which readers should view the book as a whole and meditate on it. This is encouraged by the 'historical' headings of some psalms, which relate them to incidents in the life of David. These prompt readers to find in them guidance for their own righteous behaviour in accordance with the Torah when they meet personal situations comparable with David's.

Wilson stressed the importance of discovering the 'seams' that join different groups of psalms and so create the unity of the whole book. These 'seams' were needed because the final editor had to work with existing groups of psalms, which he could not or did not want to break up. Again he took up a point that had been noted previously by Childs and Westermann, that Book 1 begins with a Royal Psalm (Ps. 2, assuming Ps. 1 is an introduction to the whole Psalter) and Books 2 and 3 end with Royal Psalms (Pss 72; 89). This, he suggests, makes the Davidic covenant, and its failure, a theme of these books. He sees Psalm 89 as marking its failure. There are a few royal psalms in Books 4 and 5 but Wilson sees these as overshadowed by the portrayal of Yahweh's kingship, particularly in Psalms 93—99 and 145. In a later essay Wilson identified a 'royal covenantal frame' to the Psalter in Psalms 2, 72, 89 and 144, and a 'final wisdom frame' in Psalms 1, 73, 90, 107 and 145 (the first psalms of Books 1, 3, 4 and 5, along with the last psalm of Book 5 proper). In his view the wisdom frame takes precedence, so that what is emphasized is trust in Yahweh rather than the power of human kings. The Psalter is then ultimately a book of wisdom containing Yahweh's instruction for the righteous, and emphasizing his kingship.

Nancy deClaissé-Walford has built on Wilson's work. In a study that concentrates on the opening and closing psalms of each of the five books she seeks to show how the Psalter was shaped to meet the needs of the post-exilic Jewish community in Judea. She argues that the community struggled with two questions: 'Who are we?' and 'What are we to do?' After the trauma of the exile it needed to answer the first question in order to establish its stability. It needed to answer the second question in order to adapt to the situation in which it found itself. In her view, Book 1 of the Psalms celebrates the reigns of David and Solomon. However, Book 2 reminds the reader/hearer that even in that period all was not well. Book 3 deals with the dark days of the exile in Babylon, when the covenant with David seemed to have failed. The only source of hope that remained was the presence of Yahweh. The theme of Book 4 is the kingship of Yahweh. Although there is no longer an earthly king on the throne of David, Israel still has a king, the king it has always had since Yahweh brought them out of Egypt. The way forward for the post-exilic community is to go back to the time when Israel relied on Yahweh alone. Book 5 continues the theme of Yahweh's kingship. However, it contains a notable concentration of psalms ascribed to David (15). There is only one Davidic psalm in Book 3 and only two in Book 4. According to deClaissé-Walford this is evidence that the post-exilic community retained its hope for a return to full nationhood, on the basis of Yahweh's covenant with David. This is an interesting and suggestive exercise in showing how the post-exilic community might have found the theological basis for its survival in the Psalter. Perhaps inevitably, it falls short of demonstrating that it is the only, or even the most likely, way of understanding the present shape of the Psalter.

ESCHATOLOGICAL INTERPRETATIONS

Wilson's interpretation of the shaping of the Psalter sees an eschatological slant in it. Books 1—3 present the historical failure of the Davidic monarchy. Book 4 responds to this with the message that Yahweh is Israel's true king and ends with a plea for him to restore the nation (Ps. 106:47). Book 5 shows that this plea will be answered provided the people trust God (Ps. 107) and live according to his Law (Ps. 119).

David C. Mitchell has argued that the Psalms present an essentially eschatological theology centred around the figure of the Davidic king. In his view an eschatological hope in a messianic figure is to be found throughout the Psalter, and indeed is its central purpose. He bases his case on a detailed study of individual psalms in which he seeks to link them with particular events and with the eschatological programme of Zechariah 9—14. Central to his argument are the Psalms of Asaph and the Songs of Ascents. Several scholars have concluded that the Asaphites were a group of levitical prophet-musicians. On the basis of references to Asaph and Asaphites in the Hebrew Bible, Mitchell argues that the Asaphites were associated with the ancient holy war rite of 'reminding' Yahweh of his people's plight at times of foreign invasion and calling on him to deliver them. He also sees them as linked with the theme of the 'gathering' of Israel for war. The name Asaph means 'gather', and Mitchell suggests that its use in psalm headings is a deliberate wordplay ('for the ingathering') referring to the eschatological 'ingathering' of Israel. He relates this to the prophetic motif of the ingathering of Israel prior to the eschatological battle with the nations (as depicted in Zech. 9—12). Mitchell takes the Songs of Ascent as referring to pilgrimage to the temple in Jerusalem, especially for the Feast of Booths. He links this with the eschatological Feast of Booths depicted in Zechariah 14:1–19 and the establishing of God's kingship on earth. Mitchell accepts that further work needs to be done to show how psalms other than those of Asaph and the Songs of Ascent can be related to the 'eschatological programme' he finds in Zechariah 9—14.

PSALMS AS INSTRUCTION

J. C. McCann has developed the idea that the book of Psalms has been edited to encourage the reading of it as a source of God's instruction, *torah*, for righteous living. Like other scholars he sees Psalm 1 as being deliberately placed to provide an introduction to the whole book of Psalms. It invites the reader to regard all that follows as instruction. The theme of the importance of *torah* is developed further by Psalms 19 and 119. He points to verbal links between these psalms. Perhaps most notably Psalm 119:1 can be seen as a positive restatement of Psalm 1:1.

He also sees literary links between Psalms 1 and 2. In particular he points to the use of 'blessed/happy' at the start of Psalm 1 and the end of Psalm 2 as an *inclusio*, which binds the two psalms together. He thinks that the real message of Psalm 2 is Yahweh's sovereignty, not that of the Davidic king. This psalm introduces the essential content of the instruction given in the psalms: 'the Lord reigns!'. The theme is affirmed at the end of Book 2 (Ps. 72) and Book 3 (Ps. 89) and given further emphasis in Book 4 in the enthronement psalms (Pss 93; 95—99). It is because the Lord reigns that all living creatures, but humans in particular, are called on to praise the Lord (Ps. 150:6). Praise is the true goal of all human life.

However, praise does not always come easily. McCann sees the central position of Psalm 73, the opening psalm of Book 2, in the Psalter as significant. There are echoes of Psalm 1 in its opening verse and of Psalm 2 in its final verse. He argues that it marks a theological turning point. The psalm focuses on the problem of the suffering of the righteous in the face of the apparent prosperity of the wicked. This is resolved by a recognition that it is possible to endure suffering while remaining faithful to the notion of suffering as a punishment for sin. The psalm gives new meaning to the concept of 'pure in heart'. To be pure in heart is to continue to obey, serve and praise God even in the midst of trouble and suffering.

BOUNDED BY OBEDIENCE AND PRAISE

Psalm 73 also plays a crucial role in Walter Brueggemann's understanding of the theological message of the book of Psalms taken as a whole. His approach is a much more general one than that of either Wilson or McCann. For him the crucial psalms are Psalms 1, 73 and 150. He sees a theological progression from obedience to praise mapped out by them. Both Psalm 1 and Psalm 150 are 'innocent'. By this he means that they are confident and untroubled. However, there is an important difference in the nature of the 'innocence' in the two psalms. Psalm 1 expresses a simple confidence that the righteous will flourish through their obedience and that the wicked will perish. Its intention is to encourage a new interpretation of the psalms that follow in terms of trusting, joyous community. But these psalms reflect the fact that the real world involves suffering, and therefore many of them are laments. What hymns there are express the hope and trust that suffering will be overcome through faith and obedience. Psalm 73 marks a transition. It moves beyond the simple faith of Psalm 1 to a recognition that knowing God's presence and enjoying communion with God outweighs all the concerns about the suffering of the righteous and the prosperity of the wicked. There are far fewer laments and many more hymns after Psalm 73 than before it. This leads to the 'innocent' outburst of praise in Psalm 150, which is possible because the lessons of life have been learned. The duty of obedience, which is taught in Psalm 1, does not need to be mentioned because it has been subsumed in the pure joy of being in God's presence.

MACROSTRUCTURE AND MICROSTRUCTURE

The studies surveyed so far have concentrated on the 'macrostructure' of the book of Psalms, its overall structure and message. Their argument has been based primarily on the presence and placing of relatively few of the psalms. Some scholars have approached the study of the book of Psalms from the other direction, looking for connections between pairs or small groups of psalms, which might demonstrate the internal coherence of the collection. Their hope is that this will give clues as to the nature and purpose of the editing of the book.

Examples of proposed 'paired psalms' are:

- Psalms 65 and 66. A psalm that extols God's goodness displayed in creation is followed by one that extols his goodness displayed in Israel's history.
- Psalms 78 and 79. Both of these are recitals of history. The first covers the period from the Exodus to David. The second refers to the destruction of Jerusalem in 587/6 BC. It may be significant that Psalm 77 refers to the exodus, as the basis of a plea for God's deliverance from trouble. Also Psalm 80 seems to refer to the destruction of Jerusalem, as does Psalm 79. The original pair may have 'attracted' the psalms that precede and follow them.
- Psalms 105 and 106 is another pair of recitals of history. It may be deliberate that they are prefaced by a 'creation psalm'. The Creator is Lord of history.

It has been argued that Psalms 3—8 form a coherent group. Psalms 3—6 can all be seen as evening or morning prayers, with their mention of 'sleep', 'morning', 'night'. Although these words do not occur in Psalm 7, Psalm 8 meditates on the night sky. All these psalms express trust in God's protection in various ways. He is a 'shield' (3:3; 5:12; 7:10), enables the psalmist to 'lie down and sleep in peace' (3:5; 4:8), can be relied on as a refuge (5:11; 7:1), and is a protector against enemies (3:7; 5:8; 6:10; 7:1; 8:2). The links suggested here are a mixture of themes and 'keywords'. Some scholars have majored on looking for linguistic links between adjacent psalms and groups of psalms. David Howard has done a very detailed study of Psalms 93—100. He analysed every lexeme in every possible relation with every other one in order to uncover significant links. Most of these are of the 'keyword' type between adjacent psalms; others are thematic links.

> **Think about**
> **PSALMS 15—24**
>
> Psalms 15—24 may form another distinct group. It begins and ends with 'gate liturgy'. Both 15:1 and 24:3 raise the question of who is worthy to 'dwell' or 'stand' in 'the hill of the LORD'. This raises the question of 'belonging' or 'being at home' in the presence of God. This has been seen as a theme that runs through these psalms, moving from longing to rest. Can you trace this progression in these psalms?

A CRITICAL RESPONSE

Norman Whybray has subjected the thesis that, in its final form, the Psalter was intended to be read as a 'book' to a critical assessment. In response to the claim that Psalm 1 provides the 'hermeneutical spectacles' through which the book of Psalms should be read he argues that, if this was the intention of the final editors, then this should be evident from the positioning of what he calls 'pure' torah and wisdom psalms and also the interpolation of torah and wisdom material in other psalms.

Apart from the three widely recognized 'torah psalms' (Pss 1; 19; 119) the word 'torah' occurs in only six psalms (Pss 37; 40; 78; 89; 94; 105). Whybray concludes that it might have been interpolated in Psalms 37:30–31; 40:6–8; 78:5–10. As we have noted already, there is considerable disagreement among scholars as to which

psalms are 'wisdom psalms'. Whybray accepts the following: Psalms 8, 14, 25, 34, 39, 49, 53, 73, 90, 112, 127, 131 and 139. He finds wisdom material interpolated in Psalms 27:11; 32:8–9; 86:11; 92:6–7, 12–14; 94:8–15; 105:45; 107:43; 111:2, 10; 144:3–4; 146:3–4.

Whybray cannot discern any significant pattern in the torah and wisdom interpolations. The distribution is a bit uneven, with somewhat more in Books 3 and 5. He notes that Psalm 1, a pure torah psalm, is in a significant position and that the pure wisdom psalms – Psalms 73, 90 and 107 – stand at the beginning of books. However, if this is a deliberate editorial strategy it is odd that there is not a wisdom or torah psalm at the start of Book 2. The placing of Psalms 19 and 119 is hard to understand if they are intended to encourage a torah interpretation of the whole book of Psalms. As a whole the pure torah and wisdom psalms are concentrated in Books 1 and 5. It is unclear, says Whybray, whether this is evidence of a desire to put emphasis on wisdom/torah at the beginning and end of the Psalter, or the result of a failure to impose a wisdom/torah theme on the Psalter as a whole. He concludes that there is no evidence of a comprehensive editing of the Psalter to produce a collection that could be read as a coherent book of piety or instruction.

Whybray also studied the Royal Psalms. He found no evidence of systematic editing of these, either by their position or by interpolations. He concluded that, while they would have helped to keep alive the hope of a restored Davidic monarchy during the post-exilic period, this could not be said to be a major concern of the Psalter. In fact, he points out, in the post-exilic period messianism was not generally compatible with a wisdom/torah theology.

There have been two kinds of response to Whybray's study by those whose work he critiques. One is that he undervalues, in fact largely ignores, the significance of Wilson's work on the kinds of organizing principles used in the Mesopotamian and Qumran collections of hymns. The other is that it is still early days for the study of the Psalter as a 'book' and that it is too soon to evaluate the value of this approach properly.

A SAMPLER OF PSALMS

The psalms in this 'sampler' have been chosen for two reasons. Some are included because they have been at the centre of recent discussion about the structure of the Psalter as a book (Pss 1; 2; 73; 150). The others are examples of the various types of psalms discussed in the study of psalm types.

Before studying this section you will probably find it helpful to skim-read Chapter 2 on Hebrew Poetry in order to get a grasp of the main points in it.

PSALM I

As we have seen, this psalm is regarded as an introduction to the whole Psalter. In some manuscripts of the book of Psalms it was either not numbered, or was combined with Psalm 2. This is why some texts of Acts 13:33 introduce a quotation from Psalm 2 as from 'the first psalm'. Its structure is simple:

vv. 1–3 A portrait of the righteous.
vv. 4–5 A portrait of the wicked.

v. 6   The contrast between the righteous and the wicked.

This psalm does not fit into any of the major literary types. Its meditative nature and some of its language leads it to be classed as a 'wisdom psalm' by some scholars. Others are more specific and classify it as one of the 'torah psalms' because of Psalm 1:2 (Pss 19 and 119 being the others).

vv. 1–2

The opening words, 'Happy are those' (or, to give a more literal translation, 'Happy is the one') is a formula that is found mainly in the Psalms and in the book of Proverbs. It is seen as an expression that is at home in the Wisdom Literature. The traditional translation of the opening word is, 'blessed'. However, this can lead to confusion of the formula used here with the Hebrew invocation, 'blessed be . . .', which uses a different word. The opening of Psalm 1 is not a prayer for the righteous to be blessed, but a statement of their situation, hence the more recent translations' use of 'happy'.

The 'righteous' are first of all defined negatively, by what they do not do (v. 1). The three clauses form a synonymous parallelism. It is doubtful whether there is any 'grading' intended in the three words used for the 'unrighteous'. In the Psalms 'the wicked' are usually those who are opposed to God, and so to his people. 'Sinners' are those who 'miss the mark' of, or deviate from, God's standards. The primary characteristic of the 'scoffers' is their self-sufficient pride, which leads them to refuse to accept instruction. They appear quite often in Proverbs. In contrast to the scoffers in particular, the 'righteous' delight in God's instruction and meditate on it. 'Instruction' is the meaning of *torah*, the Hebrew word generally translated as 'law' in v. 2. Here it probably has the wider sense rather than referring specifically to the Law of Moses.

v. 3

The righteous are depicted as a luxuriant, well-watered tree. This picture is found elsewhere in the Hebrew Bible (i.e. Ps. 92:12–14; Jer. 17:7–8; Ezek. 19:10). The verbal parallels with Jeremiah 17:7–8 are notable, and lead some to suggest that the psalmist has based this verse on that passage.

vv. 4–5

The picture of the righteous is one of permanence: a flourishing tree. The wicked are depicted as 'chaff'. This imagery conveys the idea of something worthless (what is left over from the procedure of winnowing to get the worthwhile grain) and impermanent (the chaff is blown away by the wind during winnowing).

There is debate about the meaning of 'the judgement' in v. 5. Does it refer to the wicked not being given a place among those who have influence in society, or to them not being able to stand before God's judgement? The parallelism between the two halves of the verse does not settle the issue. Probably, in the light of v. 6, it should be taken in the sense of God's judgement, which leads to the wicked being excluded from God's people.

v. 6

This picture of the two ways has echoes in the book of Proverbs, e.g.

For the LORD gives wisdom . . . preserving the way of his faithful ones (Prov. 2:6a, 8b)

The way of the wicked is an abomination to the LORD (Prov. 15:9)

PSALM 2

This is clearly a Royal Psalm, and the great majority of scholars see it as specifically a coronation psalm. Its overall structure is clear.

vv. 1–3   The futile conspiracy of the nations against the Lord and his anointed.
vv. 4–6   The Lord's response of derision.
vv. 7–9   The Lord's decree.
vv. 10–12 A warning to the rulers of the earth.

There is a predominantly 3:3 metre throughout the psalm. The psalm has a dramatic quality about it, and if it was part of a coronation liturgy one can imagine different voices speaking the different sections of it, with the king speaking vv. 7–9.

There has been an increasing tendency to regard this psalm, with Psalm 1, as part of a 'double introduction' to the whole Psalter. It introduces the theme of kingship, both human and divine, which is a theme that runs through the whole book. The fact that it ends with a formula that echoes Psalm 1:1 encourages the idea that this is an *inclusio*, which binds the two psalms together. It is the reason why some rabbis treated the two psalms as one, and is probably why some manuscripts of the Psalms treat the two as one psalm.

vv. 1–3

The change of ruler in an empire was often the occasion for vassal nations to rebel in an attempt to regain their independence. The reference to 'bonds' and 'cords' in v. 3 is no doubt intended to conjure up the picture of a yoke, a symbol of subjection. The only time when Israel could be said to have had anything like an empire was during the rule of David and Solomon. David has extended his rule over the surrounding nations. However, it is unlikely that any specific historical occasion lies behind these verses. More to the point, they are expressing a theological conviction. If Yahweh is 'a great God and a great King above all gods' (Ps. 95:3) then all nations should bow to his sovereign rule. The agent of that rule on earth is the Davidic king, and so all rulers should acknowledge him as their overlord.

vv. 4–6

When the psalmist says that Yahweh 'sits' in the heavens, he means that he is 'enthroned' there. He is the ultimate sovereign and all rebellion against his rule is laughable. He chooses who should represent his rule on earth, and he declares that it is the king whom he has established in Zion. This became another name for Jerusalem, though originally Zion was a hill within the city.

vv. 7–9

The king now announces 'the decree of the LORD'. The words in v. 7 clearly refer back to Nathan's words (spoken on behalf of Yahweh) recorded in 2 Samuel 7:14. They are an 'adoption formula'. They do not imply that the king was deified in any way. Among all the criticisms that the Hebrew prophets make of the kings of Israel and Judah, they never accuse them of claiming divinity. What they do imply is that the king is brought into a special relationship with Yahweh so that, like an only son, he

can act for his father, with his authority. Like an only son he also inherits his father's possessions. In this case, this is the earth (v. 8). Yahweh also declares that the king will be able to subdue his rebellious enemies (v. 9).

vv. 10–12

An ultimatum is addressed to the rulers of the earth. If they want to avoid destruction they must 'Serve the LORD with fear'. This is the 'wise' thing to do (vv. 10–11a). Note the echo here of the 'motto' of the book of Proverbs, 'The fear of the LORD is the beginning of wisdom' (Prov. 1:7; 9:10).

The meaning of vv. 11b–12a is unclear. The MT reads, 'and rejoice with trembling. Kiss the son.' There are three problems with this.

- It makes a poor parallel with v. 11a.
- The combination of 'rejoicing' and 'trembling' is odd.
- The word used for 'son' is the Aramaic one (*bar*) and not the Hebrew word (*ben*) used in v. 7.

Some scholars retain the MT despite these problems, seeing here a command to express the fear of the Lord by doing homage to the newly installed king. Kissing in this context was an act of self-humiliation and homage. Most, however, emend the text to give the reading found in the NRSV, 'with trembling kiss his feet', i.e. express their fear of the Lord by doing homage to him. Of course, in practice this would mean doing homage to the Davidic king, so in the end the meaning is much the same, only the emphasis is a bit different. A primary reference to Yahweh in v. 12a gives a smoother transition to the rest of the verse, in which he is clearly the subject.

In v. 12b there is a kind of parallel to the 'two ways' ending of Psalm 1. Rulers who oppose Yahweh will 'perish in the way' but those who take refuge in him will be 'happy'. We've noted that the use of 'happy' here echoes its use in Psalm 1:1.

The fall of the Davidic monarchy and the Judean state required some radical rethinking within ancient Judaism after the return from exile. One strand of thought that arose was based on the eternal nature of the covenant with David. This was taken to mean that one day a 'new David' would arise to establish Yahweh's rule over all the earth. This was the 'messianic' hope. The word 'messiah' means 'anointed' (the word used in v. 2). In the New Testament, Psalm 2 is used to express the belief that Jesus is the expected Messiah. The words 'You are my son' in Psalm 2:7 are echoed in the voice from heaven at Jesus' baptism and transfiguration (Mark 1:11; 9:7). Psalm 2:7b is applied to Jesus in Acts 13:33 and Hebrews 1:5; 5:5.

PSALM 13

This psalm is an Individual Lament. It has been called 'a parade example' of that type of psalm. It has several elements of the lament form:

v. 1   Invocation of God, 'How long, O Lord?'
vv. 1–2   Complaint
vv. 3–4   Petition.
vv. 5–6   Expression of trust.

There is no regular metre.

vv. 1–2

The fourfold repetition of the cry, 'How long?' in a series of complaints of increasing intensity drives home the psalmist's sense of desperation. The problem is threefold. God seems distant and unconcerned. The psalmist is wracked with anxiety and inner anguish. An enemy dominates the situation. In the light of v. 3b it is possible that, as some suggest, the 'enemy' here is death.

vv. 3–4

The verb translated 'consider' in the NRSV often means 'look'. That may well be the sense here, since in v. 1b the psalmist has complained that God has 'hidden his face', i.e. turned it away from him. Now he asks God to look at him and listen to him. He also asks God to act, to 'give light to' his eyes. In the Hebrew Bible, dim eyes are a sign of ill-health, grief and old age. So, to 'enlighten the eyes' is to restore someone to health and vitality. In particular the psalmist wants to be delivered from death. In v. 4 there is mention of a singular 'enemy' and also plural 'foes'. The first may be death and the second human opponents.

vv. 5–6

As was said when discussing the Laments, the sudden change of mood to trust and confidence may be the response to a salvation oracle spoken by a priest or cult prophet. Here the statement in v. 6 could be seen as a version of the vow that is made in some laments. This is especially so if the word translated 'because' in the NRSV is taken to mean 'as soon as', as some commentators argue it should.

PSALM 19

In his *Reflections on the Psalms*, C. S. Lewis wrote of this psalm, 'I take this to be the greatest poem in the Psalter and one of the greatest lyrics in the world.' It is generally described as a 'wisdom poem', and more specifically as a 'torah psalm'. In terms of subject matter and style it falls into two parts. The first part (vv. 1–6) is a hymn of creation, with special emphasis on the sun. It is written predominantly in a 4:4 metre. The second part (vv. 7–14) is a meditation on the law of the Lord and has a predominant 3:2 metre. In the first part God is referred to using the general term *el* but the divine name Yahweh is used in the second part. These differences have led some scholars to divide the psalm into two distinct poems. Others argue that the psalmist has taken an existing creation hymn and expanded it. Whether the poem was originally a single composition, or is an expansion of a previously existing one, there is good reason to treat it as a single poem now because there are conceptual links between the two halves. In the ancient Near East, the sun god was regarded as the upholder of justice and the law. The stele which contains the famous Babylonian 'Laws of Hammurabi' has carved on it a picture of the sun god Shamash giving the laws to King Hammurabi. Second, the purpose of laws is to produce a society that is ordered in a way that is good for its citizens and pleases God. The order displayed in the regular movement of the heavenly bodies created by God provides an analogy to this.

A more detailed outline of the psalm is:

vv. 1–6   The glory of God in creation.
vv. 7–14   A meditation on the law of the Lord.

vv. 7–10   Praise of the law.
vv. 11–13 Prayer for forgiveness and protection.
v. 14   Dedicatory formula.

v. 1

The Hebrew text of this verse contains a feature that is fairly common in Hebrew poetry: a chiastic arrangement of the main terms. This is the pattern A:B:B':A'. In this verse it is: the heavens:God's glory:his handiwork:the firmament. It is not easy to reproduce this in English translation. The psalmist declares that the creation, God's handiwork, displays God's glory, but he concentrates on one part of it, the heavens.

vv. 2–4b

The poet plays on the paradox of 'inaudible speech'. The existence and nature of the created world witnesses to God in a kind of fountain of unspoken communication. The implication is that receipt of this communication depends on the perception of the observer.

vv. 4c–6

Attention now fixes on the sun. No doubt this is partly because 'glory' is often depicted in terms of bright light. Two similes are used to depict the sun's glorious emergence at dawn: a bridegroom resplendent in his finery and a warrior exulting in the display of his strength. The description finally focuses on three things that provide a strong link with what is to follow. The first is the regular pattern of the sun's motion. The second is the 'all-seeing eye' nature of the sun. This probably contributed to the personification of the sun as the god of justice in ancient Near Eastern mythology. Third there is the heat of the sun. This, like justice, can be both life-giving and death-dealing, depending on the situation.

vv. 7–10

In vv. 7–9 there is a carefully constructed comprehensive description of the Law of the Lord. The Law is referred to by six terms, each linked to a specific attribute and effect.

- Law – perfect – reviving the soul.
- Decrees – sure – making wise the simple.
- Precepts – right – rejoicing the heart.
- Commandments – clear – enlightening the eyes.
- Fear – pure – enduring for ever.
- Ordinances – true – righteous altogether.

The section ends with a statement that the Law of the Lord is more precious than the finest gold and more enjoyable than the best honey. This may seem a strange sentiment today when law is often seen as a restrictive thing, a necessary evil. However, the psalmist is talking about the Creator's 'instruction' on how to live life in the best way possible within the created order. It is about getting the most out of life.

vv. 11–13

Faced with the righteousness of the law, the psalmist is aware of his imperfection. He therefore prays for forgiveness for, and protection from, sin. The word translated 'the insolent' by the NRSV in v. 13a is translated as 'presumptuous sins' by other versions. If the NRSV is correct, the psalmist is referring to both inner (v. 12b) and outer (v. 13a) pressures to sin.

v. 14

The psalm ends with a kind of dedication. This might be a variant of the formula used when presenting a sacrifice in the temple. The poet offers his poem as a kind of sacrifice to God. He uses two metaphors to describe God. In the Hebrew Bible 'rock' is often used as a symbol of both support (something firm and strong) and security (a safe place to hide). The term used here for 'redeemer' (*go'el*) refers to the nearest kinsman, whose duty it was to look after the well-being and interests of his less fortunate family members.

PSALM 23

This psalm of confidence or trust is probably the best known, and most loved, psalm in the Psalter. It speaks of Yahweh by the use of two metaphors, those of the caring shepherd (vv. 1–4) and the gracious host (vv. 5–6). Although some commentators see the shepherd metaphor as running through the whole psalm, this gives a rather forced interpretation to the imagery of vv. 5–6. The second metaphor may point to the setting in which the psalm was used. The 'thanksgiving offering' was one form of the 'sacrifice of well-being' in which only part of the animal was burnt on the altar and the rest cooked and eaten at the sanctuary by the offerer and guests. Such an occasion would be an appropriate one for reciting this psalm, which in its expression of confidence in God is also an implicit expression of thanks.

vv. 1–4

The metaphor of 'shepherd' was a rich one in ancient Israel. In what was a largely agricultural society, everyone knew about the ways of sheep and the responsibilities of shepherds. Because of the very seasonal nature of the rains there were times of year when good pasture was hard to find, and it was the shepherd's duty to find it for the sheep. Since the pasture was out in the open country, the shepherd had to protect the sheep from predators. So, shepherding was about *provision* and *protection* for the flock. In the ancient Near East, 'shepherd' was a title applied to leaders. Both gods and kings were spoken of as shepherds of their people. The shepherd's mace (rod) and crook (staff) were often used as symbols of office. Through the metaphor of 'shepherd' this section of the psalm speaks of Yahweh as the one who can be relied on to provide for, and protect, the one who trusts in him.

In v. 4a the Hebrew adjective that is used to describe the 'valley' can be interpreted as a word meaning 'darkness', or as a compound word meaning 'shadow of death'. Even in the second case, the sense may be metaphorical, 'deepest darkness', but the mention of death gives the added element of a sense of fear.

vv. 5–6

The metaphor now changes to that of a host and his guest. Perfumed oils were used at times of rejoicing. The overflowing cup is a symbol of the host's generosity. Although the idea of generous *provision* is the dominant one in these verses, the idea of *protection* is still there in the reference to the psalmist's enemies. Whoever they are, they can only look on enviously, powerless to do harm.

PSALM 33

This is a hymn of praise. It has the typical three-part structure of the hymns: call to praise (vv. 1–3), main section giving the reasons for praising God (vv. 4–19) and a concluding section (vv. 20–22). In this case the conclusion is a variation on the normal renewed call to praise. It is an expression of trust in Yahweh. The more detailed structure is set out below. There is a predominant 3:3 metre.

vv. 1–3	Call to praise the Lord.
vv. 4–19	Reasons to praise the Lord.
	vv. 4–5 The character of the Lord.
	vv. 6–9 The creative word of the Lord.

Think about
METAPHORS

When we use a metaphor we say that something is something else that it obviously and literally is not. However, we are implying that there is some point, or points, of correspondence between the two things. A metaphor is a kind of verbal 'lens', which focuses attention on that point of comparison. Like a lens, it can help us spot something about the thing we are looking at that we've not seen before. However, a metaphor can become an 'opaque' lens when the source of the comparison is something that lies outside our experience, like shepherds for most people who live in an urban, industrialized society. For such people the metaphor lacks the richness that it had in ancient Israel. When that happens we need to think about the possibility of replacing the old 'opaque' metaphor with a new 'clear' one that will convey at least something of the same meaning. Can you think of an appropriate alternative metaphor to 'shepherd' that would convey the same ideas of provision and protection to people in an urban, industrialized society? Could you expand it into a short psalm of confidence?

vv. 10–12 The counsel of the Lord.

vv. 13–19 The Lord's care of humans.

vv. 20–22 Concluding expression of confidence in the Lord.

The fact that this psalm has the same number of verses as the number of letters in the Hebrew alphabet (though it is not an acrostic poem) leads some to suggest that it is intended to be seen as an 'A to Z' of reasons to praise God.

vv. 1–3

The call to praise asserts that it is 'right and proper' for the people of God to praise him. In Israel praise was expressed with both musical instruments and the human voice. The psalmist urges that it should be done 'skilfully' (NRSV) or 'beautifully' (as some commentators translate it).

The significance of the reference to 'a new song' is unclear. It could mean that this is a newly composed song. Some commentators take it to indicate that this psalm was to be used at the New Year Festival or a renewal of the covenant. Alternatively it may be a way of expressing the idea that Yahweh's goodness always calls for new, fresh expressions of praise.

vv. 4–5

The qualities attributed to Yahweh here are ones that are commonly attributed to him in the Hebrew Bible.

- Upright. The word means 'straight, not crooked'. Yahweh's word is 'upright' because he means what he says.
- Faithfulness. He is utterly reliable.
- Righteousness. This is a relationship word, denoting the kind of behaviour

that serves to maintain the covenant relationship by faithfulness to its obligations.
- Justice. This means treating the covenant partner rightly in accord with the terms of the covenant.
- Steadfast love. This means loyal commitment to the covenant partner.

vv. 6–9

This speaks of the awe-inspiring creative activity of Yahweh. There are echoes here of the creation story in Genesis 1. The idea of creation by means of the divine word is not completely unique to Israel, but it is developed in a unique way in Genesis 1.

vv. 10–12

Yahweh is not only the Lord of nature, he is the Lord of history. Moreover, he has a plan and purpose for it. His chosen people are at the centre of this.

vv. 13–19

Yahweh is not an 'absentee landlord'. He is concerned about, and cares for, humankind. In particular, he takes care of 'those who fear him', i.e. those who show reverence and obedience towards him.

vv. 20–22

The expression of trust in Yahweh moves into a prayer for his continuing care and protection.

PSALM 49

Most scholars agree that this is a Wisdom Psalm. There are similarities in purpose, content and vocabulary with the books of Proverbs, Job and Ecclesiastes. Its main theme is the inequalities of life seen in the context of the inevitability of death. The problem is that the oppressive rich seem to avoid misfortune while the righteous poor remain poor and oppressed. Both die without the inequality having been righted.

The psalm has a threefold structure. There is an introduction (vv. 1–4) and then two sections marked out by the refrains in v. 12 and v. 20. It has a predominant 3:3 metre.

vv. 1–4   Introduction.
vv. 5–12   The limitations of wealth.
vv. 13–20   Two destinies.

vv. 1–4

The opening call has similarities to that of the wisdom teacher in Proverbs (1:8; 4:1) to his 'children' or pupils. Here, however, the audience is universal, including people of all nationalities and all social classes. The word translated 'proverb' has a wide range of meanings. A 'riddle' is a perplexing problem. In the context of this psalm it may be the problem implied in the refrain, 'Are humans any different from animals?' There is no other mention in the Hebrew Bible of meditation or instruction being accompanied by music. It was used to induce prophetic ecstasy (1 Sam. 10:5; 2 Kgs 3:15).

vv. 5–12

In these verses the wisdom teacher declares the perspective on life to which his meditation has brought him. There is really no reason for the poor to be more fearful in times of trouble than the wealthy. All the wealth of the rich cannot ultimately save them from death. All humans are destined to die and leave whatever wealth they have behind them. His meditation centres around the concept of 'ransom'. In the ancient world this would often mean 'buying freedom' from slavery or captivity. Israelite law also allowed 'ransom' from capital punishment in certain cases (Exod. 21:28–30) but not others (Num. 35:30–32). However, says the psalmist, no one is able to pay the price to ransom themselves from death ultimately.

vv. 13–20

In vv. 13–14 the psalmist describes those who trust in their prosperity as like mindless sheep who are being shepherded to Sheol, the realm of the dead, by death. The crux of the psalm is v. 15, but its meaning is debated. A few scholars regard it as a presumptuous utterance of the wealthy. However, this gives little basis for the assurance given in vv. 16–20. Most commentators see in v. 15 a personal statement of the psalmist of confidence in God, but differ about its exact nature. Some see it as a reference to deliverance from present trouble or an untimely death. Others think that the flow of the whole psalm suggests that it goes beyond this to a confidence that God *will* ransom the psalmist (and, by implication, the righteous in general) from Sheol – not in the sense that they will not die, but that their ultimate fate will be different from that of the rich who oppress them. Some support for this is found in the phrase 'for he will receive me'. The verb 'receive' here is the same one that is used of God 'taking' Enoch and Elijah (Gen. 5:24; 2 Kgs 2:11) to be with him. What kind of ultimate destiny the psalmist had in mind is not stated. Perhaps he did not know. The main thing was that he would continue to exist in a relationship with God. In the light of that confidence, the psalmist urges his hearers not to fear the rich because their only destiny is the grave.

SELAH

This term occurs 71 times in 39 psalms. It never comes at the beginning of a verse, but always in the middle or at the end. The occurrences are concentrated in Psalms 1—89. Exceptions are Psalms 109, 139 and 140. It also occurs three times in the psalm in Habakkuk 3. Despite the frequency of its use, there is uncertainty about its meaning.

- The commonest understanding of it is that adopted by the LXX translators. They translated it by *diapsalma*, meaning 'a pause'. This would imply that it indicates a pause in the singing of the psalm, perhaps an instrumental interlude.
- Most ancient Jewish traditions take it to mean 'always, everlasting, for ever'.
- Some modern scholars suggest that it comes from the root *sll*, 'to lift up'. It may be an instruction to sing, or play, louder. Alternatively it may indicate some liturgical action.
- Another suggestion is that it comes from the root *slh*, 'to bend, bow down'. If so, it might indicate the points at which the congregation would bow down or prostrate themselves in worship.

PSALM 60

This is a communal lament uttered at a time of national distress, apparently the result of military defeat. In the light of v. 9 it is possible that the enemy concerned was Edom. The structure of the psalm is:

v. 1   Invocation: 'O God'.

vv. 1–4   Complaint.

v. 5   Petition.

vv. 6–8   Answering oracle.

vv. 9–10   Complaint.

v. 11   Petition.

v. 12   Expression of trust.

The metre is predominantly 3:3.

vv. 1–4
The nation has suffered a calamity. The reference to broken defences (v. 1a) suggests that this involved military defeat. The disaster is described by using the metaphor of a great earthquake. The shocked state of the people is compared to a tottering drunk. Behind v. 3a is probably the idea of the cup of God's wrath (Ps. 75:8). The meaning of v. 4 is unclear. If it is part of the complaint, it probably refers to the raising of a signal flag on the wall of a city as a warning of impending attack. This would be the sign for those outside the city to flee to it for protection. Of course, they may then have to face the horrors of a long siege. The psalmist attributes the disaster to the action of God. He assumes that he is in control of the destiny of his people. He does not protest that the people do not deserve it.

v. 5
This is a plea for God to act and reverse the situation.

vv. 6–8
These verses also occur in Psalm 108, which is a prayer of thanksgiving made up of Psalm 57:7–11 plus Psalm 60:5–12. This suggests the oracles might be preserved and reused, and not always be a fresh, spontaneous utterance. The reference in v. 6 to dividing up and portioning out land is a claim to ownership of the territory concerned. It echoes the tradition of the Promised Land being apportioned to the tribes by lot (Josh. 18:8–10). The calling of Ephraim God's 'helmet' and Judah his 'sceptre' indicates their importance to him. In vv. 6–7 there is an alternation of territory to the west and east of the Jordan:

Shechem, Succoth; Gilead and Manasseh, Ephraim and Judah. There is also a chiasm here, west:east:east:west (part of Manasseh was, like Gilead, east of the Jordan). The nations mentioned in v. 8 are traditional enemies of Israel. God claims them as his in language that seems to be somewhat contemptuous. The casting of a shoe may be an action indicating ownership (e.g. Ruth 4:7; Deut. 25:8–9).

vv. 9–10

The questions in v. 9 are probably spoken by the king, or some other national leader. Taken with v. 10 they imply that God has failed to give his people the victory in battle they expected.

v. 11

The fresh complaint leads to another plea for help. Only God can deliver his people. Human help is worthless.

v. 12

Like many Laments, this one ends with an expression of trust in God, in this case that he will give Israel victory over their foes.

It is impossible to identify with certainty the historical situation behind this psalm. The superscription links it to David's war against the Aramean kingdoms and Edom, recorded in 2 Samuel 8:3–14; 10:6–18; 1 Chronicles 18:3–13; 19:6–19. However, there are differences between what is said in the superscription and in these narratives. The differences in the numbers of Edomites killed (2 Sam. 8:13 and 1 Chr. 18:12 say 'eighteen thousand' rather than the 'twelve thousand' here) may be the result of a textual error. Numbers were usually represented by letters of the alphabet, and these seem to have been particularly prone to copying errors. 1

Samuel 8:13 attributes the victory to David, 1 Chronicles 18:12 attributes it to Abishai, the son of Zeruiah, whereas the superscription attributes it to Abishai's brother, Joab. The attribution to David is explicable as the ascription to a commander-in-chief of the action of one of his subordinates, a common feature of ancient (and some modern) records of warfare.

The linking of this psalm to David's campaigns is probably secondary (though some modern scholars defend it). There is nothing in the narratives about it to explain the situation of distress described in the psalm. One would have to postulate some major defeat preceding those victorious campaigns, not mentioned in the surviving record, to which they were a response. The singling out of Edom in v. 9 is reminiscent of the virulent attacks on Edom for the part she played at the time of the downfall of Judah (e.g. Ps. 137:7; Lam. 4:21–22; Obad.), which leads some to see that event as the background to this psalm.

This psalm shows the freedom the ancient Israelites felt about complaining to God, but also the robustness of their faith, which enabled them to continue to trust him even in desperate situations.

PSALM 73

This psalm is hard to classify. Its meditative style, its concern with the problem of the prosperity of the wicked and sufferings of the righteous, and the likelihood that it begins with a proverbial statement leads most scholars to classify it (with some hesitation) as a Wisdom Psalm. However, others see in it elements of the Individual Thanksgiving, or the

Individual Lament, or the Psalm of Confidence.

There is also disagreement about the detailed structure of the psalm. The Hebrew word *'ak* ('truly, surely, indeed') begins vv. 1, 13 and 18, suggesting that these are major break-points in the psalm. There is general agreement that v. 17 is the centre and turning point of the psalm. One possible structure is given below. The metre is predominantly 3:3.

v. 1   A proverbial saying.

vv. 2–3   The psalmist's plight.

vv. 4–12   The psalmist's problem: the prosperity of the wicked.

vv. 13–16   The psalmist's complaint: an insoluble problem.

v. 17   The turning point.

vv. 18–20   A new perspective on the wicked.

vv. 21–26   The psalmist's relationship with God.

vv. 27–28   Concluding confession of faith.

v. 1

The opening verse may be a kind of 'title', summing up the message of the psalm. However, it may well be a proverbial saying, meditation on which, in the face of the apparent contradiction of it by the prosperity of the wicked, provoked the psalmist to doubt. The traditional rendering of the opening line is 'Truly, God is good to Israel'. However, the letters can be divided differently (in early manuscripts the letters are not divided into words by spaces) to read, 'Truly, God is good to the upright'. This is adopted by many modern translations because it gives better parallelism with the second line.

vv. 2–3

The psalmist's attitude of envy and resentment nearly led to disaster. The reference is probably to a collapse of faith.

vv. 4–12

The cause of his envy was the apparent prosperity of the wicked. Both their prosperity and their wickedness is described in graphic terms. They seem prosperous and trouble free (vv. 4–5). They flaunt their wickedness (vv. 6–8). Their prosperity leads people to fawn on them (v. 10, though the meaning of this verse is unclear and disputed). They are contemptuous of God (v. 11). The psalmist sums up his (previous) view of them in v. 12.

vv. 13–16

The cause of his resentment was that all his piety seemed to be in vain (vv. 13–14). He found himself in a quandary. On the one hand he did not want to put himself outside the community of faith by giving way to his doubts (v. 15). On the other, he could not find a satisfactory answer to them (v. 16).

v. 17

This is clearly the turning point of the psalm. Something happened to the psalmist in the context of worship (no doubt in the temple in Jerusalem). We are not told what happened, but what follows suggests that it was some kind of encounter with God.

vv. 18–20

The psalmist now has a radically different view of the state of the wicked. He sees the transitory nature of their prosperity and success. Death suddenly sweeps it away (v. 19; Job 18:14 calls death 'the king of terrors').

vv. 21–26

Looking back, the psalmist now sees the stupidity of his envy and resentment. The reason for this change is that he realizes that he has the most valuable thing possible for a human being – an intimate, continual relationship with God.

The meaning of v. 24b is a much debated issue. Does the 'afterward' mean 'after these present distresses', or 'at the end of life', or 'after death'? The contrast with the fate of the wicked in v. 20 suggests that the second or third of these possibilities is more likely. What then does, 'you will receive me with honour [or "glory"]' mean? Some take it to mean that his life will come to an honourable end. Others argue that he is indeed looking beyond death, sure that in some, unspecified way, his relationship with God will survive it and will continue. Two things are suggested in support of this. The first is that the verb translated as 'receive' is, as in Psalm 49:15, the one used of God 'taking' Enoch and Elijah to be with him. Second, v. 26 seems to lend support to this since it seems to say that his relationship with God will survive the demise of his body. The description of God as 'my portion' is interesting. It refers to the apportioning of the Promised Land among the tribes by lot. The Levites were not given a portion of land as their source of economic support. Their 'portion' was Yahweh (Deut. 10:9). By using this term the psalmist is expressing his special relationship with Yahweh and his total dependence on him.

vv. 27–28

The psalmist now sums up what he has learnt by contrasting the true state of the wicked, as he now sees it, with his own state. He has learnt that nothing is better or more valuable than to be 'near God'.

The recent trend to read the Psalter as a coherent book, and not just a loose anthology of poems, highlights the importance of this psalm. It is almost at the centre of the Psalter's 150 psalms, and stands at the beginning of Book 3. The significance of the second point is that most of the Laments in the Psalter come in Books 1 and 2. The 'tone' of the Psalter changes after Psalm 73, moving more towards thanksgiving and praise. This psalm gives a theological motive for this change – a recognition of the inestimable value of an intimate and continual relationship with God. The psalm shows that this recognition is no shallow optimism, but is hard-won in the face of the inequities and complexities of life.

PSALM 84

This is a Song of Zion. These Songs do not have any common form. Although this one is predominantly an expression of joy and praise, there is an element of lament (v. 2) and a prayer for the king (vv. 8–9). It has no consistent metre. One way of structuring it is as follows:

vv. 1–4   The psalmist's longing to be in the temple.

vv. 5–7   The happiness of the pilgrims to Zion.

vv. 8–9   A prayer for the king.

vv. 10–12 The blessedness of being with God.

vv. 1–4

The psalmist is clearly among those Israelites who lived at a distance from the temple and normally only visited it at one of the pilgrimage festivals. He expresses his longing to be there, and contemplates the happy state of those who 'live in your house', namely the priests and Levites.

vv. 5–7

These verses give a picture of the joy of the pilgrims as they travel towards the temple. The Hebrew of v. 5b does not have the word 'Zion', saying simply, 'in whose heart are the highways'. This probably means, 'whose heart is set on pilgrimage'. The meaning of v. 6 is unclear. The 'valley of Baca' is not mentioned anywhere else in the Hebrew Bible. One explanation of this verse is that the reference is to an arid place that was transformed by the autumn rains. These may have begun to fall at about the time of the pilgrimage to the Feast of Booths. The beginning of the rains, seen as a sign of blessing from God, encourages the pilgrims on their journey as they draw nearer to Zion.

vv. 8–9

Some commentators find the presence of this prayer odd. However, there is some rationale for it. The pilgrims are heading for Zion, the seat of the Davidic king as well as the home of the temple. Indeed, the temple was a royal sanctuary, built and maintained by the kings of Judah. Second, as Psalm 72 expresses very clearly, the well-being of the people was seen as tied up with that of the king.

vv. 10–12

Although the more thoughtful Israelites realized that Yahweh was not 'confined' to the temple in any way (1 Kgs 8:27), nevertheless the temple was the place where they expected to encounter him in a special way. Therefore the temple was a source of blessing. The psalmist expresses his wish that he could remain there

enjoying that blessing. However, the psalm ends with a declaration that God's blessing is not limited by geography; it is given to all those, everywhere, who 'walk uprightly' (i.e. in obedience and faithfulness to God) and trust in God.

PSALM 96

This is one of the group of psalms that celebrate Yahweh's kingship (Pss 47; 93; 96—99). They are united by their common theme and do not have a common form. All except Psalm 98 contain the phrase, 'Yahweh/God is king!' Psalms 97 and 99 have the threefold structure of the hymnic General Praises. The others vary in form. Psalm 96 has a shortened version of the General Praise form (no concluding call to praise), repeated.

vv. 1–3   Call to praise the Lord.

vv. 4–6   Main section: reasons to praise the Lord.

vv. 7–9   Call to praise the Lord.

vv. 10–13 Main section: reasons to praise.

The metre of the psalm is irregular.

vv. 1–3

In vv. 1–2 there is a type of parallelism that is sometimes called 'staircase parallelism'. Each line begins with the same phrase, but the second half changes, moving the thought forward. Here, as in Psalm 33, the reference to a 'new song' may be a way of expressing the idea that God's goodness always calls for new, fresh expressions of praise. In v. 3 the Israelites are called upon to share their knowledge and experience of Yahweh with all nations.

vv. 4–6

This section asserts the kingship of Yahweh over all creation. 'Honour and majesty' (v. 6a) is a pair of words that is used to describe royal dignity (e.g. Ps. 21:5). The statement that Yahweh 'is to be revered above all gods' (v. 4) no doubt had its origins at the time when the Israelites did not deny the existence of other gods but simply worshipped Yahweh alone. It seems to have become a traditional liturgical statement of praise. Certainly here v. 5 implies that all other claimed gods are simply human creations. By contrast, Yahweh is the Creator.

vv. 7–9

Once again there is 'staircase parallelism' in vv. 7–8. The 'offering' may refer to the tribute that subjects would bring to their ruler. The worship of v. 9 can also be seen as the homage rendered to a king. As in v. 3 there is a universal note here. All the earth, not just Israel, should do homage to Yahweh.

vv. 10–13

The universal note continues. Someone (presumably Israel) is to proclaim to all the nations that 'Yahweh is king!'

The phrase translated as, 'The LORD is king!' in the NRSV has been the centre of much debate. Mowinckel suggested that it should be translated, 'Yahweh has become king.' He believed that the psalms with this phrase were used in the Autumn Festival, in which Yahweh was annually ritually 'enthroned'. The psalms celebrated that ritual event. Against this translation it has been pointed out that in 2 Samuel 15:10 and 2 Kings 9:13, where the context does seem to require the translation 'Absalom/Jehu *has become* king', the name of the ruler comes after the verb in Hebrew. In the psalms the name comes before the verb. It is therefore argued that the emphasis in the psalms is different – expressing the ongoing reign of Yahweh: he *is* king. Since this argument rests on only two examples, it has to be treated with caution. However, Mowinckel's translation rests on a hypothetical ritual act. Few scholars adopt it nowadays.

In the ancient Near East the king was also the supreme judge of his nation. This section of the psalm asserts that Yahweh is the supreme judge of the earth, and calls upon all people, all sea creatures, all land creatures and all the trees to rejoice in this fact. The reason they should rejoice is that he judges with 'equity' (v. 10c, 'fairness'), 'righteousness' and 'truth' (v. 13b).

The statement that he is 'coming' to judge can be taken in three possible ways.

- It could refer to his ongoing acts of judgement in history.
- It could be looking forward to a final judgement at the end of history.

COMPARING PSALMS 96, 97, 98 AND 99

Psalm 96	Psalm 97	Psalm 98	Psalm 99
A new song All the earth called to praise Yahweh Yahweh's coming to judge the world	The Lord is king Thanksgiving to Yahweh Zion His holy name	A new song The sea and the world called to praise Yahweh Yahweh's coming to judge the world	The Lord is king Exaltation of Yahweh Zion His holy mountain

- It could refer to his coming experienced in the context of worship.

These may not have been mutually exclusive meanings in the context of Israel's faith.

Psalms 96—99 seem to form a coherent group of two pairs. Psalms 96 and 98 both begin with the phrase, 'O sing to the LORD a new song.' Psalms 97 and 99 both begin with the phrase, 'The LORD is king.' They both have the form of a General Praise. There are also other similarities, which are set out in the table 'Comparing Psalms 96, 97, 98 and 99' on p. 48.

PSALM 101

Luther called this psalm, 'David's mirror of a monarch'. There is a general consensus that it is a Royal Psalm, even though there is no explicit reference to the king. The actions the psalmist pledges to carry out in vv. 5–8 make sense only if he is the king. In particular, v. 8 refers to the execution of justice in Jerusalem ('the city of the LORD'). The psalm is generally taken to be a vow concerning the nature of his rule made by the king at his coronation. It may have been repeated each year at the anniversary of his coronation. The psalm falls into two parts: vv. 1–4 are about the character of the king and vv. 5–8 about the character of his rule. The metre is almost uniformly 3:2.

vv. 1–2a

It is probably Yahweh's 'loyalty and justice' of which the king says he will sing, not his own. He is saying that he will praise Yahweh because of his moral attributes. The translation of v. 2a is problematic. The NRSV understands it as the king's response to Yahweh's character. He will seek to emulate it. This requires an emendation of the text in the second line of v. 2a. The Hebrew has, 'When will you come to me?' A few scholars argue that the verb in the first line translated 'I will study' can be taken to mean 'I will compose a song about'. They then take this line as a continuation of praise of Yahweh's character. This would lead fairly naturally to the question, 'When will you come to me?' But what then does the question mean? Some take it as a prayer for Yahweh to be with him as he rules. A few take it as a plea for deliverance, and then take the psalm to be a kind of lament. The king is in distress and cries out for Yahweh's intervention on the basis of Yahweh's own character (vv. 1–2a) and his own innocence (vv. 2b–8). This seems a rather forced interpretation of the psalm.

vv. 2b–4

The basic commitment to integrity in v. 2b is expanded by what is said in vv. 3–4. The word translated 'base' means 'worthless'. In Hebrew idiom the heart is primarily the centre of the reason and will. The commitment in v. 4a is therefore about an attitude of mind, or way of thinking.

v. 5

Sins of speech are among those condemned most frequently in the Hebrew Bible (e.g. in the 'gate liturgies' of Pss 15 and 24). No doubt this is because they are very disruptive of the harmony of a community. Also, honesty in speech is vital for the proper administration of justice; hence the prohibition of 'false witness' in the Ten Commandments.

v. 6

This verse describes the kind of people whom the king will gather around him as courtiers and servants. There are verbal links here with v. 2. As well as the phrase 'the way that is blameless', and the verb 'walk', the Hebrew word translated 'integrity' in v. 2b comes from the same root as the word for 'blameless'.

v. 7
This is an antithesis of v. 6 in its statement of those who will not have a place in the royal court.

v. 8
The reference here is to the administration of justice. This usually took place in the morning, with the king dealing with the more difficult cases (2 Sam. 15:2; Jer. 21:12).

This psalm gives us an insight into the ideal of kingship in ancient Israel. We've seen that Psalm 2 presents the Davidic king as Yahweh's representative on earth. Here we see that the king is expected to reflect Yahweh's moral character in his person and in the way he rules.

PSALM 124
There is some dispute among scholars whether or not there are any genuine Communal Songs of Thanksgiving in the Psalter. This is one psalm that most scholars do put in that category. It has elements that are found in the Individual Thanksgivings: a description of the situation of distress (vv. 2b–5); an account of Yahweh's act of deliverance (vv. 6–7). However, its basic structure is threefold:

vv. 1–5   A reflection on what they have been saved from.
vv. 6–7   Gratitude for their deliverance.
v. 8   An expression of trust in Yahweh.

The metre is irregular. The psalm is notable for its vivid imagery.

vv. 1–2a
The repetition in these lines is clearly intended for the sake of emphasis. There may be an echo here of Jacob's words in Genesis 31:42.

vv. 2b–3
The language used in these verses suggests that the peril that the community had faced was military, but it is too general for it to be possible to relate it to any particular known situation in the history of Israel and Judah.

vv. 4–5
The imagery changes from that of a ravening beast to that of a destructive flood. Behind it is the experience of the flash floods that occur in the wadis after heavy rain. There may also be an allusion to the common ancient Near Eastern imagery of the waters of chaos, which were subdued by the creator god.

vv. 6–7
These verses express gratitude to Yahweh for his deliverance of the people. That deliverance is expressed in terms of a bird being freed from a hunter's snare.

v. 8
The psalm ends with an expression of trust in Yahweh. The phrase 'the name of the LORD' may have its background in the phrase, 'to call on the name of the LORD'. This means to cry out for Yahweh's deliverance (Joel 2:32). Note the link here between the confidence in Yahweh's power to save and the belief in him as Creator.

PSALM 138
Most scholars regard this as an Individual Thanksgiving. A few suggest that, because of the mention of the 'kings of the earth' in

v. 4, the speaker is the king, and so it is really a Communal Thanksgiving. However, this argument has not found general acceptance. Its structure is a variant on the usual form of an Individual Thanksgiving.

vv. 1–2   Introduction. Invocation of Yahweh and expression of thanks.
v. 3   An account of Yahweh's act of deliverance.
vv. 4–6   An exhortation to the kings of the earth to praise Yahweh.
vv. 7–8a   An expression of confidence in Yahweh.
v. 8b   A concluding prayer.

There is no consistent metre.

vv. 1–2

The MT does not have the invocation 'O Lord', but it is found in some Hebrew manuscripts, including one from Qumran (11QPs[a]), and in the oldest translations of the Hebrew Bible. Reference to doing things with 'the whole heart' is particularly common in Deuteronomy, as well as being found in some other psalms (e.g. 111:1; 119:2). Since in Hebrew idiom the 'heart' is primarily the centre of the mind and the will, doing things with 'the whole heart' means doing them with a sincerity of purpose.

The word translated 'gods' in the phrase, 'before the gods I sing your praise' can mean simply 'heavenly beings'. However, in view of the summons to the kings of the earth in v. 4, the psalmist may well have in mind the gods that the other nations worship. He does not debate the reality, or otherwise, of their existence, but simply asserts that by his actions Yahweh has shown that he is supreme over 'everything'.

v. 3

Yahweh's act of deliverance is reported, but no details of it are given.

vv. 4–5

The usual summons to the congregation to praise Yahweh is replaced by a summons to 'all the kings of the earth'. If, as v. 2 may suggest, the psalmist is thinking of Yahweh as the supreme ruler of the earth, this summons to the kings is an appropriate way of calling the whole earth (i.e. the kings and the nations they rule) to praise Yahweh. It does not necessarily imply that the psalmist is speaking as a king to kings.

v. 6

The psalmist makes the point that despite his exalted status, Yahweh is neither too proud nor too distant to help the lowliest of his creatures.

vv. 7–8a

The expression of confidence is more commonly a feature of the Individual Lament, but is found in a few other Thanksgivings (Pss 18:28–29; 118:6–7). It might be an indirect way of referring to the psalmist's previous state of distress, which is a common element in Individual Thanksgivings.

v. 8b

The usual concluding exhortation to praise is replaced by a prayer.

PSALM 150

This is the last of the five 'Hallel Hymns' (Pss 146—150), each of which begins and ends with the cry 'Hallelujah!' ('Praise the Lord!' in the NRSV). This cry is made up of the command *hallelu* ('praise') and the short form of the divine name, *yah*. Psalm 150 has rightly been described by J. L.

Mays as 'the liturgical cry, Hallelujah, turned into an entire psalm'. The usual statement of the reason for giving praise is incorporated into the summons to praise in v. 2. The point of vv. 3–5 is that all types of instrument, and hence instrumentalists, are to play their part in praising Yahweh. The normal identification of those to whom the summons to praise is addressed is delayed until the end (v. 6). With its universal call to praise Yahweh for his 'surpassing greatness', it is a fitting doxology with which to end the Psalter.

The Hallel Hymns bring to a climax the trend in Books 4 and 5 of the growing dominance of psalms of praise. This gives rise to a movement within the Psalter from a dominance of lament and prayer in the first half to a dominance of praise in the last third. Some see this as a consequence of the move from meditation on the historical failure of the Davidic kings to the recognition of Yahweh's kingship and the expectation of the consummation of his universal rule. Others see the movement in terms of a more general spiritual journey, from the simple trust in Yahweh and his sovereignty expressed in Psalms 1—2, through grappling with the vicissitudes of life to a deeper, more mature trust, which is expressed in unfeigned praise.

THEOLOGY IN THE PSALMS

Since the Psalter is a collection of poems coming from a variety of periods in Israel's history, we must be wary of seeking to impose a systematic theology on the book, but rather be prepared to recognize some diversity of outlook in the expressions of faith that are to be found in it. We will not attempt an exhaustive study of the theology expressed in the psalms, but pick out some major themes.

THE UNDERSTANDING OF GOD
Practical monotheism
Psalm 81:9–10 clearly echoes the beginning of the Ten Commandments.

> There shall be no strange god among you;
> you shall not bow down to a foreign god.
> I am the LORD your God,
> who brought you up out of the land of Egypt.

> I am the LORD your God, who brought you out of the land of Egypt, out of the house of slavery; you shall have no other gods before me. (Exod. 20:2–3)

This is a practical monotheism. The existence of other gods is not denied. Whatever reality they may or may not have, the Israelites are to have nothing to do with them. It is the same kind of practical approach to theology that is expressed when the psalmist reports 'fools' as saying, 'There is no God' (Pss 14:1; 53:1). This is not an attribution of philosophical atheism. Rather, as the content of what follows indicates, it is saying that these people live as if God did not exist. Unlike those who 'act wisely', they do not 'seek after God'. As a result they are corrupt. It is against the background of practical monotheism that we can understand statements such as: 'For the LORD is a great God, and a great King above all gods' (Ps. 95:3); and 'The LORD is king! . . . all gods bow down before him' (Ps. 97:1a, 7c). These emphasize Yahweh's incomparability and superiority without denying the existence of other gods. Psalm 82 depicts Yahweh as presiding in the council of the gods and sentencing all the other gods to death for failing to uphold justice. Perhaps this is one way of expressing the move from practical to absolute monotheism! Belief in absolute monotheism, that Yahweh is the only God, is clearly expressed in the attacks on the idols of the nations in Psalms 115:4–7; 135:13–18.

> Our God is in the heavens;
> he does whatever he pleases.
> Their idols are silver and gold,
> the work of human hands.
> They have mouths, but do not speak;
> eyes, but do not see.
> They have ears, but do not hear;
> noses, but do not smell.
> They have hands, but do not feel;
> feet, but do not walk;
> They make no sound in their throats.
>   (Ps. 115:4–7)

Creator

The creation of the world by Yahweh is a repeated theme in the Psalter. It is sometimes expressed by use of the imagery of Yahweh's conflict with the chaos waters or dragon. This is so in some Laments, where it is appealed to as a reminder of Yahweh's past triumphs (e.g. Pss 74:12–17; 89:9–13). In Psalm 74:14 the dragon is named as Leviathan, a name found in the Canaanite texts from Ugarit as that of a creature defeated by Baal. More commonly the psalms speak of Yahweh subduing the sea or waters at creation (e.g. Pss 65:6–7; 93:3–4; 104:5–9). In the Ugaritic texts Baal does battle with Prince Sea, but this is not linked with the creation of the world. In Psalm 33:6–7 the subduing of the waters has lost the idea of a mythic struggle and become simply one of the acts of creation, as in Genesis 1. Psalm 104 extols Yahweh by describing the wonders of his creation. This psalm has a good deal in common with Pharaoh Akhenaten's 'hymn to the sun' and also with Genesis 1. It is particularly in the hymns in the Psalter that Yahweh's creation of the world is alluded to because, as Psalm 19:1 says, 'The heavens are telling the glory of God; and the firmament proclaims his handiwork.' Psalm 8:5–8 expresses the same understanding of God's purpose in creating humans as does Genesis 1:26, and the language is similar.

Think about
BORROWED IMAGERY

The imagery of Yahweh's conflict with the chaos waters or the dragon (sometimes named Leviathan or Rahab) is found in Hebrew poetry outside the psalms: Job 7:12; 26:12–13; Isaiah 27:1; 51:9. This imagery is found in the Babylonian creation story *Enuma Elish*. In this story Marduk, the god of Babylon, has to defeat the powers of chaos (depicted both as the waters of chaos and as sea monsters) before creating the world. As noted in the main text, similar imagery is used of the Canaanite god Baal, though in this case it is not linked with creation, though it may be linked with the cycle of the seasons. The Babylonian and Canaanite traditions pre-date the Hebrew traditions. So, the Hebrew poets have taken imagery from the cultures around them and used it in a polemical way to declare (by implication) that it is Yahweh, not Marduk or Baal, who is the Creator and the one who guarantees its stability. Is there imagery that could be taken from the secular culture of today and used to express beliefs about God?

Lord of history

Yahweh is not only the Lord of nature, he is also Lord of history. His mighty deeds in history are another theme of the Psalter. The most frequently mentioned of these is the exodus, the liberation of the Hebrew slaves from oppression in Egypt in the time of Moses (e.g. Pss 77:11–20; 78:13, 53; 80:8; 81:5; 114:1, 3, 5; 135:8–9; 136:10–15). There is also often mention of the events which followed this, the wilderness wanderings (e.g. Pss 68:7–8; 78:14–31; 81:7; 114:4, 6, 8; 136:16) and the settlement in Canaan (e.g. Pss 78:54–55; 114:2, 5; 135:10–12; 136:17–22). This whole complex of events is the theme of a few psalms, such as Psalms 78, 105, 106 and 136. Even the exile in Babylon is seen as one of Yahweh's deeds, an act of judgement on the nation's sin. It is the background of Psalms 74 and 79, which lament the destruction of the temple, and Psalm 137. The restoration from exile is the theme of Psalm 126.

Descriptions of Yahweh

One of the commonest images used of Yahweh in the psalms is that of king (e.g. Pss 24:7–10; 48:2; 95:3; 96:10; 97:1; 98:6; 99:1). In some cases his kingship is associated with subduing the waters (Pss 29:10; 74:12–15; 93:1–4). There is a parallel to this in the Ugaritic texts where Baal's victory over Prince Sea leads to him being declared king. As king, Yahweh is spoken of as enthroned on the cherubim (Pss 80:1; 99:1). This was represented by the cherubim that were with the Ark of the Covenant in the Holy of Holies of the temple in Jerusalem. In Psalm 132:7 the Ark is called 'his footstool' (see also Ps. 99:5). It contained the tablets with the Law inscribed on them. In the ancient

Near East important documents were sometimes kept in a container under the throne. One of the functions of kings in the ancient Near East was to act as a judge, the final court of appeal. Therefore reference to Yahweh as 'judge' is another way of speaking of his kingship (e.g. Pss 58:11; 94:2; 96:10, 13; 98:9). The same is true of the image of 'shepherd' (e.g. Pss 23:1; 80:1).

Yahweh is given a number of titles in the Psalter. One of these is 'the Most High'. This divine title goes back to pre-Israelite times in Jerusalem (Gen. 14:18–22), so it is not surprising that it occurs in two of the Songs of Zion (Pss 46:4; 87:5) as well as others (Pss 47:2; 50:14; 73:11; 78:17, 35, 56; 82:6; 83:18; 97:9). This title expresses Yahweh's greatness. In the psalms, as elsewhere in the Hebrew Bible, Yahweh is spoken of as a holy God (e.g. Pss 22:3; 99:3, 5, 9). He is sometimes given the title 'the Holy One of Israel' (Pss 71:22; 78:41; 89:18). This title is particularly associated with the book of Isaiah, and it has sometimes been suggested that the prophet Isaiah coined the title. However, the title occurs in Psalm 78. This psalm contains a polemic against the northern kingdom of Israel, yet does not mention its troubled final years and downfall. It seems, therefore, to pre-date that period, and so to have been composed before Isaiah's time. This suggests that both the psalm and Isaiah are reflecting the language of the Jerusalem cult when they speak of 'the Holy One of Israel'.

Yahweh's steadfast love

The nearest thing there is to a 'definition' of Yahweh in the Hebrew Bible is the statement:

But you, O LORD are a God merciful
and gracious,
slow to anger, and abounding in steadfast
love and faithfulness. (Ps. 86:15)

This statement, with some variations, is
found in: Exodus 34:6; Numbers 14:18;
Nehemiah 9:17; Psalm 103:8; Jonah 4:2.
Presumably all these passages reflect a
traditional liturgical form of words that
was used in worship in the Jerusalem
temple. One term in this 'definition',
'steadfast love' (*hesed* in Hebrew) is used
over 100 times of Yahweh in the Psalter.
The English translations of this word vary
considerably: e.g. steadfast love, loving
kindness, loyalty, mercy. It is difficult to
translate because it is so tied up with
Yahweh's covenant relationship with
Israel. The word denotes his attitude of
faithful, loving commitment to them. For
this reason it is both the basis of calls to
praise Yahweh (e.g. Pss 117, 136) and the
ground of appeals to him to deliver his
people (e.g. Pss 36:10; 89:49; 90:14).

> **Digging deeper:**
> **THE ATTRIBUTES OF YAHWEH**
>
> Consult one or two Bible dictionaries (such as
> *NIDOTTE*, the *Anchor Bible Dictionary*) to study
> the other attributes of Yahweh that are
> mentioned in the 'definition' in Psalm 86:15:
> mercy, grace, slowness to anger, faithfulness.

Because of his steadfast love, Yahweh
could be relied on to deliver his people,
both individually and as a nation.
Sometimes this deliverance is expressed by
the verb 'save' (*yasha'* in Hebrew). This is
especially the case in the Laments, when it
is used in the imperative form to appeal to

God (e.g. Pss 7:1, 22:21; 28:9). On other
occasions the verb 'redeem' is used to
describe Yahweh's action. There are two
different Hebrew verbs that can be
translated as 'redeem'. One (*padah*, e.g. Pss
25:22; 26:11; 71:23; 78:42) has its
background in commercial transaction.
The other (*ga'al*, e.g. Pss 74:2; 106:10;
107:2; 119:154) relates to family law, where
the *go'el* ('redeemer') was a relative who
redeemed another family member from
slavery (Lev. 25:47–55), or bought back
family land lost because of debt (Lev.
25:23–34). It therefore has warm personal
connotations, and is also particularly
appropriate in the covenant context.

The presence of Yahweh

Psalm 11:4 expresses a tension that lies at
the heart of the Hebrew understanding of
Yahweh,

> The LORD is in his holy temple;
> the LORD's throne is in heaven.

This is the tension between the
transcendence and immanence of God. It
is expressed even more sharply in
Solomon's prayer at the dedication of the
temple. At the opening of the prayer he
says,

> I have built you an exalted house,
> a place for you to dwell in for ever.
> (1 Kgs 8:13)

Yet later on in the prayer he says, 'But will
God indeed dwell on the earth? Even
heaven and the highest heaven cannot
contain you, much less this house that I
have built!' (1 Kgs 8:27)

From early Israelite times the Ark of the
Covenant (which, as we've noted above,

came to be understood as the footstool of Yahweh's throne) was seen as the symbol, maybe the sacrament, of Yahweh's presence with the people (Num. 10:35–36). The bringing of the Ark to Jerusalem by David (2 Sam. 6) and then the building of the temple by Solomon to house it, resulted in Yahweh's presence becoming associated with Mt Zion. This close association is the basis of the Songs of Zion in the Psalter. Some of the psalms express the experience of a special sense of God's presence in the worship in the temple, which is sometimes expressed in terms of 'seeking' or 'beholding the face of' Yahweh (e.g. Pss 24:6; 27:4; 42:1–2; 84:7).

Yahweh and the nations

Belief in Yahweh as the Creator of the world and the King above all gods (and eventually as the only God) leads naturally to the belief that he is not only God of Israel, but of the whole world. This is expressed in two ways in the psalms. First, there are exhortations to 'all you peoples' (Ps. 47:1), 'all the earth' (Ps. 66:1), the 'kingdoms of the earth' (Ps. 68:32) etc. to praise Yahweh. Second, there are allusions to the time when the other nations will turn to and/or submit to Yahweh (e.g. Pss 22:27–28; 47:9; 65:2; 86:9; 102:15–22).

THE UNDERSTANDING OF HUMANITY

One of the clearest statements in the Hebrew Bible of the dignity and role of humans is Psalm 8:3–8. It has much in common with Genesis 1:26–28. Alongside this there is expression of the transitoriness of human life by the image of the withering of grass or wild flowers (Pss 90:5–6; 102:11; 103:15–16) or the comparison of human life with breath (Pss 39:5; 62:9) or a shadow (Ps. 102:11). As elsewhere in the

Hebrew Bible the weakness of humans in comparison with God can be expressed by referring to them as 'flesh' (Pss 56:4; 78:39).

The Hebrews did not think of the human person as an immaterial soul contained in a material body, but more holistically as an animated body. Although the Hebrew word *nefesh* is often translated 'soul' in English versions of the Bible, it does not mean 'soul' in a dualistic sense. In fact the word has a range of meanings, depending on its context. What may be its earliest meaning, 'neck/throat', is found in Psalm 69:1,

> Save me, O God,
> for the waters have come up to my neck.

Perhaps because one breathes through the neck/throat, *nefesh* can mean 'breath' (Job 41:22), and quite often means 'life', as in Psalm 38:12,

> Those who seek my life lay their snares,
> those who seek to hurt me speak of ruin,
> and meditate treachery all day long.

On many occasions it seems to mean 'living being/person'. When God breathes into a form that he has made out of the 'dust of the earth', what results is not a person with a 'soul' but a 'living *nefesh*', i.e. a 'living person'. In the psalms, phrases such as 'my soul', 'his soul', etc. are often best translated as 'I', 'me', 'myself', etc., as seems appropriate.

> Come and hear, all you who fear God,
> and I will tell what he has done for me
> ['my soul']. (Ps. 66:16)

However, there are times when it refers to the inner seat of feelings and desires.

My soul [*nefesh*] is cast down within me.'
  (Ps. 42:6)

Do not let them say to themselves,
Aha, we have our heart's desire [*nefesh*].'
  (Ps. 35:25)

The psychosomatic unity of the human person in Hebrew thought is evidenced in the way that various parts of the human body are used to refer to aspects of the human personality. A literalistic translation of Psalm 26:2 is, 'Examine me, O Lord, and test me, judge my kidneys and my heart.' The *Good News Bible* translation gives the right sense of the second line when it says, 'judge my desires and thoughts'.

LIFE AFTER DEATH

The realm of the dead is referred to in a variety of ways in the psalms. In Psalm 30 it is referred to twice by words that mean 'pit' (*bor* in v. 3; *shahat* in v. 9) and once by the word Sheol (possibly meaning 'destruction'). Of these terms, Sheol is the most common. It is a place of darkness (Ps. 88:6) and silence (Ps. 115:17) located in 'the depths of the earth' (Pss 63:9; 86:13). In some psalms those in Sheol are said to be cut off from Yahweh (Pss 6:5; 88:10–12), but there is evidence of some development of thought since in Psalm 139:8 the psalmist says, 'If I make my bed in Sheol, you are there.' A careful reading of the psalms makes it clear that in them death and Sheol are not just an event at the end of life and the place where the dead go. They are spoken of as powers that threaten the living. Many of the references to the danger of, or deliverance from, death and Sheol are to situations of distress and suffering of various kinds.

Existence in Sheol hardly qualifies to be described as 'life after death'. However, there are three psalms that many commentators think reflect an emerging belief in a worthwhile afterlife. M. J. Dahood, in his commentary on Psalms, finds many more references to immortality, but his interpretations have failed to convince many other scholars.

In Psalm 16 the psalmist expresses his joyful confidence in Yahweh. His relationship with Yahweh means more to him than anything else. The psalm ends with the words,

> Therefore my heart is glad, and my soul rejoices;
> my body also rests secure.
> For you do not give me up to Sheol,
> or let your faithful one see the Pit.
> You show me the path of life.
> In your presence there is fullness of joy;
> in your right hand are pleasures for evermore. (vv. 9–11)

Scholars are divided over whether these verses are expressing confidence of a secure and happy life, as long as it lasts, or expressing confidence that not even death will end the psalmist's fellowship with Yahweh. Its openness to the second interpretation led the early Christians to apply it to the resurrection of Jesus (Acts 2:25–28; 13:35).

Psalm 49 is a wisdom poem that reflects on the problem of the prosperity of the wicked and the suffering of the righteous. Death is seen as the great leveller (vv. 10–12). The fate of those who disregard God (vv. 13–14) is contrasted with that which the psalmist expects, 'But God will ransom my soul from the power of Sheol, for he will receive me' (v. 15). This might refer simply to deliverance from an untimely death, but coming after vv. 10–14 it seems much more likely that the psalmist is expressing confidence in a worthwhile existence with God after death. It has been pointed out that the verb used here for 'receive' (*laqah*) is used of God 'taking' Enoch (Gen. 5:24) and Elijah being 'taken up' (2 Kgs 2:3, 5). Perhaps the psalmist expected to pass unscathed through death as these two seemingly did.

Psalm 73 is another meditation on the problem of the inequalities of life. While worshipping in the temple the psalmist found the answer to his problem (v. 17). The prosperity of the wicked evaporates in the face of death (vv. 18–20) but his fellowship with God will not (vv. 23–24),

> Nevertheless I am continually with you;
> you hold my right hand.
> You guide me with your counsel,
> and afterwards you will receive me with
> honour.

It is possible that 'afterwards' here means 'after my present troubles', but it seems much more likely that it means 'after death' in view of vv. 18–20. Again, as in Psalm 49, the verb for 'receive' is *laqah*, which might support this interpretation.

If these interpretations are correct, the thread that runs through all these three psalms is the psalmist's sense that his relationship with Yahweh is so real and deep that not even death will be able to end it.

Think about
RESURRECTION

Because of the holistic view of the human person in Hebrew thought, when belief in a meaningful life after death did arise, it was thought of in terms of resurrection of the body rather than the survival of a disembodied soul or spirit. In Ezekiel 37:11–14 the picture of bodily resurrection is used metaphorically of the restoration of the nation from exile. In Isaiah 26:19 it is also probably being used as a metaphor for the restoration of the nation, though some scholars think that here it does refer to the resurrection of individuals. The one place in the Hebrew Bible that does speak of the resurrection of individuals is Daniel 12:1–3. Although there is no explicit mention of the body here, the phrase 'the dust of the earth' in v. 2a clearly harks back to the story of the creation of Adam in Genesis 2:7, implying a kind of 're-creation' of humans in a bodily form. However, for the righteous this is a transformed body (v. 3).

SACRIFICE

Since, as we have seen, most of the psalms were used in worship in the temple in Jerusalem it is not surprising that there are many references to sacrifice in the Psalter. A number of different sacrifices are mentioned.

- The word that is normally translated 'sacrifice' in the psalms (*zevah*, e.g. Pss 4:5; 27:6; 54:6; 116:17) probably refers to the *sh^elamim zevah*, which is variously translated as 'peace/communion/well-being offering'. It seems to have been one of the most common forms of sacrifice in pre-exilic times. The fat of the sacrificed animal was burnt on the altar and the rest of it was cooked and eaten by the worshippers and priests at the sanctuary. The basic idea seems to have been that of communion between the worshippers and God.

- In the case of the 'burnt offering' or 'whole offering' (*'olah*, Pss 20:3; 51:19; 66:13, 15) all of the animal was burnt on the altar, except the hide, which went to the priest. This offering seems to have been regarded as a gift to God.
- The purpose of the 'thank-offering' (*todah*, e.g. Pss 56:12; 107:22; 116:17) is indicated by its name. It was a specific form of the communion offering.
- The 'freewill offering' (*n^edavah*, Ps. 54:6) was also a form of thank-offering.
- The fulfilment of vows (Pss 22:25; 50:14; 56:12; 61:5, 8; 65:1; 66:13; 76:11; 116:14) would usually involve the offering of an animal sacrifice as a thank-offering.
- The Hebrew word *minhah* (Pss 20:3; 96:8) originally meant a sacrificial offering of any kind, but later became restricted to cereal offerings and oil.

Like the rest of the Hebrew Bible, the Psalter assumes the existence of the sacrificial system without providing any theological explanation of the meaning of the sacrifices or how or why they were thought to be effective.

Within the Psalms there are some passages that can be seen as critical of animal sacrifices (Pss 40:6–8; 50:8–15; 51:16–17; 69:30–31; 141:2). These have some similarity to passages in the prophets that are critical of sacrifice (1 Sam. 15:22; Jer. 7:21–23; Hos. 6:6; Amos 5:21–24; Mic. 6:6–8). Although these passages have sometimes been understood as rejecting sacrifice altogether, most scholars regard them as asserting that moral righteousness

and obedience are more important than the ritual of sacrifice, and that without these as their background, sacrifices are worthless. It is also important to bear in mind the tendency in Hebrew to say 'X not Y' when the sense intended is 'X rather than Y'. This is illustrated by the parallel clauses of Hosea 6:6,

> For I desire steadfast love and not sacrifice,
> the knowledge of God rather than burnt offerings.

Here it is clear that 'and not' is parallel to 'rather than' and has the same meaning. So, when the psalmist says, 'Sacrifice and offering you do not desire, but you have given me an open ear' (Ps. 40:6ab), he is probably saying that hearing and obeying God is more important than offering sacrifices. In the oracle in Psalm 50:8–15 God initially expresses acceptance of the people's sacrifices (v. 8) but then goes on to refute any idea that he needs them. This may be a polemic against the view that sacrifice is a way of bribing or manipulating God to do what the offerer wants. Psalm 51:16–17 declares,

> For you have no delight in sacrifice;
> if I were to give a burnt-offering, you would not be pleased.
> The sacrifice acceptable to God is a broken spirit;
> a broken and a contrite heart, O God, you will not despise.

Here the author is probably saying that *in his case* sacrifice is inappropriate because he has committed a grievous sin (possibly murder, v. 14) for which the Law did not provide any sacrifice as a means of atonement. All he could do was throw himself on Yahweh's mercy in abject penitence. Psalm 141:2 may reflect a situation in which the psalmist was unable to offer a sacrifice and so offered what was possible – prayer: 'Let my prayer be counted as incense before you, and the lifting up of my hands as an evening sacrifice.'

The polemic of the prophets against a merely ritualistic view of sacrifice, which separated it from the need to live in obedience to Yahweh's moral laws, highlights a real danger attached to the sacrificial cult. However, these 'critical' passages in the psalms show that within the cultic establishment itself there was an awareness of this danger. This is underlined by the two 'gate liturgies' in Psalms 15 and 24. They remind the worshippers that the prerequisite for acceptable sacrificial worship in the temple is a life lived in obedience to Yahweh's moral demands.

> **Think about**
> **SACRIFICE AND OBEDIENCE**
>
> What would be a modern equivalent of the danger of 'a merely ritualistic view of sacrifice, which separated it from the need to live in obedience to Yahweh's moral laws'? Can you think of some modern version of the Hebrew 'gate liturgies' that might be used to counter this danger?

IMPRECATIONS IN THE PSALMS

For many modern readers one of the disturbing features of the psalms is the way in which a psalm can move from the sublime to the vengeful. Psalm 139 is a classic example of this. After a moving meditation on Yahweh as his omniscient (vv. 1–6) and omnipresent (vv. 7–12) Creator (vv. 13–18) the psalmist bursts out, 'O that you would kill the wicked, O God, and that the bloodthirsty would depart from me' (v. 19). He goes on to express his hatred for 'those who hate you, O LORD' (v. 21). Similar sentiments are expressed in: Psalms 58:6–11; 69:22–28; 83:9–18; 109:6–20; 137:7–9; 149:5–9. Christians tend to feel uncomfortable with these passages because they seem incompatible with Jesus' teaching about loving one's enemies (Matt. 5:43–48; Luke 6:27–31). In the eighteenth century, John Wesley forbade his followers to sing the imprecatory passages in the psalms. Modern versions of the psalms intended for use in Christian worship often omit these passages.

In the face of this modern discomfort with the imprecations, some scholars have argued for their theological importance. Erich Zenger is an example. He argues that Christians cannot simply dismiss these passages as 'sub-Christian'. The fact is that they express a truth about God that is affirmed in both the Old and New Testaments. God has not only created the world, he is also the Lord of its history and will have the final word about its history as its Judge. In a world marred by sin and evil, God's coming in judgement is a source of hope, not fear, because this coming will be in order to establish justice, to make everything 'as it should be'. The imprecations in the psalms are the expressions of someone who is suffering from oppression and longs passionately for justice to be done by God. No doubt the lack of any concept of a worthwhile afterlife adds urgency to the psalmists' pleas for action by God *now*, in this life. Zenger argues that the concentration of modern Western theology on personal sin, and a consequent tendency to ignore issues of social injustice and the suffering it brings (issues of which the Hebrew prophets were very aware) is part of the reason why Western Christians find the imprecations uncomfortable reading. One of the values the imprecations have today is that they expose the reality of violence and oppression in human experience. They both give the victims a means of expressing their suffering and challenge those who are comfortable to identify with the victims.

Zenger emphasizes that these are poetic prayers and as a result use strong, even stark, images that would not be appropriate in prose. He also stresses that it is theologically important to recognize that the psalmists are appealing to a God whom they regard as personal and just. They are not calling for vengeance to fall in an automatic way. They express their deepest feelings of hatred and aggression and then leave everything in God's hands. It is notable that Psalm 139 ends with the psalmist asking God to examine him and his thoughts and to remove what is evil in him (vv. 23–24) – at least being open to the possibility that this might include his own feelings of hatred. Zenger suggests that to lose this kind of praying, in which we may say literally anything to God, is to lose something valuable. On the other hand, he accepts that in a liturgical context these kinds of passages need to be balanced with other biblical texts that speak of non-violence as the way to overcome evil, and that present the vision of an end to all violence in the coming of the kingdom of God.

Think about
IMPRECATIONS IN THE PSALMS

What do you think about Zenger's 'defence' of the use of the imprecations in the psalms in public worship today?

The imprecations are usually found in Laments (Ps. 139 may be an exception, it is hard to classify). Some modern scholars, most notably Claus Westermann and Walter Brueggemann, have drawn attention to the pastoral importance of the Laments, which make up about one-third of the Psalter. They point out that the use of Laments in worship prevents worship becoming purely 'upbeat' and triumphalistic in a way that detaches it from the reality of many people's lives, with their struggles and sufferings. Seen as human words that may be expressed to God in the context of worship, rather than as an immediate verbal communication from God, the Laments give those who are suffering both the 'permission' and the vehicle to express their raw feelings to God as they call for justice to be done by God.

THE UNDERSTANDING OF KINGSHIP
The psalms are our main source for understanding the ideology of kingship in Judah, centred on the house of David. As we have seen, there is some debate over which psalms should be classified as 'Royal Psalms'. However, if we start with the core of undisputed Royal Psalms and also consider those that explicitly mention the

king (even if he is not the speaker) we have a firm base for exploring the ideology of kingship in Judah.

A major reason why the rule of King David and his descendants persisted in Jerusalem throughout the existence of Judah as an independent state was the belief that David and his heirs were chosen by Yahweh to rule his people. This was expressed in Yahweh's covenant with David (2 Sam. 7:1–17). Psalms 89:28–37 and 132:11–12 refer to this covenant explicitly, and it is alluded to in Psalm 18:50. There is a difference of emphasis between Psalm 89 and Psalm 132. Psalm 89:30–37 speaks of Yahweh punishing kings who forsake his Law, but says that David's line will continue for ever. Psalm 132:11–12 seems to make continuance of the line dependent on the kings keeping the Law. In Psalm 132 the choice of David is linked with the choice of Zion as Yahweh's 'resting place'. This is clearly a reference to the bringing of the Ark of the Covenant to Jerusalem.

Perhaps the most important point theologically about the ideology of kingship in the psalms is that Davidic rule is understood as exercised within the overall rule of Yahweh. The Davidic king is considered to serve Yahweh, representing his rule on earth. Yahweh is, and always remains, the active King of all, not least of Judah. Davidic rule is his instrument. This point of view dominates the coronation psalms (Pss 2; 110). Psalm 89:18 says, 'For our shield belongs to the LORD, our king to the Holy One of Israel.' In Psalm 59:13 the speaker, who may be the king, calls on Yahweh to overcome his enemies because, 'Then it will be known to the ends of the earth, that God rules over

Jacob.' It is notable that in the Royal Psalms the people are not referred to as belonging to the king ('my people' or 'his people') but as 'your [Yahweh's] people' (Ps. 72:2).

An immediate consequence of the fact that the Davidic king rules as Yahweh's representative is that he is to promulgate and uphold the laws of Yahweh, which he himself is bound to keep (Pss 89:30–32; 132:11–12). When the people pray for the king they ask that he will be given God's justice and righteousness so as to rule rightly (Ps. 72:1–2). Psalm 101 is probably a form of 'coronation oath' in which the king declares his intent to live a life of integrity before God and to rule justly. In Psalm 18:22 he recognizes that his deliverance by God is a reward for keeping God's ordinances and statutes.

Because he is the representative of God's rule on earth, the king is assailed by the evil-doers who oppose God. This is probably how we should understand the 'enemies' in Psalms 2 and 110. Of course it would be tempting to equate all the enemies of the king with the enemies of God. On the whole the Royal Psalms avoid this by stressing that it is when the king is trusting in God that his enemies will be overcome (Ps. 21:7–12). He cannot count on automatic divine help in battle.

Psalm 72 clearly links the divine blessing the king enjoys with the welfare of the people he rules. He is the mediator of divine blessing to them. The nation prays for him because its well-being depends on him and his relationship with Yahweh.

In Psalm 110:4 the king is called 'a priest for ever according to the order of Melchizedek'. This was probably a purely titular office inherited from the previous Jebusite kings of Jerusalem (see Gen. 14:18–20).

There is no mention of the Spirit of God in relation to the king in the psalms, but he is referred to several times as the anointed one (Pss 2:2; 18:50; 20:6; 28:8; 89:20). It is very likely that was understood as a sign of endowment with the Spirit of Yahweh.

The Royal Psalms clearly present the king as having a unique relationship with Yahweh. This is expressed in three ways. First, he is called Yahweh's 'servant' (Pss 89:3, 20, 39, 50; 132:10; 144:10 and the heading of Ps. 18). This, of course, indicates his subordination to Yahweh, but to be a servant of a great person is an honour, how much more to be the one who rules as the servant of Yahweh!

Second, he is called Yahweh's 'son'. Here Psalm 2:7 is central. The formula used, 'You are my son; today I have begotten you', is an adoption formula. On the day of his coronation the king becomes Yahweh's adopted son. In Psalm 89:27 the king is described as Yahweh's 'firstborn'. The description of Israel as Yahweh's 'firstborn son' in Exodus 4:22 shows that this way of describing the king does not necessarily imply deification or some kind of quasi-physical relationship. It means that the king entered into a relationship of unique intimacy and privilege, which is what gave him the right to rule in Yahweh's name over Yahweh's people. Some scholars have seen in Psalm 110:3b a reference to Canaanite mythical ideas of the king as the son of the goddess Dawn. Even if this is

granted, it does not follow that the psalmist uses the imagery as anything more than metaphorical language. However, it is more likely that the whole verse refers not to the king but to his subjects (as in the NRSV), and v. 3b to the vigour and vitality of the young men among them.

> Your people will offer themselves
>   willingly,
> on the day you lead your forces
> on the holy mountains.
> From the womb of the morning,
> like dew, your youth will come to you.
>   (Ps. 110:3)

It is possible that in Psalm 45:6 the king is referred to as 'God'. However, there are several possible ways of construing this verse.

- 'Your throne, O God, endures for ever and ever' (NRSV text). In this case the king is addressed as 'god'. However, since he is not referred to as divine elsewhere in the psalms, or the rest of the Hebrew Bible, this must be taken as hyperbole, extreme court rhetoric (cf. v. 2a, it is, after all, a wedding psalm!). All it means is the flattering statement that the king is 'godlike' in his regal majesty.
- 'Your throne is a throne of God, it endures for ever and ever' (NRSV margin). This makes good sense. In 1 Chronicles 29:23 Solomon is said to have 'sat on the throne of the LORD'. This is another way of expressing what is said in Psalm 110:1, that the Davidic king sits at Yahweh's right hand.
- 'Your divine throne endures for ever and ever'. This means much the same as the previous translation.

● 'Your throne is like that of God, it endures for ever and ever'. This translation sees here a Hebrew idiom such as is used in Song of Songs 1:15, 'Your eyes are [like those of] doves'. If this is so, the stress is on the promise of enduring Davidic rule in Jerusalem.

The messianic hope

The ideology of kingship represented in the psalms was the origin of Jewish, and then Christian, messianism. As king after king failed to live up to the glowing picture and high ideals of this ideology, the hope grew that one day a king would come who would live up to them. The downfall of Judah could have brought these hopes to an end but, encouraged by some of the pronouncements of the prophets (e.g. Jer. 23:5–6; Ezek. 34:23–24), they became stronger and, for some in Judaism at least, contributed to keeping the Jewish faith alive through times of trouble.

> **Think about**
> **THE MESSIANIC HOPE**
>
> Compare what is said about the king in the Royal Psalms and in two other passages which contributed to the 'messianic hope': Isaiah 9:2–7; 11:1–5.

About one-third of the quotations from the Old Testament in the New Testament are from the Psalter. Particularly important among these are quotations from Psalms 2:7; 110:1, 4; which are given a messianic sense and applied to Jesus. Although not classified as a Royal Psalm, Psalm 118:22–23 was interpreted in a messianic way by some Jews:

The stone that the builders rejected has become the chief cornerstone. This is the LORD's doing; it is marvellous in our eyes.

In the New Testament these words are quoted on a number of occasions and applied to Jesus' rejection and vindication (Matt. 21:42; Mark 12:10–11; Luke 20:17; Acts 4:11–12; 1 Pet. 2:7). The messianic overtones are clear in the quotation from Psalm 118:25–26 at the time of Jesus' entry into Jerusalem on an ass (Matt. 21:9; Mark 11:9–10; Luke 19:38; John 12:13).

FURTHER READING

Items marked * are considered first ports of call, while others are more complex or relate to specific issues.

COMMENTARIES

Anderson's commentary is a good 'first port of call' because it strikes a good balance between brevity and detail. It is also well-balanced in its discussion of problems of interpretation. Kidner's commentary suffers from its brevity, but is still valuable for its theological insights. Weiser's commentary is also often theologically insightful. It is marked by a tendency to attribute as many psalms as possible to a Covenant Renewal Festival. Dahood's commentary needs to be used with care because of his proneness to rewrite the Hebrew text in the light of supposed Ugaritic parallels. Craigie was also a Ugaritic specialist, but used his knowledge more judiciously. His commentary, and the other two in the WBC series, are good scholarly works. Kraus' commentary is very technical. Mays concentrates on the literary features and theological message of the psalms. He also reflects the recent interest in the structure of the Psalter as a book. Like the other volumes in the DSB, Knight's has a Christian devotional emphasis.

L. C. Allen *Psalms 101–150*. WBC. Waco, TX: Word Books, 1983.

* A. A. Anderson *Psalms*. NCB. London: Oliphants, 1972; 2 vols.

P. C. Craigie *Psalms 1–50*. WBC. Waco, TX: Word Books, 1983.

M. J. Dahood *Psalms*. AB. Garden City, NY: Doubleday, 1965, 1968, 1970; 3 vols.

* D. Kidner *Psalms*. TOTC. London: IVP, 1973, 1975; 2 vols.

G. A. F. Knight *Psalms*. DSB. Edinburgh: St Andrews, 1982; 2 vols.

H.-J. Kraus *Psalms*. Minneapolis, MN: Augsburg, 1988/1989; 2 vols.

* J. L. Mays *Psalms*. Interpretation. Louisville, KY: John Knox, 1994.

M. E. Tate *Psalms 51–100*. WBC. Waco, TX: Word Books, 1990.

A. Weiser *The Psalms*. OTL. London: SCM, 1962.

OTHER BOOKS AND ARTICLES

* P. R. Ackroyd *Doors of Perception: A Guide to Reading the Psalms*. London: SCM, 1978.

* B. W. Anderson with S. Bishop *Out of the Depths: The Psalms Speak for Us Today*. Louisville, KY: Westminster John Knox Press, 2000 (3rd edn).

W. Brueggemann *The Message of the Psalms: A Theological Commentary*. Minneapolis, MN: Augsburg, 1984.

W. Brueggemann 'The Costly Loss of Lament', *JSOT* 36 (1986), 61–65.

W. Brueggemann 'Bounded by Obedience and Praise: The Psalms as Canon', *JSOT* 50 (1991), 63–92.

W. Brueggemann *The Psalms and the Life of Faith*, ed. P. D. Miller. Minneapolis, MN: Fortress, 1995.

B. S. Childs *An Introduction to the Old Testament as Scripture*, Philadelphia: Fortress, 1979.

D. J. A. Clines 'New Year' in *The Interpreter's Dictionary of the Bible, Supplementary Volume*. Nashville, TN: Abingdon, 1976, 627–628.

F. Colquhoun *Hymns that Live*. London: Hodder & Stoughton, 1980.

* J. L. Crenshaw *The Psalms: An Introduction*. Grand Rapids, MI: Eerdmans, 2001.

* J. Day *Psalms*. OT Guides. Sheffield: JSOT Press, 1992.

* N. L. DeClaissé-Walford *Reading from the Beginning: The Shaping of the Hebrew Psalter*. Macon, GA: Mercer University, 1997.

E. S. Gerstenberger *Psalms*. FOTL 14, Part 1. Grand Rapids, MI: Eerdmans, 1988.

E. S. Gerstenberger *Psalms with Lamentations*. FOTL 14, Part 2. Grand Rapids, MI: Eerdmans, 2001.

* S. E. Gillingham *The Poems and Psalms of the Hebrew Bible*. Oxford: OUP, 1994.

M. D. Goulder *The Psalms of the Sons of Korah*. JSOTSup 20. Sheffield: JSOT, 1982.

M. D. Goulder *The Prayers of David (Psalms 51–72)*. JSOTSup 102. Sheffield: JSOT, 1990.

M. D. Goulder *The Psalms of Asaph and the Pentateuch*. JSOTSup 233. Sheffield: Sheffield Academic Press, 1996.

M. D. Goulder *The Psalms of the Return*. JSOTSup 258. Sheffield: Sheffield Academic Press, 1998.

H. Gunkel and J. Begrich *An Introduction to the Psalms*. Macon, GA: Mercer University Press, 1998 (original German edn, 1933).

W. L. Holladay *The Psalms through Three Thousand Years: Prayerbook of a Cloud of Witnesses*. Minneapolis, MN: Fortress, 1993.

D. M. Howard, Jr *The Structure of Psalms 93–100*. Winona Lake, IN: Eisenbrauns, 1997.

H.-J. Kraus *Worship in Israel*. Oxford: Blackwell, 1966.

* J. C. McCann *A Theological Introduction to the Book of Psalms*. Nashville, TN: Abingdon Press, 1993.

J. C. McCann (ed.) *The Shape and Shaping of the Psalter*. JSOTSup 159. Sheffield: JSOT Press, 1993.

J. M. Miller 'The Korahites of Southern Judah', *CBQ* 32 (1970), 58–68.

D. C. Mitchell *The Message of the Psalter: An Eschatological Programme in the Book of Psalms*. JSOTSup 159. Sheffield: Sheffield Academic Press, 1997.

S. Mowinckel *The Psalms in Israel's Worship*. Oxford: Blackwell, 1962; 2 vols.

E. Routley *An English-Speaking Hymnal Guide*. Collegeville, MN: Liturgical Press, 1979.

* K. Seybold *Introducing the Psalms*. Edinburgh: T. & T. Clark, 1990.

C. Westermann 'The Role of the Lament in the Theology of the Old Testament', *Interpretation* 28 (1974), 20–38.

C. Westermann *Praise and Lament in the Psalms*. Edinburgh: T. & T. Clark, 1981.

N. Whybray *Reading the Psalms as a Book*. JSOTSup 222. Sheffield: Sheffield Academic Press, 1996.

G. H. Wilson *The Editing of the Hebrew Psalter*, SBLDS 76, Chico, CA: Scholars Press, 1985.

G. H. Wilson 'The Qumran Psalms Scroll (11Qps[a]) and the Canonical Psalter', *CBQ* 59 (1977), 448–464.

E. Zenger *A God of Vengeance?*. Louisville, KY: Westminster John Knox Press, 1996.

Chapter 2

HEBREW POETRY

What is poetry? Most people think that they can tell the difference between poetry and prose. It may therefore seem surprising that there is disagreement over what constitutes poetry in the Hebrew Bible. To see that this is the case it is necessary only to compare different modern English translations of the Bible in editions that set out what the translators regard as poetry differently from prose. They will be found to differ in various places in the books of the Hebrew prophets. Moreover, behind this disagreement is the fact that the Hebrew text itself does not set these passages out as poetry in the way we find it set out in other books, such as the Psalms and Job. So how are we to recognize Hebrew poetry? We will survey the main issues that have featured in recent discussion before drawing some conclusions.

PARALLELISM

Much modern discussion of Hebrew poetry has built on the work of Robert Lowth in the mid-eighteenth century. He argued that the essential feature of Hebrew poetry is what he called 'parallelism'. By

this he meant the occurrence of pairs of lines in which the words or phrases in one line correspond in some way to those in the other. He identified three main types of parallelism.

- *Synonymous parallelism*. This is when the same idea that is expressed in the first line is repeated in the second, but in a different way. For example, in Psalm 33:10–11 there are two pairs of lines, each pair demonstrating synonymous parallelism:

    The LORD brings the counsel of the
       nations to nothing;
    he frustrates the plans of the peoples.
    The counsel of the LORD stands for
       ever,
    the thoughts of his heart to all
       generations.

- *Antithetic parallelism*. In this case what is said in the second line contrasts what is said in the first line in some way. For example, in Psalm 30:5 there is a pair of such contrasting lines:

    For his anger is but for a moment;
    his favour is for a lifetime.

Weeping may linger for the night,
but joy comes with the morning.

- *Synthetic parallelism*. Under this category Lowth included all those pairs of lines in which the second line did not either repeat or contrast the first. He divided it into several subcategories.

Many scholars have accepted Lowth's basic position, but the 'catch-all' category of synthetic parallelism is obviously unsatisfactory. T. H. Robinson tried to sharpen it up by suggesting that the second line must, in some way, satisfy the 'expectation' raised by the first.

Think about PARALLELISM

Read through Psalms 6, 12 and 30 and assign each pair of lines to one of Lowth's three types of parallelism. Take note of the relative frequency of the different types.

The most thorough critique of parallelism as *the* characteristic of Hebrew poetry has been expressed by James Kugel. He argues that the attempt to classify all poetic lines into just three types does not really work. Psalms 23 and 122 are examples of psalms in which nearly the whole poem consists, in Lowth's terms, of synthetic parallelism, but in which there is no clear consistency in the kind of relationship between the lines in each pair. Kugel puts forward the very broad definition of parallelism as a rhetorical device in which two lines state that 'A is so, and what's more B'. He describes B as 'seconding' the thought of A in some way. Partly because of what he

sees as the broad character of parallelism, Kugel denies that there is any sharp poetry/prose distinction to be made in Hebrew, and prefers to speak of 'elevated prose' rather than poetry.

Many scholars have accepted that Kugel has made a good case against seeing parallelism, as defined by Lowth, as *the* criterion of Hebrew poetry. They also accept that he has shown that the poetry/ prose distinction is not a sharp one. However, few accept the conclusion that therefore it is not possible to recognize a form of Hebrew literature that can be classified as 'poetry' rather than 'prose'. What has become clear is that it is necessary to look for a variety of characteristics rather than a single defining feature. In particular, it has been pointed out that one weakness in the approach of Lowth and those who followed him was a concentration simply on the semantic aspect of poetry, the meaning of the lines. This has been expressed in terms of Hebrew poetry depending primarily on 'thought patterns'. There is some truth in this, as indicated by Lowth's classes of synonymous and antithetical parallelism, but it is not the whole story.

LINGUISTIC APPROACHES

Since the late 1970s a number of scholars have used linguistic methods in the attempt to understand the workings of Hebrew poetry. Michael O'Connor has tried to describe Hebrew poetry strictly in terms of the way in which sentences are structured as far as their grammar is concerned. The study of the grammatical structure of sentences is called 'syntax'. O'Connor argues that Hebrew poetry can

Digging deeper:
O'CONNOR'S 'CONSTRAINTS'

In order to understand O'Connor's 'constraints', or rules, for the syntactical structure of Hebrew verse it is necessary to understand his terminology. He uses three terms to refer to various constituents of a *line* (the basic unit of poetry in his view).

- *Unit*. Most words count as individual *units*. However, in Hebrew there are some words called 'particles' (these often depend on other words), which O'Connor does not count as units.
- *Constituent*. This is a word or phrase that has a specific grammatical function in a line. For example, the first line of Psalm 106:7 can be divided into four constituents (each is indicated by the words joined by hyphens):

> Our-ancestors, when-they-were-in-Egypt, did-not-consider your-wonderful-works

The first constituent is the grammatical 'subject' of the line, the third is the action carried out by the subject, and the fourth is the grammatical 'object' of the line. The second is a phrase that defines when the action of the verb took place. The next line has only two constituents:

> they-did-not-remember the-abundance-of-your-steadfast-love

The first is the action (there is no separate word for 'they' in the Hebrew, it is expressed in the form of the verb) and the second the grammatical 'object' of the action.

- *Clause predicators*. The most common of these is a verb. In the examples already given from Psalm 106:7, the clause predicators in the two lines are the verbs 'consider' and 'remember'.

O'Connor's first four 'constraints' are fairly straightforward, the other two are more complex.

1. A line contains from zero to no more than three clause predicators. It is the absence of a clause predicator in the second line of a pair that produces 'gapping'.
2. A line contains at least one and no more than four constituents.
3. A line contains at least two, and no more than five, units.
4. A constituent may contain no more than four units.
5. If a line contains three clause predicators it cannot contain a dependent noun or noun phrase, and if it contains two clause predicators only one of them may have a dependent noun or noun phrase.
6. If a line contains one or more clause predicators it cannot contain a noun or noun phrase that is not dependent on one of them.

For a more detailed, but still fairly accessible, account of O'Connor's work see W. L. Holladay's article, 'Hebrew Verse Structure Revisited (I): Which Words "Count"?' (1999).

be defined in terms of 'syntactical patterns', the various ways in which sentences are structured. He argues that it is the existence of limitations of the kinds of patterns that occur, what he calls 'syntactical constriction', that is the fundamental feature of Hebrew poetry which distinguishes it from Hebrew prose.

O'Connor takes the basic unit of Hebrew poetry to be what he calls the 'line'. Most Hebrew poetry consists of pairs of lines. It is this feature that Lowth recognized and which led to his analysis of Hebrew poetry in terms of parallelism. Other scholars use the term 'colon' for what O'Connor calls a 'line', and then refer to a pair of lines as a 'bicolon' (of which the plural is 'bicola'). On the basis of his analysis of various pieces of Hebrew poetry, O'Connor identified six 'constraints' or rules, which limit the structure of poetic lines. These have to be stated in rather technical grammatical language, and to appreciate them fully it is necessary to have a reasonable knowledge of Hebrew. The 'Digging deeper' box gives a very simplified account of O'Connor's rules.

O'Connor also identifies some patterns in the way in which the lines of Hebrew poetry are interrelated. Probably the most significant of these is 'gapping', or the ellipsis (omission) of words. A common example of this is when the second line of a verse omits the verb used in the first line, although it is clearly required by the sense, e.g.

> May the Lord cut off all flattering lips,
> the tongue that makes great boasts.
> (Ps. 12:3)

> You have set our iniquities before you,
> our secret sins in the light of your
> countenance. (Ps. 90:8)

> The mountains skipped like rams,
> the hills like lambs. (Ps. 114:4)

O'Connor claims that 'gapping' is a major feature of Hebrew poetry and does not occur in prose. Although he has thrown much new light on Hebrew poetry, his syntactic approach has its limitations. It is concerned solely with the 'substructure' of the poetic lines. It does not deal with the *meaning* of a poem nor address the question of the artistry of poetry.

Adele Berlin builds on this linguistic approach of O'Connor and other scholars (Collins, Geller). She sees parallelism and 'terseness' (which is sometimes the result of gapping) as *the* two markers of Hebrew poetry. Against the traditional view of parallelism she argues that it has many aspects, and cannot be limited to just a few 'types'. In response to some of the syntactical studies she argues that parallelism operates on many different levels, and that no one level is 'fundamental'. She discusses how it is manifest at a number of levels.

- *Grammatical parallelism: morphology.* This is parallelism at the level of individual words. Parallelism can be produced by replacing one word by another that serves the same syntactic function. For example, a noun may be replaced by a pronoun:

> Let all the earth fear *the Lord*;
> let all the inhabitants of the world
> stand in awe of *him*. (Ps. 33:8)

A feminine word may be replaced by a masculine one (or vice versa):

> The sacrifice acceptable to God is a broken (*fem.*) spirit;
> a broken (*masc.*) and contrite heart, O God, you will not despise. (Ps. 51:17)

A perfect form of the verb may be replaced by its imperfect form.

> The LORD sits (*perf.*) enthroned over the flood;
> the LORD sits (*imperf.*) enthroned as king for ever. (Ps. 29:10)

- *Grammatical parallelism: syntax.* Here Berlin is concerned with the surface structure of the sentence, not the deep structure as explored by Collins or Geller. She points out that a number of 'transformations' can be used to produce parallelism between the lines of a poetic sentence. A noun clause may be replaced by a verbal one:

> *I will bless the* LORD at all times,
> *his praise* shall continually be in my mouth. (Ps. 34:1)

The mood of a verb may be changed:

> For in death there is no remembrance of you;   (*a statement*)
> in Sheol who can give you praise?'   (*a question*)
> (Ps. 6:5)

The subject of one line may become the object of the next:

> You (*subj.*) are my son;
> today I have begotten you (*obj.*).
> (Ps. 2:7)

- *Lexical (word) parallelism.* A major aspect of this is the use of 'word pairs' such as man/woman, earth/heaven, loyalty/truth, etc.

> In my distress I *called* upon the LORD;
> to my God I *cried* for help. (Ps. 18:6)

> The *heavens* are the LORD's heavens,
> but the *earth* he has given to human beings. (Ps. 115:16)

Berlin argues that these word pairs are the result of the wider phenomenon of 'word association', which occurs in all cultures, being 'activated' by the poetic use of parallelism. She discusses some of the 'rules' that operate with regard to word association in general and that help to explain the pairings that are actually found in poetry.

- *Semantic (meaning) parallelism.* This is the relationship between one line and its parallel line. Berlin does not want to define this as closely as Lowth's synonymous and antithetic parallelism, nor as broadly as Kugel. She sees it in terms of the two lines containing 'a semantic continuation, a progression of thought'.
- *Phonological (sound) parallelism.* By this Berlin means the occurrence of sound pairs in the two lines. There may be more than one pair. These 'sound parallelisms' will, of course, only be noticeable in the Hebrew text.

> Happy are those whose transgression is forgiven (*n^e suy*).
> Whose sin is covered (*k^e suy*). (Ps. 32:1)

Berlin emphasizes that although there is often an interdependence of parallelism on different levels, it can exist on one level without existing on others.

METRE

One mark of poetry in many cultures is the presence of 'metre', a regular rhythmic sound pattern. There has been, and continues to be, considerable debate about whether or not this is a feature of Hebrew poetry and, if it is, what form it takes.

In the 1890s E. Sievers argued that a key feature of Hebrew poetry is the presence of lines that contain two unstressed syllables followed by a stressed syllable. This is called an *anapaestic metre*. An English example is (stressed syllables in italics):

> And the *sheen* / of their *spears* / was like *stars* / on the *sea*.

In the twentieth century, first G. Hölscher, and then S. Mowinckel argued against this and in favour of the characteristic metre of Hebrew poetry being an alternation of unstressed and stressed syllables, an *iambic metre*. An English example is (stressed syllables in italics):

> The *cur*-few *tolls* the *knell* of *part*-ing *day*.

All these scholars recognized that there is sometimes a variation of metre within a Hebrew poem. However, there was a tendency to explain this by appeal to textual errors or later revision and rewriting of the poems.

Other scholars have argued that what is important in Hebrew poetry is not the pattern of stressed syllables, but the number or length of syllables. D. Freedman and M. Dahood have both argued for the importance of the number of syllables in each line form. They also look for a balancing of the number of syllables between adjacent lines. Their view is influenced by the fact that they believe these to be characteristic features of Ugaritic poetry. Not all Ugaritic scholars agree with them about this.

There are scholars, most notably J. Kugel and M. O'Connor, who deny that there is any regular metre in Hebrew poetry. As we have seen, for them the key features of Hebrew poetry lie elsewhere. Kugel argues that whatever approximate regularity there may be in the metre of a poem arises from the balancing of ideas that is a feature of parallelism as he defines it. Because parallelism is very flexible, there is no regular metre.

Because biblical Hebrew stopped being a living language over 2,000 years ago we face inevitable uncertainties about how it was spoken, and about intonation and stress. This makes attempts to reconstruct metrical patterns problematic. The same, of course, is true to an even greater extent with Ugaritic, even if we assume the validity of using Ugaritic poetry as a model for Hebrew poetry. However, many scholars agree with Wilfred Watson that metre is a feature of Hebrew poetry, but that it is used flexibly. As a result, it is rare for there to be a regular, fixed metre throughout any one poem. Nevertheless there are some consistent regular patterns of stress in the psalms, such as the pattern of three stresses in one line followed by two in the next (3:2), which was recognized long ago as a feature of many Laments, though it does also occur in other types of poem. A clear example is the opening lines of Psalm 5.

Give-ear-to my-words, O-LORD;
give-heed-to my-sighing.
Listen to-the-sound-of my-cry,
my-King and-my-God.

The words joined by hyphens represent single words in Hebrew, and each has one stressed syllable, hence the pattern of stress is 3:2:3:2.

The occurrence of such patterns is not surprising if most of the poems were intended to be sung or chanted. S. Gillingham notes that the most common patterns of stress are: 2:2, 3:3 (especially found in hymnic psalms), 4:4 and 3:2 (found in many Laments). Here are examples of the 2:2, 3:3 and 4:4 patterns (an example of 3:2 has been given above).

2:2 Do-not-be-far from-me,
      for-trouble is-near
      and-there-is-no-one to-help.
         (Ps. 22:11)

3:3 The-earth is-the-LORD's and-all-
         that-is-in-it,
      the-world, and-those-who-live in-it.
         (Ps. 24:1)

4:4 God is-in-the-midst-of-the-city;
         it-shall-not be-moved;
      God will-help-it when-the-morning
         dawns. (Ps. 46:5)

Gillingham, like Adele Berlin, prefers to speak of 'rhythm' rather than 'metre' as a feature of Hebrew poetry, because rhythm is more dynamic and fluid. It can have discernible, but changing patterns.

RECOGNIZING HEBREW POETRY

The discussion so far indicates that there are few scholars who agree with Kugel that it is not possible to distinguish Hebrew poetry from prose. One of Kugel's reasons for saying this is that Hebrew has no word for poetry. In response to this Francis Landy points out that this is not because the Hebrews had no concept of poetry, but because they had several words for it, with some being more specific than others. Moreover, as Robert Alter points out, the introduction to a piece of text may indicate that something other than prose follows. For example, in Exodus 15:1 we read 'Then Moses and the Israelites sang this song to the LORD ...' This leads us to expect that what follows will be different from the normal prose of speech. In fact the word for 'song' in Hebrew can refer to a wide range of things: prayer (Ps. 42:9), the ditties of fools (Eccl 7:5), the Song of Songs. Landy defines the difference between poetry and prose as being that between 'marked' and 'unmarked' texts. What are the 'marks' of poetry?

We have noted above that Berlin regards parallelism (as she defines it) and terseness as *the* marks of Hebrew poetry. Other scholars (Gillingham, Miller, Watson) give longer lists. The following features are selected from these lists, as seeming to be the more important ones.

● *Parallelism*, as defined by Berlin.
● *Terseness*. Two particular ways in which this is achieved are by 'gapping' and by the omission of various Hebrew particles that are common in prose, such as the Hebrew marker of the definite object,

HEBREW AND UGARITIC POETRY

In the 1920s a French team of archaeologists began excavations at a site in northern Syria called Ras Shamra. They unearthed the remains of a Canaanite city that flourished from about the fourteenth to the twelfth centuries BC, and was known as Ugarit. Numerous clay tablets were found in the city. They are written in an alphabetic script derived from the cuneiform script used in Mesopotamia. When this had been deciphered it became clear that the language used (now called Ugaritic) is closely related to Hebrew. Many of the texts are written in prose: letters, legal documents, financial and administrative records. However, most of the texts are written in poetry and deal with religious and mythological themes. They provide a major insight into Canaanite culture and a valuable background against which to understand aspects of the history and religion of ancient Israel.

A number of comparisons can be made between Ugaritic and Hebrew poetry. A major difference is in the content of the poems. Much of the Ugaritic material consists of long verse narratives concerning the gods and legendary human heroes. These have all the elements we associate with story-telling, such as descriptions of people, events and scenery. There is a mixture of narration and dialogue. The poetry of the Hebrew Bible has nothing like this. Even the so-called historical psalms (Pss 78; 105; 106) and poems like the Song of the Sea (Exod. 15:1–18) and Deborah's Song (Judg. 5) do not tell a story in the same way as the Ugaritic poems. They summarize, or allude to, events that the hearers are expected to be aware of already. The primary concern of the poet is not with telling the story, but in evoking a religious response of some kind – praise, thanksgiving, penitence, etc. In the Hebrew Bible it is prose, not poetry, that is the medium used for narratives of various kinds. The reason for this difference between Ugaritic and Hebrew literature is a matter of debate. Some have suggested that the ancient Hebrew poets avoided verse narrative just because of its associations with pagan religious mythology. Others have suggested that the Hebrew writers discovered and exploited the greater flexibility and subtlety of prose as a medium for story-telling.

Despite this major difference in content, there are several similarities between Hebrew and Ugaritic verse. The most obvious of these is the use of pairs of words of the same grammatical class (noun, verb, etc.) in parallel lines of verse. Many word pairs that are common in Ugaritic poetry occur also in Hebrew poetry. Scholars have listed over one hundred such pairs. It is notable that word-pairing is very rare in Ugaritic prose, but does feature significantly in Hebrew prose. This leads to a sharper poetry/prose distinction in Ugaritic. It may be that this is a result of the function of prose documents from Ugarit, which are primarily 'informational' rather than 'literary'.

Metre seems to have been a feature of Ugaritic poetry, though there is some disagreement among scholars about its nature. The 3:3 rhythm that is popular in Hebrew is also found in Ugaritic verse, though it is less predominant there.

---

the prefix that in Hebrew indicates 'the', and the word for 'who/which'.
- *The use of word pairs*. This contributes to parallelism.
- *Rhythm*. As we have seen, this is fluid rather than fixed.
- *Unusual word order*. Sometimes this seems to be the result of seeking to sustain a particular rhythm.
- *Unusual vocabulary, including archaisms*.
- *A concentration of figurative language*.

Think about
COMPOSING HEBREW POETRY

Try composing some 'Hebrew-style' poetry (in English!) incorporating as many as possible of the features that are listed as being the more important ones.

Landy argues that poetry is not constituted merely by a concentration of such features. Rather, they are part of what makes poetry a language that is of a different order from prose. He highlights the following more general characteristics as 'markers' of poetry and prose.

- There is a difference in the sense of time in poetry and prose. Prose generally assumes sequential time. Poetry has an air of timelessness, being concerned with recurrent patterns and stillness.
- In prose the distinctions between the writer, the subject matter and the readers are usually clearly preserved. However, in poetry the writer's feelings and sensations are expressed in a way that seeks to draw the readers in to share them.
- Prose is usually concerned with everyday life, activities and speech. Poetry is used to speak about liminal situations.
- Prose presents the world through relationships of nearness, time and space. Poetry presents the world through relationships of likeness and difference.

It has to be said that, in the end, the judgement that a particular piece of Hebrew text is poetry rather than prose will always have an element of subjectivity about it. However, consideration of the characteristics listed above does provide some objective basis for the judgement.

VERSE, STROPHE AND STANZA

J. P. Fokkelman thinks that Hebrew poems contain structures at levels above the basic unit of the bicolon or tricolon. He calls these basic units 'verses', and argues that groups of two or three (or occasionally more) verses form distinct strophes. A strophe has an 'internal cohesion', which may take a number of forms. He gives the following examples of possible forms of cohesion.

- The strophe may be formed by a compound sentence that extends over two or more bicola.
- The strophe may formulate or explain one thought.
- The cola in it may form a clear series of some kind.
- The strophe may be an embedded speech, such as a quotation.
- The strophe may present or work out a metaphor or simile.
- The strophe may be demarcated by an *inclusio*.

The move from one strophe to another is often marked by a change in the subject matter, the mode of the sentence (statement, question, command, wish), the form of the verbs (tense, the grammatical person: 'I', 'you', 'they', etc.), and so on.

Psalm 13 provides an example of how strophes may be recognized.

Strophe 1   v. 1   How long, O LORD? Will
you forget me for ever?
How long will you hide
your face from me?

v. 2 How long must I bear pain
in my soul,
and have sorrow in my
heart all day long?
How long shall my enemy
be exalted over me?

Strophe 2   v. 3 Consider and answer me,
O Lord my God!
Give light to my eyes, or
I will sleep the sleep of
death,

v. 4 and my enemy will say, 'I
have prevailed';
my foes will rejoice
because I am shaken

Strophe 3   v. 5 But I trusted in your
steadfast love;
my heart shall rejoice in
your salvation.

v. 6 I will sing to the Lord,
because he has dealt
bountifully with me.

The first strophe is clearly marked out by the series of four questions, each beginning, 'How long'. Strophe 2 is a single compound sentence, and is also marked by a change from question to command or plea. The final strophe is marked by a change from plea to an expression of trust in God.

Fokkelman argues that often, especially in longer poems, there are stanzas. These are usually composed of two or three (though occasionally more) strophes. He admits that it is not always easy to recognize stanzas. The kind of criteria that he uses is illustrated by his division of Psalm 103 into three stanzas:

Stanza 1 vv. 1–8   The end of this stanza is marked by the 'definition' of the nature of Yahweh in v. 8. This is prepared for by the use of the key words 'mercy' and 'steadfast love' in v. 4.

Stanza 2 vv. 9–16   There is a kind of *inclusio* here, formed by the negatives 'not . . . nor' in vv. 9–10 and the negative 'no more' in v. 16 ('it is gone' in the NRSV can be rendered as 'is no more').

Stanza 3 vv. 17–22   This stanza is given coherence by the theme of Yahweh's rule (vv. 19, 22) and the use of the verb 'to do' (vv. 18, 20, 21).

Digging deeper:
IDENTIFYING STROPHES

Fokkelman identifies the following strophes in Psalm 103: vv. 1–2, 3–5, 6–8, 9–10, 11–13, 14–16, 17–19, 20–22. Can you understand the bases on which he does this?

FURTHER READING

The items marked with * are considered suitable as first ports of call, while others are more complex or relate to specific issues.

In the introduction to his commentary on Psalms 101—150, Dahood discusses the relationship between Ugaritic and Hebrew poetry. Mowinckel has a chapter on metre in Hebrew poetry in vol. 2 of his book on *The Psalms in Israel's Worship*. Holladay's article '*Hebrew Verse Structure* Revisited (I)' provides a good introduction to O'Connor's work.

* R. Alter *The Art of Biblical Poetry*. New York: Basic Books, 1985.

S. E. Balentine and J. Barton (eds.). *Language, Theology, and the Bible: Essays in Honour of James Barr*. Oxford: Clarendon Press, 1994.

A. Berlin *The Dynamics of Biblical Parallelism*. Bloomington, IN: Indiana University Press, 1985.

T. Collins *Line-Forms in Hebrew Poetry*. Rome: Pontifical Biblical Institute, 1978.

M. Dahood *Psalms 101–150*. AB. Garden City, NY: Doubleday, 1970.

* J. P. Fokkelman *Reading Biblical Poetry: An Introductory Guide*, Louisville, KY: Westminster John Knox Press, 2001.

D. N. Freedman 'Pottery, Poetry and Prophecy: An Essay on Biblical Poetry', *JBL* 96 (1977), 5–26.

S. A. Geller *Parallelism in Early Biblical Poetry*. HSM 20. Missoula, MT: Scholars Press, 1979.

* S. E. Gillingham *The Poems and Psalms of the Hebrew Bible*. Oxford: OUP, 1994.

W. L. Holladay 'Hebrew Verse Structure Revisited (I): Which Words "Count"?', *JBL* 118 (1999), 19–32.

W. L. Holladay 'Hebrew Verse Structure Revisited (II): Conjoint Cola, and Further Considerations', *JBL* 118 (1999), 401–416.

J. Kugel *The Idea of Biblical Poetry*. New Haven, CT: Yale University Press, 1981.

F. Landy 'Poetics and Parallelism: Some Comments on James Kugel's *The Idea of Biblical Poetry*', *JSOT* 28 (1984), 61–87.

R. Lowth *Lectures on the Sacred Poetry of the Hebrews*. London: T. Tegg and Son, 1835 (originally published 1753).

P. D. Miller 'The Theological Significance of Hebrew Poetry', in S. E. Balentine and J. Barton (eds.) *Language, Theology, and the Bible: Essays in Honour of James Barr*. Oxford: Clarendon Press, 1994, 213–230.

S. Mowinckel *The Psalms in Israel's Worship*. Oxford: Blackwell, 1962; vol. 2.

M. P. O'Connor *Hebrew Verse Structure*. Winona Lake, IN: Eisenbrauns, 1980.

T. H. Robinson *The Poetry of the Old Testament*. London: Duckworth, 1947.

G. W. E. Watson *Classical Hebrew Poetry*. JSOTSup 26. Sheffield: JSOT Press, 1986 (2nd edn).

Chapter 3

WISDOM AND WISDOM LITERATURE

THE WISDOM LITERATURE

Within the Hebrew Bible there are three books that, despite their diversity, have so much in common that scholars have come to regard them as representing a distinct type of literature. Moreover, this literature is taken to reflect a particular strand of Israelite religion and culture. The books concerned are: Job, Proverbs and Ecclesiastes (called Qoheleth in Hebrew Bibles).

One way of expressing what these books have in common is to say that they are all concerned with 'wisdom'. This can be justified simply at the level of vocabulary. Various forms of the Hebrew root *hkm*, meaning 'wisdom', occur relatively frequently in them, as the table 'Occurrence of *hkm*, "wisdom", in Proverbs, Job and Ecclesiastes' below shows.

Taken together, these three books account for the majority of occurrences of the root *hkm* in the Hebrew Bible. There are other words that are characteristic of these books but not common outside of them. Some have meanings that are aspects of 'wisdom' (e.g. *binah*, 'understanding'; *navon*, 'intelligent'; *'arum*, 'cunning'), or of its opposite (e.g. *k*e*sil*, 'stupid'; *lets*, 'scoffer, arrogant person', *ʳᵉwil*, 'fool').

> **Think about WISDOM**
>
> What does the term 'wisdom' mean today? How is it related to such things as: knowledge, understanding, intelligence, experience?

OCCURRENCE OF *HKM*, 'WISDOM', IN PROVERBS, JOB AND ECCLESIASTES

	Proverbs	Job	Ecclesiastes
hokmah (wisdom)	39	18	28
hakam (wise)	47	8	21
hakam (to be wise)	12	2	4
hokmot (wisdom)	3		

Although a shared vocabulary is one of the most obvious things that links these books, more important than this is a common approach to reality. This is 'humanistic' in the sense that it is concerned with what is good for men and women. It is also 'experiential' in that what the authors say is rooted in careful observation of life, especially the consequences of particular patterns of human behaviour. Although each of the books has its own emphases, there are shared themes such as: the value of wisdom, the power of speech, the inequities of life, the problem of suffering, the finality of death. Another striking similarity that they share is the absence of many of those things that are normally seen as distinctively Israelite. There is no mention of the great moments of Israel's history, of the Sinai covenant or the covenant with David. The temple, its sacrificial system and calendar of feasts gets barely a mention. Neither prophet nor priest gets a mention alongside 'the wise' and 'the fool'. Besides such similarities of approach to reality and content, these books (especially Proverbs and Ecclesiastes) share specific literary forms that mark them off from other biblical books. These will be discussed in detail later.

Job, Proverbs and Ecclesiastes are not unique within either the corpus of surviving early Jewish literature or the literature that has survived from the wider world of the ancient Near East. There are two apocryphal or deuterocanonical books that can be classed as Jewish 'wisdom literature'. They are the Wisdom of Jesus Ben Sirach (or Ecclesiasticus) and the Wisdom of Solomon. Ben Sirach wrote his book in Hebrew in Palestine early in the second century BC. His grandson later translated it into Greek for the benefit of the Jews in Alexandria. The Wisdom of Solomon was probably written in Alexandria sometime in the first century BC, and was composed in Greek. These two books show us how the ideas and themes found in the wisdom literature of the Hebrew Bible were developed among the more conservative Jews of Palestine (Ben Sirach) and among the Greek-speaking diaspora Jews.

A good deal of literature that has survived from ancient Egypt and Mesopotamia has come to be called 'wisdom literature' because of its comparability to the biblical 'wisdom' books. There is a wider diversity among these texts than among the three biblical books, and they clearly bear the distinctive marks of their own cultures. This leads some scholars to be hesitant about giving them the label 'wisdom literature'. However, despite their diversity, these texts from Egypt, Israel and Mesopotamia still have enough in common for most scholars to be reasonably happy with the common classification. As long as the Egyptian and Mesopotamian material is used with care, it provides a helpful wider context within which to understand the biblical books.

THE NATURE OF WISDOM

In the Hebrew Bible in general, 'wisdom' refers to particular skills, both physical and intellectual. People who possess these skills are described as 'wise'. So, in the account of the construction of the tabernacle God says to Moses, 'I have given skill ["wisdom"] to all the skilful ["wise of heart"], so that they may make all that I have commanded you' (Exod. 31:6). These skills include artistic design, metal work, work with precious stones and woodwork (Exod. 31:3–5, where Uri is said to be endowed with 'ability', i.e. 'wisdom', to do these things). They also encompass spinning (Exod. 35:25, done by skilful, i.e. 'wise of heart', women), embroidery and weaving (Exod. 35:35). Elsewhere it is used of cunning or craftiness (2 Sam. 13:3), political pragmatism (1 Kgs 2:6), professional mourning (Jer. 9:17), sailors and shipbuilders (Ezek. 27:8–9).

Within the wisdom literature the meaning of 'wisdom' becomes somewhat narrower. Speaking of the book of Proverbs in particular Whybray says,

> Elsewhere in the Old Testament *hokmah* means something like 'skill': practical knowledge in any sphere, from that of the artisan to that of the politician. But in Proverbs *hokmah* is always *life*-skill: the ability of the individual to conduct his life in the best possible way and to the best possible effect. (1994, p. 4)

Alongside this narrowing of meaning there is another one. In the wisdom literature *hokmah* is often coupled with other words meaning 'understanding' (*binah*, *t^evunah*), or 'knowledge' (*da'at*). This gives it a more 'intellectual' slant. As a result wisdom is seen as 'an intellectual quality which provides the key to happiness and success, to "life" in its widest sense' (Whybray, 1974, p. 8). This is a narrowing of meaning, not a change in meaning, as shown by the idiomatic phrase 'wise of heart' noted above in texts outside the wisdom literature. In Hebrew the heart is primarily the centre of reasoning and the will, not of the emotions as in English.

The wisdom literature is predicated on the assumption that wisdom can be acquired. Thus we are told that the purpose of the book of Proverbs is 'for learning about wisdom and instruction' (Prov. 1:2). It is not only 'the simple' and 'the young' who can benefit from this: 'Let the wise also hear and gain learning' (Prov. 1:5). The opening verses of Proverbs also make it clear that gaining wisdom is not just acquiring a body of knowledge. It is learning how to behave, how to live, 'gaining instruction in wise dealing, righteousness, justice and equity' (Prov. 1:3), and has to do with 'shrewdness' and 'prudence' as well as 'knowledge' (Prov. 1:4).

**Think about
WISDOM LITERATURE TODAY?**

Read the 'prologue' of the book of Proverbs (Prov. 1:2–6) with its statement of the purpose of the book. Can you think of any comparable modern forms of 'wisdom literature'?

WISDOM IN ISRAEL – A FOREIGN IMPORT?

Through much of the twentieth century there was a general scholarly consensus that the wisdom literature of the Hebrew Bible represented a tradition that was a 'foreign import' into Israelite culture. A number of things encouraged this conclusion. One is, as we have noted, the absence from this literature of much that is distinctively Israelite, such as references to its history, the covenants, its religious institutions. Then there is the fact that in Egypt and Mesopotamia wisdom literature pre-dates that of the Hebrew Bible by many centuries. Of particular importance was the publication in 1923 of an Egyptian work, the *Instruction of Amenemope*, which is usually dated to the twelfth century BC. It was soon realized that there are significant similarities between this work and Proverbs 22:17—24:22. It is possible that both Proverbs and *Amenemope* are drawing on a common source, but the majority of scholars concluded that the compiler(s) of Proverbs 22:17—24:22 were dependent on *Amenemope*. Finally, there is the existence within Proverbs of a number of pairs of proverbs in which one is 'secular' and the other 'theological' in tone. An example of this is:

> The teaching of the wise is a fountain of life,
> so that one may avoid the snares of death. (Prov. 13:14)

> The fear of the LORD is a fountain of life,
> so that one may avoid the snares of death. (Prov. 14:27)

W. McKane appealed to this phenomenon to support the argument that wisdom was originally imported into Israel as something that was pragmatic and secular. It was only gradually assimilated to Israel's Yahwistic faith. These pairs of proverbs are evidence of that process of assimilation.

If wisdom was imported into Israel, when did this occur? The most likely time seemed to be the reign of Solomon. He would have needed to establish quite a complex bureaucracy to support his activities as described in 1 Kings 1—11.

These included establishing 12 tax districts that supplied the provisions for the court on a monthly basis; numerous major building projects, which required the use of forced labour gangs based on a conscription system; the setting up of a standing army, including for the first time chariot forces, which were stationed in a number of cities throughout the kingdom. From where did Solomon get the trained bureaucrats he needed? It was suggested that he adopted and adapted the training system used in Egypt, based on temple and court schools, which made use of works like the *Instruction of Amenemope*. After all, it was argued, he married an Egyptian princess and imported his chariots from Egypt. After being the consensus view for some decades, various aspects of this scenario have been called into question during the last 20 years or so.

WISDOM SCHOOLS

In both Egypt and Mesopotamia there were professional teachers, sages, who built up and preserved the traditional wisdom material. Their sphere of activity was what scholars now call 'wisdom schools'. In them young men were taught to read and write, and were trained as administrative officials for both the temples and the royal court. Were there such schools in ancient Israel? Scholarly answers range from a definite 'No' (Weeks) through a qualified 'Yes' (Davies) to a firm 'Yes' (Lemaire). The fact is that there is no unambiguous reference to a wisdom school in Israel until Jesus Ben Sirach's 'house of instruction' in the early second century BC (Sir. 51:23). A few passages in the Hebrew Bible have been seen as indirect evidence of schools. Isaiah 28:9–10 has been taken as a complaint by the prophet's opponents that he is treating them like little children who have to be taught by rote. In vv. 11–13 the prophet responds that this is how God will deal with them. In vv. 10 and 13b two short monosyllables (*saw, qaw*) are repeated several times, which might be a parody of children learning by rote. However, these are not the names of any of the letters of the Hebrew alphabet. Isaiah 50:4–9 is the third of the 'Servant Songs'. It speaks of the relationship between God and the Servant in terms of a teacher–student relationship. This, however, is not clear evidence of a 'school' setting for education. Similarly Proverbs 5:13 refers to 'teachers' and 'instructors', but the setting in which they operated is not specified. The similarities between Proverbs 22:17—24:22 and *Amenemope* can be taken to imply that both were used in the same kind of setting, that of a wisdom school. The biblical evidence is clearly inconclusive.

Another line of evidence is a number of texts from Israel of the kind called 'abecedaries'. They consist of strings of letters, sometimes written singly and sometimes in groups of the same letter. These may be writing exercises done by students learning their letters. There are other texts that look like practice exercises in the learning of the Egyptian hieratic numerals that were used in ancient Judah. However, none have been found in a context that is clearly a 'school'. There is clear evidence, both biblical and archaeological, of literacy in ancient Israel, especially from the eighth century onwards. The Gezer Calendar (tenth century), the Siloam Tunnel Inscription (eighth century) and the Lachish Letters (eighth century) are notable examples. The question is how literacy was acquired. It has been argued that the cumbersome

nature of the Egyptian and Mesopotamian scripts meant that a prolonged educational process was needed if they were to be mastered. However, the alphabetic Hebrew script of only 22 letters can be learnt quite quickly at home or in the workplace and so there was not the pressure in Israel for a school system. In response to this it is argued that the schools in Egypt and Mesopotamia taught a lot more than literacy. They passed on a good deal of other 'technical' and 'professional' knowledge and skills. The archaeological evidence for schools in ancient Israel is suggestive and not conclusive.

Digging deeper:
WISDOM SCHOOLS IN ANCIENT ISRAEL?

In his essay, 'Were There Schools in Ancient Israel?' Davies (1995) comes to a cautiously positive conclusion, whereas in Chapter 8 of his book *Early Israelite Wisdom* (1994) Weeks comes to a negative conclusion. Read their arguments and draw your own conclusion.

SOLOMON'S BUREAUCRACY

Archaeology has not produced much evidence of the great wealth and major building projects attributed to Solomon. This is partly explicable by the fact that Jerusalem has suffered serious destruction and rebuilding, and that some of the areas that archaeologists would like to explore are now inaccessible under built-up areas. In a socio-archaeological study Jamieson-Drake has argued that under the early monarchy Israel had the character of a 'tribal chiefdom' and that it was only in the eighth century that Judah became a 'bureaucratic kingdom'. His work has been appealed to by some as undermining a major argument put forward to support the existence of schools in early Israel. Others have criticized his work quite strongly. They point out that he used data from southern Palestine only, ignoring possible evidence of Solomonic activity in the north. Moreover he does not even give a complete account of the evidence from the south, again ignoring some evidence from the tenth century. It is also argued that he exaggerates the contrasts between Israel and its large neighbours and between situations in Palestine in the tenth and eighth centuries, turning what are differences of degree into absolute differences.

PROFESSIONAL 'WISE MEN'
Jeremiah 18:18 has been a key text in the debate about whether, and when, there were professional wisdom teachers (sages) in Israel.

> Then they said, 'Come, let us make plots against Jeremiah – for instruction shall not perish from the priest, nor counsel from the wise, nor the word from the prophet. Come, let us bring charges against him, and let us not heed any of his words.'

Traditionally this has been taken to refer to three recognized professional groups (priests, sages, prophets) each with its own expertise (instruction [*torah* in Hebrew], counsel and the word of Yahweh). However, this verse lacks a narrative context to aid in its interpretation. It is pointed out that in Jeremiah 4:9 'the king and officials' are linked with the priests and prophets. Moreover, in Ezekiel 7:26 there is a close parallel to Jeremiah 18:18: 'They shall keep seeking a vision from the

prophet; instruction shall perish from the priest, and counsel from the elders.' Here 'counsel' is linked with 'the elders'. So, it is arguable that if 'the wise' in Jeremiah 18:18 are a distinct group, they are more likely royal advisors, politicians, than professional wisdom teachers. Of course, some of these advisors could have been professional sages, but the text does not demand that interpretation.

In Jeremiah 8:8–9 the prophet seems to attack in the same breath those who claim to be wise and some scribes. Are these one and the same group? If so there is a possible link between the 'wise' and those who are involved with literate activity. However, the change from second person address in v. 8a ('you say') to third person reference in v. 8b ('the false pen of the scribes') suggests that the prophet has two different groups in mind.

As with schools, there is no clear reference to professional wisdom teachers in Israel until Jesus Ben Sirach in the early second century BC.

SECULAR WISDOM
The study of Egyptian literature since the publication of *Amenemope* has increasingly shown that it is incorrect to label any of it as 'secular'. Not all of it, especially the earlier *Instructions*, expresses personal religious commitment in the way that *Amenemope* does. Nevertheless, from the earliest examples, the teaching of the *Instructions* is based on the fundamentally religious concept of Maat. This is often rendered as 'order', 'justice', 'truth', but was not just an abstract principle, but a divine entity. This undermines one aspect of the consensus view, but still leaves open the fundamental question of whether wisdom

came into Israel from Egypt, or elsewhere, or was of basically Israelite origin.

CONCLUSIONS

The debates surveyed above have led some scholars to abandon the older consensus view altogether. Others have continued to hold to it in modified forms, while recognizing more clearly the degree to which it depends on analogies and suppositions that are open to question. They argue that whenever one may date the development, during the monarchical period in Israel and Judah a state apparatus run by officials did grow up and some system of training would have been needed. Even if the analogy with Egypt and Mesopotamia has been over-pressed in the past, it is unlikely that Israel would have a system of government and education that owed nothing to its neighbours. The pattern may not have been taken directly from Egypt, but may have been adopted from the Canaanite city-states (of which Jerusalem was one). They had been under Egyptian influence for centuries and seem to have been finally absorbed into Israel during the early monarchy. Also, it is argued that the linking of Solomon with wisdom should not be lightly dismissed as purely 'back-projection' from later times. There must be *some* reason for linking Solomon with wisdom. What is said of his 'wisdom activity' in 1 Kings 4:32–33 goes beyond what one might expect simply from a desire to find an author for Proverbs, Ecclesiastes and the Song of Songs.

WISDOM IN ISRAEL – HOME GROWN?

In Egypt the *Instructions* are mostly presented as the teaching given by a father to a son who is to succeed him in office in the royal court. As part of the consensus view discussed above, it was generally assumed that wisdom teaching in ancient Israel was closely connected with the court. Critics of the consensus point out that very little of the material in Proverbs speaks directly of the king and his court: Proverbs 8:15–16; 14:28, 35; 16:10, 12–15; 17:7, 26; 19: 6, 10, 12; 20:2, 8, 26, 28; 21:1; 22:11, 29; 23:1; 24:21; 25:1–7, 15; 28:2, 15, 16; 29:4, 12, 14, 26; 31:1–9. One response to this is to argue that since, in its present form, Proverbs is a post-exilic compilation, its editors may have selected their material from earlier collections to provide a more general 'training for life' in the changed circumstances of Judah no longer being a monarchical state. An alternative approach argues that simply counting the explicit references to 'king', 'prince' or 'ruler' does not give a true picture. For example, a number of commentators have seen Proverbs 28—29 as 'a sort of manual for a monarch' (Fox, 2000, p. 10). There are references to rulers at the beginning and end of these chapters, with others scattered throughout. However, examinations of the contents of Proverbs have led to suggestions that much of the material originated somewhere other than the royal court.

FOLK WISDOM

Whybray has argued that if one puts aside the presupposition of a court context, the proverbs about rulers make good sense if seen as the observations of ordinary people. People do not have to be courtiers to have opinions on how their rulers should and shouldn't behave and about their duties and responsibilities. F. W. Golka's comparative study of African and biblical proverbs lends support to this view. African proverbs coined by the ordinary people express their views of the king or chief and of courtiers. These views may be critical or sympathetic in tone. It should be noted that Golka has his own presupposition (or 'methodological principle'), namely that 'among all peoples popular origin of proverbs has to be assumed until there is proof to the contrary' (Golka, 1993, p. 27). From their studies of proverbs about wealth and poverty both Whybray and Golka conclude that the sentence proverbs in Proverbs 10—29 (i.e. excepting 22:17–24:22) reflect the setting of farmers of moderate means farming their own land. It is perhaps worth noting here that Job and his friends are not depicted as 'sages' but as moderately well-off farmers.

Golka was consciously taking further the arguments of his teacher Claus Westermann that the roots of Israelite wisdom are to be found in 'folk wisdom', the observations on life of the ordinary people. He sums up the world he sees reflected in the sentence proverbs of Proverbs 10:29.

> It is the world of the farmer, the tiller of the soil, and the tradesman that opens before our eyes in these comparisons. It is the realm of the simple person and his everyday life out of which the proverbs have grown. (Westermann, 1995, p. 60)

Westermann thinks that the proverbs originated among preliterate people as short, one-part sayings. These were then extended to form the two-part comparisons and antitheses that are characteristic of the extant sentences. He thinks that it is possible to discern the simpler sentences behind some of the antitheses in particular.

Although he accepts that many of the sayings in Proverbs are in origin oral folk sayings, and that some may have originated in village communities, M. V. Fox argues that the proponents of the folk origin of the biblical proverbs have tended to overlook clues to an urban setting. Among those he cites are references to working with precious metals (Prov. 17:3; 27:21), fine jewellery (25:11–12), and messengers (25:13). Also, references to slaves are from the point of view of their (relatively wealthy) owners (29:21). Fox contends that at least some of the proverbs about the king do make best sense as the reflections of courtiers (e.g. 25:6–7). He disagrees with Golka that proverbs that are critical of the king must come from common people rather than courtiers. In any case, he argues that the proverbs that Golka classes as 'critical' are not 'deeply critical' of kingship but recognize the power that kings have to do damage without criticizing kingship itself. He therefore argues for the court as 'the decisive locus of Wisdom creativity'.

FAMILY WISDOM

In the *Instructions* and also in Proverbs (especially, but not exclusively, chs 1—9) the teacher addresses the teaching to 'my child ["son" in Hebrew]'. The teacher–student relationship is depicted as a father–son relationship. Is this a real family relationship? Some scholars give a positive answer to this since on a few occasions the mother is explicitly mentioned as the teacher (Prov. 1:8; 6:20; 30:17, 31:1–9, 26). Here mention needs to be made of the existence of 'wise women' in ancient Israel (2 Sam. 14:2; 20:16). So, Fontaine puts some emphasis on the oral origins of wisdom and the home as the setting for instruction, though allowing the possibility of later instruction within schools. Other scholars too (Crenshaw, Fox, Golka) recognize the probable role of the family in instruction and the creation of proverbial wisdom. Given the nature of Israelite society, a sharp distinction cannot be made between 'family', 'clan' and 'tribe' as sources of wisdom.

CONCLUSIONS

It is certainly the case that breaking free from the presuppositions of the consensus has led scholars to uncover evidence for 'home-grown' wisdom in Israel arising from the experience of ordinary people. This was no doubt passed on informally, with the home as an important place where this was done. However, this does not rule out the possibility of influence from outside Israel playing a significant role in the development of education and of 'wisdom teaching' in particular.

CONTEXTS OF LEARNING IN ANCIENT ISRAEL

There seems no good reason why the different 'roots of wisdom' advocated by recent scholars should be considered as exclusive of each other. Crenshaw speaks of three main contexts, or fundamental settings, of learning in ancient Israel: the family, the school and the court. This seems a reasonable scenario. As he observes, the sentences fit well into a family or folk context of instruction. The more complex instruction form, found particularly, but not exclusively, in Proverbs 1—9 is more likely the product of professional teachers. There is no good reason to discount the reference in Proverbs 25:1 to the activity of royal officials in compiling collections of proverbs. Also, Fox has made a good case for seeing a greater relevance of at least some of the material in Proverbs to courtiers than allowed by advocates of the folk wisdom origin of proverbs. He argues that while the sayings in Proverbs are drawn from different social groups, including the small farmer, the courtier and the literati, it was in the end a series of learned clerks, some at least 'king's men', who made collections that became part of Israel's wisdom heritage and literature. These learned clerks, some possibly being professional wisdom teachers, were no doubt aware of the wider wisdom literature of the ancient Near East and drew on it as well as on native Israelite wisdom.

WISDOM 'INFLUENCE' IN THE HEBREW BIBLE

Job, Proverbs and Ecclesiastes are not the only places in the Hebrew Bible where scholars have discerned evidence of the approach to life that is characteristic of these books. Whybray (1974) has done the most thorough investigation of the presence of 'wisdom influence' outside the 'core' books. Using the criterion of the

> **Digging deeper:**
> **WISDOM 'INFLUENCE' IN THE HEBREW BIBLE**
>
> Read Deuteronomy 32, Psalms 37 and 49 and Ezekiel 28. Can you discern the features in these passages that led Whybray to include them in his list of those passages that exhibit something of the ethos and vocabulary of 'wisdom'?

EGYPTIAN WISDOM TEXTS

The Instruction of Ptahhotep (c. 2400)
Ptahhotep was a vizier of a pharaoh of the fifth dynasty of the Old Kingdom. It provides instruction for his son, who is to succeed him in office.

The Instruction of Merikare (c. 2100)
Merikare reigned in the First Intermediate Period. In the *Instruction* his father gives him advice on the conduct of the daily affairs of state.

The Instruction of Amenemhet
This purports to be the (posthumous) advice given by Pharaoh Amenemhet I to his son, who succeeded him after he had been assassinated c. 1960 following a conspiracy in his harem. Its main message is a warning against placing trust in anyone. The work was certainly in existence prior to 1100.

The Instruction of Ani (c. 1580–1080)
Ani is a minor official who provides advice for his son as he is about to venture out into the world. The supreme virtue commended is self-control. This is evidenced by control of the tongue, secretiveness, deference to betters and avoidance of sexual indiscretion.

The Instruction of Amenemope (c. 1200)
Amenemope was among the lower ranks of agricultural officials. The purpose of the work is clearly set out in its introduction, namely to provide training in how to be successful in the royal civil service. There is more obvious expression of piety in it than in the earlier works.

The Instruction of Onchsheshonqy (c. 400)
unlike the other texts this one does not come from the circle of royal officials, even though it claims to be the work of a man who was imprisoned after being implicated in a palace revolt. It addresses the populace in general rather than any elite circle. It presupposes a rural background and expresses deep religious sentiments.

The Dispute over Suicide (c. 2100)
An Egyptian work having the form of a dialogue between a man who is weary of life and his *ka* (inner being, soul).

The Song of the Harper (c. 2100)
A piece of Egyptian 'protest literature', which urges the enjoyment of life now, since you cannot take anything with you when you die, and no one has ever returned from the grave. It gives the shocking (because contrary to the accepted traditional view) advice, 'Do not control your passion until that day of mourning comes for you.'

The Satirical Letter of Hori (c. 1580–1080)
This takes the form of a satirical reply from a teacher of apprentices in the Office of Writings to a pompous letter from a military scribe. As it points out muddles and errors in the letter it provides model lessons for the apprentices.

N.B. All the dates given above are BC.

---

occurrence of distinctive 'wisdom vocabulary' he detected this influence in the following fairly extensive sections of the Hebrew Bible.

- Genesis 2—3
- The Joseph Story (Gen. 37—50)
- Deuteronomy 1—4
- The Song of Moses (Deut. 32).
- The Succession Narrative (2 Sam. 9—20; 1 Kgs 1—2)
- The History of Solomon (1 Kgs 3—11)
- Psalms 1; 19:8–15; 37; 49; 51; 73; 90; 92; 94; 104; 107; 111; 119
- Isaiah 1—39
- Jeremiah

MESOPOTAMIAN WISDOM TEXTS

The Instruction of Shurrupak (c. 2000)
A Sumerian work purporting to be by the survivor of the great flood.

Lamentation of a Man to His God (c. 2000)
A Sumerian work in which a sufferer, who thinks he is facing undeserved suffering, details its nature and calls out to his god for a hearing and relief. When the sufferer accepts that no one is sinless and makes confession, his god is pleased and restores him.

The Counsels of Wisdom (c. 1500–1200)
A collection of Babylonian sayings, which have the instruction form. They are explicit in urging the claims of piety.

I Will Praise the Lord of Wisdom (c. 1300)
A ruler recounts how he has suffered various disasters and was eventually restored by Marduk.

The Dialogue of Pessimism (c. 1200)
A satirical dialogue between a master and his slave, which implies that life is meaningless and ends with the slave advocating suicide.

The Babylonian Theodicy (c 1000)
An acrostic dialogue of 27 stanzas of 11 lines each, between a sufferer and a friend. The friend tries to defend the justice of the gods against the sufferer's complaints. He does, however, accept that the gods have made humans prone to commit injustice. The message seems to be that all the sufferer can do is continue to pray to the god who has temporarily deserted his cause.

The Words of Ahiqar (c. 500)
These are attached to the story of Ahiqar, a high official in the reigns of Sennacherib and Esarhaddon of Assyria, who was wrongly disgraced and then eventually restored to favour. Although only known in Aramaic, it was probably originally written in Akkadian. It contains a mixture of wisdom forms.

N.B. All the dates given above are BC.

- Ezekiel 28
- Daniel

The degree to which the vocabulary and ethos of 'wisdom' is present in these passages varies considerably.

FURTHER READING

Items marked * are considered suitable as first ports of call, while others are more complex, or relate to specific issues.

Heaton provides a clear statement of the older 'consensus' position. Weeks marshals the arguments against it, which are summarized briefly in the opening chapter of Martin's book.

* J. L. Crenshaw 'The Three Main Contexts of Israelite Learning', in J. G. Gammie and L. G. Perdue *The Sage in Israel and the Ancient Near East*. Winona Lake, IN: Eisenbrauns, 1990; pp. 205–216.

* G. I. Davies 'Were There Schools in Ancient Israel?', in J. Day, R. P. Gordon and H. G. M. Williamson *Wisdom in Ancient Israel*. Cambridge: CUP, 1995; pp. 199–211.

J. Day, R. P. Gordon and H. G. M. Williamson *Wisdom in Ancient Israel*. Cambridge: CUP, 1995.

J. Day 'Foreign Semitic Influence on the Wisdom of Israel and its Appropriation in the Book of Proverbs', in J. Day, R. P. Gordon and H. G. M. Williamson *Wisdom in Ancient Israel*. Cambridge: CUP, 1995; pp. 55–70.

C. R. Fontaine 'Wisdom in Proverbs', in L. Perdue, B. B. Scott and W. J. Wiseman *In Search of Wisdom*. Louisville, KY: Westminster/John Knox, 1993; pp. 99–114.

M. V. Fox *Proverbs 1–9*. AB. New York, NY: Doubleday, 2000.

J. G. Gammie and L. G. Perdue *The Sage in Israel and the Ancient Near East*. Winona Lake, IN: Eisenbrauns, 1990.

F. W. Golka *The Leopard's Spots: Biblical and African Wisdom in Proverbs*. Edinburgh: T. & T. Clark, 1993.

E. W. Heaton *The School Tradition of the Old Testament*. Oxford: OUP, 1994.

D. W. Jamieson-Drake *Scribes and Schools in Monarchic Judah: A Socio-Archaeological Approach*. Sheffield: JSOT Press, 1991.

W. G. Lambert *Babylonian Wisdom Literature*. Oxford: OUP, 1960.

* A. Lemaire 'The Sage in School and Temple', in J. G. Gammie and L. G. Perdue *The Sage in Israel and the Ancient Near East*. Winona Lake, IN: Eisenbrauns, 1990; pp. 165–181.

A. Lemaire 'Wisdom in Solomonic Historiography', in J. Day, R. P. Gordon and H. G. M. Williamson *Wisdom in Ancient Israel*. Cambridge: CUP, 1995; pp. 106–118.

W. McKane *Proverbs: A New Approach*. OTL. London: SCM, 1970.

* J. D. Martin *Proverbs*. OT Guides. Sheffield: Sheffield Academic Press, 1995.

J. B. Pritchard *Ancient Near Eastern Texts Relating to the Old Testament*. Princeton, NJ: Princeton University Press, 1969 (3rd edn).

* J. D. Ray 'Egyptian Wisdom Literature', in J. Day, R. P. Gordon and H. G. M. Williamson *Wisdom in Ancient Israel*. Cambridge: CUP, 1995; pp. 17–29.

S. Weeks *Early Israelite Wisdom*. Oxford: Clarendon Press, 1994.

C. Westermann *Roots of Wisdom*. Edinburgh: T. & T. Clark, 1995.

R. N. Whybray *The Intellectual Tradition of the Old Testament*. BZAW 135. Berlin: W. de Gruyter, 1974.

R. N. Whybray *Wealth and Poverty in the Book of Proverbs*. Sheffield: JSOT Press, 1990.

R. N. Whybray *Proverbs*. NCB. London: Marshall Pickering, 1994.

Chapter 4

PROVERBS

OVERALL STRUCTURE OF THE BOOK OF PROVERBS

There is little disagreement about the overall structure of the book of Proverbs. The book contains a number of headings that appear to divide it into several different sections. A couple of other sections are usually recognized on literary grounds. As a result a very widely accepted outline for the contents of the book is as given in the table 'Structure of the Book of Proverbs' below.

The following points are worth noting with regard to this outline.

- Proverbs 1:1–7 probably acts as an introduction the book as a whole as well as to 1:8—9:18.

- In the Hebrew text 22:17a reads, 'Incline your ear and hear the words of the wise.' The LXX has a different word order, beginning with 'The words of the wise', enabling it to be read as a title. Whether or not one takes this as a title, a change of literary style makes clear that a new section begins here.
- There is considerable debate about where Agur's words end. The most obvious break comes at 30:15 with the first of a series of numerical proverbs, but whether all of 30:1–14 is intended to be the words of Agur is widely disputed.
- 31:10–31 is clearly an independent poem using the literary form of the acrostic: 22 lines, each beginning with successive letters of the Hebrew alphabet.
- 31:1–9 forms a coherent section on its own.

	STRUCTURE OF THE BOOK OF PROVERBS
1:1—9:18	'The proverbs of Solomon son of David, king of Israel'
10:1—22:16	'The proverbs of Solomon'
22:17—24:22	'The words of the wise'
24:23–34	'These are also the sayings of the wise'
25:1—29:27	'These are other proverbs of Solomon that the officials of King Hezekiah of Judah copied'
30:1–14	'The words of Agur son of Jakeh'
30:15–33	A collection of numerical proverbs
31:1–9	'The words of King Lemuel'
31:10–31	An acrostic poem about the capable wife

We will discuss each section when discussing the compilation of the book below, noting what evidence there is of more detailed structure within them.

LITERARY FORMS

The book of Proverbs is written entirely in Hebrew poetry. In one sense this is surprising. Prose would seem to be an eminently suitable medium for giving moral and religious instruction. It is the form used for the collections of Law in the Hebrew Bible and for the exhortatory 'sermons' found in the opening chapters of Deuteronomy. Why then is Proverbs written in poetry? There is no clear answer, but plausible reasons can be suggested. The most obvious is that poetry is easier to memorize than prose. Learning by rote was part of the teaching technique used throughout the ancient Near East, and use of poetry would make this easier. Much of the wisdom literature throughout this area is poetic in form. Ease of memorizing would also be important in material that was to be passed on down the generations in oral form. Second, there is the fact that poetry, with its use of the sound of words and of imagery, often has a more powerful persuasive effect than can be achieved in prose. Much of the wisdom literature is concerned with persuading people about how, and how not, to behave. Third, the use of poetry may be intended to make a distinction between 'law' and 'wisdom', a distinction that has not always been recognized in popular piety.

The Hebrew word that is translated as 'proverb' (*mashal*) in the headings of the book of Proverbs does not designate a definite literary form. The exact sense of the word is unclear. It could be related to a verb meaning 'to rule' or to one meaning 'to be like'. Thus *mashal* might mean either 'a powerful word' or 'a comparison'. The latter sense does define a literary form, but in practice by no means all the sayings in Proverbs are comparisons. In fact the term *mashal* occurs fairly often in the Hebrew Bible and is applied to sayings that have a wide variety of literary forms. Within the book of Proverbs itself there are two main forms of literature. In Proverbs 1—9; 22:17—24:22; 31:1–9 what is called the 'Instruction' form predominates. In the rest of the book the 'wisdom sentence' form is predominant.

> **Digging deeper:**
> **THE MEANING OF *MASHAL***
>
> Use a concordance, Bible dictionary (such as *NIDOTTE*) and a Hebrew–English lexicon to study the use of the word *mashal* in the Hebrew Bible. Decide what meaning, or meanings, you think it has on the basis of the way it is used.

THE 'INSTRUCTION'

McKane carried out a detailed study of the literary form of the Egyptian and Mesopotamian *Instructions* and identified a common literary form that he called the Instruction form. He showed that this form is to be found in Proverbs in the sections listed above. The characteristics of the Instruction form are that it contains a command (positive or negative) followed by a motive clause ('because/for . . .') and occasionally also by a final or purpose clause that gives the consequence of following the advice proffered. Sometimes there is a conditional clause ('if . . .'), which defines the condition or circumstances in which the imperative applies. Proverbs 3:1–2 is a straightforward example of command followed by motive.

Command: My child, do not forget my teaching,
but let your heart keep my commandments;
Motive: for length of days and years of life
and abundant welfare they will give you.

Proverbs 1:10–19 is a rather complex example that includes the conditional clause. It begins with the conditional clause, followed by the command: 'My child, if sinners entice you, do not consent.' The nature of the enticement is then spelt out in vv. 11–14. The command is then repeated (v. 15), followed by the motive clause (v. 16).

My child, do not walk in their way, keep your foot from their paths;
for their feet run to evil, and they hurry to shed blood.

In this case vv. 17–19 can be seen as an extension of the motive clause (they begin with 'for . . .'), but they take the form of expressing the consequence of the actions of the 'sinners', so are better seen as a negative version of the consequence clause in that they give the consequence of not heeding the command.

THE 'WISDOM SENTENCE'

In Proverbs the wisdom sentence is nearly always made up of two halves. For example, Proverbs 16:18,

---

Think about
THE INSTRUCTION FORM

Try writing your own 'instructions'. You might like to use the following traditional English proverbs as the 'command' to which to add the 'motive'.

'Judge not a man at first sight.'
'Never fish in troubled waters.'
'Make hay while the sun shines.'
'Speak the truth and shame the devil.'

Now try adding purpose clauses and conditional clauses.

Pride goes before destruction, and a haughty spirit before a fall.

This is the basic unit of Proverbs 10:1—22:16 and 25:1—29:27. It has the parallelism that is a common feature of Hebrew poetry. Three types of parallelism are very common in Proverbs.

Antithetic parallelism
In this type the second half of the sentence expresses a contrast to the first half, e.g. Proverbs 12:25,

Anxiety weighs down the human heart, but a good word cheers it up.

There are two notable subgroups of this type of sentence. One contrasts something that is an 'abomination' to the Lord with what 'delights' him.

A false balance is an abomination to the LORD,
but an accurate weight is his delight.
(Prov.11:1)

The other group are the 'better . . . than' sayings.

> Better is a dinner of vegetables where
>   love is,
> than a fatted ox and hatred with it.
>   (Prov. 15:17)

Synonymous parallelism

Synonymous parallelism occurs when the second half of the sentence repeats the essential point of the first half, but in different words, e.g. Proverbs 19:5,

> A false witness will not go unpunished,
> and a liar will not escape.

The true comparisons, or similes ('Like . . . so/is . . .'), can be classed as a subgroup of this type.

> Like snow in summer or rain in harvest,
> so honour is not fitting for a fool.
>   (Prov. 26:1)

Progressive parallelism

In this type of sentence the second half builds on or extends what has been said in the first half, e.g. Proverbs 20:4,

> The lazy person does not plow in season;
> harvest comes, and there is nothing to
>   be found.

OTHER FORMS

There are a number of other, less common, forms in Proverbs. One of the most obvious is the numerical proverb, which is concentrated in the section 30:15–33. Most take the form 'three things . . . four . . .', as in Proverbs 30:18–19,

> Three things are too wonderful for me;
> four I do not understand:
> the way of an eagle in the sky,

Think about
WISDOM SENTENCES

Does your culture have a 'wisdom sentence' form of proverb? What form does the sentence take? In English most proverbs are one-part sentences, e.g.

> 'A stitch in time saves nine.'
> 'Discretion is the better part of valour.'

Note how Proverbs 16:18 (quoted in the text) has been 'anglicized' into the form, 'Pride goes before a fall.' Only a few English proverbs have the two-part structure that is typical of Hebrew proverbs, e.g.

> 'Every dog has its day,
> and every man his hour.'

> 'Marry in haste and repent at leisure;
> 'tis good to marry late or never.'

Try turning some one-part proverbs into two-part, Hebraic-style proverbs; some antithetic, some synonymous and some progressive. You might like to expand the following traditional English proverbs.

> 'God helps those who help themselves.'
> 'Honesty is the best policy.'
> 'Least said is soonest mended.'
> 'Prevention is better than cure.'

> the way of a snake on a rock,
> the way of a ship on the high seas,
> and the way of a man with a girl.

A variant on this is the simple list of four things that are 'small, yet . . . exceedingly wise' in Proverbs 30:24–28.

There are a couple of riddles (Prov. 23:29–30; 30:4). As well as the acrostic poem in praise of the capable wife (31:10–31) there is a short poem in praise of wisdom (3:13–18). There are three speeches by 'Lady Wisdom' (1:20–33; 8:1–36; 9:1–6). Two short autobiographical narratives appear in 4:3–9 and 24:30–34.

If the wisdom material was used in education, the diversity of forms to be found in Proverbs is not surprising. A good teacher uses a variety of approaches.

OTHER STYLISTIC FEATURES

In any language the sound of words is sometimes important as well as their meaning. This can affect both the impact and memorability of a saying. This is particularly important with proverbs. 'Look before you leap' sounds better, and has more impact, than 'Look before you jump' (because of the repeated *l* sound). 'He who hesitates is lost' is preferable to 'He who hesitates will lose' (because of the *ts* sound followed by *st*). This kind of 'sound effect' is important in Hebrew proverbs, but is inevitably lost in translation.

Hebrew proverbs tend to be quite terse and therefore 'punchy'. So, Proverbs 15:23 reads in Hebrew,

> Rejecter of instruction, despiser of his soul,
> but hearer of admonition, acquirer of understanding.

Something of the 'punch' is lost in the full English translation, even if its meaning is clearer,

> Those who ignore instruction despise themselves,

but those who heed admonition gain understanding.

WHAT IS A PROVERB?

We have seen that simply trying to determine the meaning of the Hebrew word *mashal* does not give much help in answering the question, 'What is a proverb?', either in terms of form or content. If, in the biblical context, we limit the use of the word 'proverb' to the 'wisdom sentence' an examination of form and content does lead to a definition of 'proverb' with which most scholars agree. These sentences seem to have the following characteristics.

- They are brief.
- They are grounded in experience.
- They often arise from careful observation of life and the world.
- They are expressed in a memorable form.
- They claim to present a valuable insight.

On this basis a biblical Hebrew proverb might be defined as 'a reflection on life crystallized in a brief, memorable sentence'.

It is important to recognize some limitations of the proverb as a means of communication and teaching, if it is not to be misused. The single wisdom sentence lacks a context, which the hearer or reader has to supply. That context is important for its meaning, since that was rooted in a specific observation or experience. The reader has to intuit an appropriate context. In certain circumstances the proverb 'Look before you leap' is an appropriate admonition; in others 'He who hesitates is lost' provides a valuable insight. Perhaps it is to remind people of this that the compilers of Proverbs occasionally put two 'opposing' proverbs together, e.g. Proverbs 26:4–5.

> Do not answer fools according to their
>   folly,
> or you will be a fool yourself.
> Answer fools according to their folly,
> or they will be wise in their own eyes.

Many biblical proverbs are simply observations of 'the way it is' and do not contain any explicit evaluation. One should not simply assume that the statement of a reality means approval of it. Once again it is important to compare proverb with proverb to get a 'rounded' view of what the wisdom teachers were saying. Hence, Proverbs 17:8 is balanced by Proverbs 17:23,

> A bribe is like a magic stone in the eyes
>   of those who give it,
> wherever they turn they prosper.

> The wicked accept a concealed bribe
> to pervert the ways of justice.

Put together, we get the point that, while bribes often work, it is wrong to use them, at least in the administration of justice. Proverbs 15:27 counsels against bribes in general,

> Those who are greedy for unjust gain
>   make trouble for their households,
> but those who hate bribes will live.

The nature of proverbs may differ somewhat from culture to culture. Many English proverbs have the nature of 'good advice'. However, if one assumes that this is the case with a Hebrew proverb that is simply a non-evaluative observation of 'the way it is' one might be badly led astray, as the example concerning bribes given above shows.

Finally, in expressing 'the way things are' proverbs are observations, not laws. They are *describing the norm*, not *expressing the inevitable*. It is generally the case that,

> A soft answer turns away wrath,
> but a harsh word stirs up anger.
> (Prov. 15:1)

However, experience teaches us that neither half of the sentence expresses what is inevitably or always the case. Life and humans are too complex for a brief sentence to sum up all the truth about a given situation. Those who are wise are aware of that and will use proverbs with due discretion.

A THEMATIC STUDY: WORDS

We have said that it is important to compare proverb with proverb to get a 'rounded' view of what the wisdom teachers were saying. One way of doing this is to carry out a thematic study. What follows is an example of such a study.

When doing a thematic study in the book of Proverbs it is important to use a bit of 'lateral thinking' to produce a list of terms that are relevant to the theme. Taking 'words' as the theme, one can produce a list of terms that relate to the physical production of words such as: speech, mouth, tongue, lips. Then there are terms that relate to the way words are used by people, such as: liar, scoffer, gossip, flatterer, whisperer, the fool, the wise.

The book of Proverbs contains a number of 'pen portraits' of different types of characters. For many of these their 'portrait' includes how they use words. For some, of course, this is the main focus of the portrait.

THE LIAR

The book of Proverbs is very clear in its condemnation of liars and lying.

> There are six things that the LORD hates,
> seven that are an abomination to him:
> haughty eyes, a lying tongue . . .
> (Prov. 6:16–17a)

> Lying lips are an abomination to the
> LORD,
> but those who act faithfully are his
> delight. (Prov. 12:22a)

Lying is characterized as a form of hatred for the victim.

> Lying lips conceal hatred,
> and whoever utters slander is a fool.
> (Prov. 10:18)

> A lying tongue hates its victims,
> and a flattering mouth works ruin.
> (Prov. 26:28)

The sage is convinced that truth will endure but lies fail.

> Truthful lips endure for ever,
> but a lying tongue lasts only a moment.
> (Prov.12:19)

This is probably a reference to the lie told on the spur of the moment to get out of an awkward situation, to save face, or to gain some temporary advantage. Sooner or later the web of deceit will fall apart.

THE WHISPERER

The whisperer is mentioned in only a few proverbs, one of which occurs twice. He is a close companion of the 'perverse person', that is someone who turns truth on its head

(Prov. 2:12–15). Such twisting of the truth poisons relationships and creates strife.

> A perverse person spreads strife,
> and a whisperer separates close friends.
>   (Prov. 16:28)

> For lack of wood the fire goes out,
> and where there is no whisperer,
>   quarrelling ceases. (Prov. 26:20)

It is a sad comment on human nature that all too often we enjoy listening to the whisperer.

> The words of a whisperer are like
>   delicious morsels;
> they go down into the inner parts of the
>   body. (Prov. 18:8; 26:22)

People enjoy a piece of juicy talebearing, and are all too ready to believe it. The danger is that once accepted and believed the whisperer's words are not easily forgotten. They remain imprinted on the mind. This is why listening to such a person is as bad as being one.

> An evildoer listens to wicked lips,
> and a liar gives heed to a mischievous
>   tongue. (Prov. 17:4)

THE GOSSIP

The gossip can be seen as an 'overt whisperer', and is linked with revealing secrets. It is best to avoid his company.

> A gossip goes about telling secrets,
> but one who is trustworthy in spirit
>   keeps a confidence. (Prov. 11:13)

> A gossip reveals secrets;
> therefore do not associate with a babbler.
>   (Prov. 20:19)

THE FLATTERER

The flatterer is literally a person 'who makes smooth his words'. He is linked with the liar and is seen as one who brings ruin and downfall to people.

> A lying tongue hates its victims,
> and a flattering mouth works ruin.
>   (Prov. 26:28)

> Whoever flatters a neighbour
> is spreading a net for the neighbour's feet.
>   (Prov. 29:5)

Boosting someone's ego falsely only sets them up for a fall. For this reason the flatterer is contrasted unfavourably with the person who is willing to tell others unpalatable truths.

> Whoever rebukes a person will
>   afterward find more favour
> than one who flatters with the tongue.
>   (Prov. 28:23)

THE SCOFFER

The characters considered so far are minor ones in the book of Proverbs. The scoffer comes in for more attention.

> The proud, haughty person, named
>   'Scoffer',
> acts with arrogant pride. (Prov. 21:24)

> A scoffer seeks wisdom in vain,
> but knowledge is easy for one who
>   understands. (Prov. 14:6)

> Scoffers do not like to be rebuked;
> they will not go to the wise. (Prov. 15:12)

> Strike a scoffer, and the simple will learn
>   prudence;
> reprove the intelligent, and they will gain
>   knowledge. (Prov. 19:25; cf. 21:11)

Condemnation is ready for scoffers,
and flogging for the backs of fools.
(Prov. 19:29)

Drive out a scoffer, and strife goes out;
quarrelling and abuse will cease.
(Prov. 22:10)

The devising of folly is sin,
and the scoffer is an abomination to all.
(Prov. 24:9)

Scoffers set a city aflame,
but the wise turn away wrath.
(Prov. 29:8)

The scoffer is characterized by pride and arrogance (Prov. 21:24). He is so sure that he is right that he is not willing to receive rebuke or seek wisdom from those who can give it (1:20–33, addressed to the 'simple'; 'scoffers' and 'fools' is an extended exposition of 14:6 and 15:12). His attitude invites harsh treatment (19:25, 29; 21:11). Although he will learn nothing from it, others will. As well as being arrogant and unteachable, and perhaps because of these traits, the scoffer is adept at causing trouble: strife, quarrelling, abuse (22:10). The trouble he causes is compared to a raging fire (29:8). No wonder he is described as 'an abomination to all' (24:9)!

THE RIGHTEOUS AND THE WICKED

The righteous and the wicked are major characters in the book of Proverbs, and usually occur together in proverbs as 'antithetical twins'. Some of those proverbs are about their use of words.

The mouth of the righteous is a fountain of life,
but the mouth of the wicked conceals violence. (Prov. 10:11)

The tongue of the righteous is choice silver,
the mind of the wicked is of little worth.
(Prov. 10:20)

The speech of the righteous is a source of health and vitality, while that of the wicked threatens destruction, hence the contrasting value put on what they say. At the root of this difference is the fact that the righteous know what is 'acceptable', probably meaning what is acceptable to Yahweh, or perhaps that they say what is appropriate to the occasion, whereas the wicked distort the truth.

The lips of the righteous know what is acceptable,
but the mouth of the wicked what is perverse. (Prov. 10:32)

THE WISE AND THE FOOL

The wise and the fool are also major characters and 'antithetical twins' in the book of Proverbs. Much of what is said about their use of words contributes to the book's general teaching about words and how they should be used.

THE WISE USE OF WORDS

Words are very powerful.

Death and life are in the power of the tongue,
and those who love it will eat its fruits.
(Prov. 18:21)

That is why it is so important that words are used wisely. In their proverbs the sages lay down three main guidelines for the wise use of words. First of all they should be used sparingly.

When words are many, transgression is not lacking,

but the prudent are restrained in speech.
   (Prov. 10:19)

Because we are imperfect people, we are bound to say something harmful or hurtful, or wrong in some other way, from time to time. The more we speak, the more we will do that. Therefore it is better to restrain ourselves from speaking unnecessarily. Other proverbs express different aspects of this theme.

   Those who guard their mouths preserve
      their lives,
   those who open wide their lips come to
      ruin. (Prov. 13:3)

   To watch over the mouth and tongue
   is to keep out of trouble. (Prov. 21:23)

Second, we should think before we speak. In Proverbs in general 'hasty' is a bad word, and this applies to the use of words.

   Do you see someone who is hasty in
      speech?
   There is more hope for a fool than for
      anyone like that. (Prov. 29:20)

The person who is in a hurry to speak may well not mean any harm, but poorly considered words can do as much harm as wildly waving a sword might.

   Rash words are like sword thrusts,
   but the tongue of the wise brings healing.
      (Prov. 12:18)

It is carefully considered and thought-out words that will bring heath and healing.

Third, and following on from the previous guidance, it is important to listen before speaking.

If one gives answer before hearing,
   it is folly and shame. (Prov. 18:13)

This proverb condemns that all-too-common failing of being a good talker but a poor listener. In the end we simply carry on a conversation with ourselves, which exposes our lack of understanding.

THE HELPFUL USE OF WORDS

The liar, whisperer, gossip, scoffer, and so on, provide examples of the unhelpful and wrong use of words. By contrast there are three ways of using words that are commended in the book of Proverbs.

Words should be 'fitting'.

   A word fitly spoken
   is like apples of gold in a setting of silver.
      (Prov. 25:11)

   To make an apt answer is a joy to anyone,
   and a word in season, how good it is!
      (Prov. 15:23)

These proverbs commend words that are 'fitting' in the way they are expressed and in their timing. A word that is poorly expressed may not be listened to or understood, however good its content. Good advice given at the wrong moment can be counterproductive.

Words should be pleasant.

   Pleasant words are like a honeycomb,
   sweetness to the soul and health to the
      body. (Prov. 16:24)

The sages are not talking here about the 'smooth words' of the flatterer. The kind of things they mean are found in the following proverbs.

A gentle tongue is a tree of life,
but perverseness in it breaks the spirit.
(Prov. 15:4)

The wise of heart is called perceptive,
and pleasant speech increases
persuasiveness. (Prov. 16:21)

The mind of the wise makes their speech
judicious,
and adds persuasiveness to their lips.
(Prov. 16:23)

Perhaps one meaning of Proverbs 16:21 is
that harsh words are unlikely to win
arguments.

The sages recognized that we cannot
always be pleasant. At times it is necessary
to use words of reproof. They did not shy
away from this. Indeed they commend it
because, rightly used and received, reproof
builds up a person's character. Note that
what is commended is a *wise* rebuke.

Like a gold ring or an ornament of gold
is a wise rebuke to a listening ear.
(Prov. 25:12)

The desire not to hurt someone by giving a
needed rebuke may cause the unloving
thing to be done.

Better is open rebuke
than hidden love. (Prov. 27:5)

In fact a rebuke given at the right time
may nip a problem in the bud.

Whoever winks the eye causes trouble,
but the one who rebukes boldly makes
peace. (Prov. 10:10)

The wise reprover may not always be
thanked, but will sometimes get due
recognition.

Whoever rebukes a person will afterwards
find more favour
than one who flatters with the tongue.
(Prov. 28:23)

**Digging deeper:
THE SLUGGARD**

The sluggard, or 'lazy person' (as many modern translations refer to him) is something of a comic character in the book of Proverbs. Some of the proverbs about him show that the wisdom teachers had a sense of humour. Using a concordance, do a thematic study of laziness and the lazy person in Proverbs. Here is a general proverb on the theme to get you started.

A little sleep, a little slumber,
a little folding of the hands to rest,
and poverty will come upon you like a robber,
and want, like an armed warrior.
(Prov. 24:33–34)

THE COMPILATION OF THE BOOK OF PROVERBS

We have seen that, taken at its face value, the evidence within the book of Proverbs shows that it is a collection of collections and that the process of its formation stretched from the time of Solomon (mid-tenth century) until at least that of Hezekiah (late eighth century). Also, some of the material is attributed to non-Israelites. It is therefore clearly difficult to speak of an 'author' and 'date' of the book in the way that is usually meant when those terms are used.

The attribution of the book (Prov. 1:1) and at least some of its contents (10:1; 25:1) to Solomon is understandable in the light of the tradition of Solomon's personal wisdom (1 Kgs 4:29–34). It is hard to think of Solomon, or anyone in the royal court, as the original creator of much of the material in the book. As we have seen in the discussion of the roots of wisdom in Israel, many of the wisdom sentences reflect the social setting of the moderately well-off rural farmer. However, in the ancient Near East the attribution of a wisdom book to someone did not mean that that person was the originator of all the material in it. In the preface of the *Instruction of Ptahhotep* it is made clear that the book includes 'the advice of the ancestors' and 'the utterances of times past' (quoted in Fox, 2000, p. 57). Wisdom teachers were collectors of material, not just creators of it. Writing more than two millennia after *Ptahhotep* Ben Sirach says to his students,

> Be ready to listen to every godly
>   discourse,
> and let no wise proverbs escape you.
>   (Sir. 6:35)

So, it would be natural to attribute Proverbs to Solomon as the one who initiated the collection of wisdom material in Israel and personally contributed some material to it.

Careful study of the major collections that are discernible in the book (see the table 'Structure of the Book of Proverbs' on p. 91) indicates that they are themselves collections of collections. A suggestive piece of evidence for this is the fact that there are some proverbs that are repeated more or less word for word (e.g. Prov.

14:12/16:25; 18:8/26:22; 20:16/27:13). This is more likely to happen when blocks of proverbs are brought together than when proverbs are selected individually for inclusion in an existing collection.

Proverbs 10:1—22:16 contains 375 sentences. All but one of these is a two-part sentence (19:7 has three parts). Scholars do not always agree about the classification of particular sentences, but about 200 of these contain antithetical parallelism. About 160 of the antithetical sentences occur in Proverbs 10—15. The difference in the predominant form of sentences is often taken as evidence that Proverbs 10—15 and 16:1—22:16 were originally separate collections. It is interesting that there is an unusual concentration of proverbs using the name Yahweh in 14:26—16:11. Is this somehow related to the joining of these two earlier collections?

Proverbs 25—29 also seems to contain two different blocks of material. In Proverbs 25—27 there are a large number of similes (comparisons using the word 'like') and metaphors (implicit comparisons) and relatively few antithetical sentences. This section also contains a concentration of short pieces of the 'instruction' form. Compared with chs 25—27, chs 28—29 have a high concentration of sentences with antithetical parallelism and progressive parallelism. There are very few comparisons. Once again, these stylistic differences might indicate two originally separate collections. The fairly lengthy piece of 'instruction' (vv. 23–27) at the end of Proverbs 27 could have been the conclusion of the first collection.

With regard to Proverbs 1—9 there is general, though not unanimous,

Digging deeper:
THE COMPILATION OF PROVERBS 25—29

Read through Proverbs 25—27 identifying the comparisons (whether similes or metaphors) and the antithetical sentences. Then read Proverbs 28—29 identifying the sentences with either antithetical or progressive parallelism and the comparisons. What percentage of proverbs in chs 25—27 are comparisons, and what is the percentage of comparisons in chs 28—29?

agreement that there are ten sections, each of which begins in the same way.

- They are all addressed (in Hebrew) to 'my son' ('sons' in Prov. 4:1) as the first or second word.
- The son is commanded to 'hear', 'receive', 'not forget', and so on, the instruction which follows (in 2:1 this is expressed in a conditional form).
- The personal authority of the speaker, the 'father', is asserted.
- The great value and utility of the father's words is asserted or implied.

The sections begin at: 1:8–9; 2:1f.; 3:1–2; 3:21–22; 4:1–2; 4:10–12; 4:20–22; 5:1–2; 6:20–22; 7:1–3. There is also a fair degree of agreement on three 'interludes' between some of the sections, and that ch. 8 is a final 'interlude' which is a counterpart to 1:20–33.

- 1:20–33 Wisdom's warning.
- 3:13–20 A poem in praise of Wisdom.
- 6:1–19   Four admonitions and warnings.
- 8:1–36   Wisdom's self-praise.

Beyond this level of agreement there is dispute over the extent to which the ten sections each form a coherent 'instruction'. Whybray sees in several of them an original core that has then undergone expansion by one or more additions. For example, in his analysis of Proverbs 3:21–35 he regards vv. 21–24, 27–31 as the original instruction. He suggests that vv. 25–26 are a secondary addition made in order to equate the father's teaching with trust in Yahweh. Since, in contrast to the specific teaching of vv. 27–31, vv. 32–34 speak only in general terms of the fates of the righteous and the wicked, they too are regarded as a secondary addition, with v. 35 added later. Fox, on the other hand, sees each 'lecture' (to use his terminology) as a cohesive unit with a threefold structure (illustrated by 3:21–35).

1. *Exordium.* The introduction, which contains,
   a. an *address*, 'my son(s) . . .';
   b. an *exhortation* (3:21);
   c. a *motivation* (3:22–26).
2. *Lesson.* The body of the teaching (3:27–32). In this case there are five admonitions, all beginning with 'Do not . . .'
3. *Conclusion.* A summary statement, which generalizes the teaching (3:33–34). It sometimes ends with a *capstone* that forms a memorable climax (3:35).

Proverbs 9 contains portraits of personified Wisdom (vv. 1–6) and Folly (vv. 13–18). These form a suitable dramatic climax to this section of the book. Scholars differ over the nature and function of vv. 7–12. There is no consensus concerning the reason for the present order of the ten instructions. No clear development of

**Digging deeper:
PROVERBS 3:21–35**

Read the relevant sections in the commentaries on Proverbs by Fox and Whybray so that you can appreciate more fully and assess for yourself their arguments, which have been summarized in this chapter.

thought or thematic arrangement is discernible.

Like chs 10—31, chs 1—9 appears to be a collection of pre-existing material. For a long time there was a general consensus that Proverbs 1—9 should be dated later than Proverbs 10—31, and well into the post-exilic period. There were two main reasons for this. The first was the belief that the extended 'discourse' form in these chapters was a literary development of the wisdom sentence. The second was the assumption that the theological portrayal of Wisdom in these chapters reflects a later, more developed, 'wisdom theology' than do the sentences. Recently the adequacy of both of these reasons has been questioned. The recognition of the instruction form in Proverbs 1—9 undercut the first reason. It is clear that this is an independent literary form that has a long history pre-dating the earliest likely date for the book of Proverbs. Second, comparison of the content of Proverbs 1—9 with that of non-Israelite material, especially Egyptian wisdom literature, has led some scholars (e.g. Kayatz, Lang) to conclude that a pre-exilic date cannot be ruled out for the theological conception of wisdom in these chapters.

Proverbs 1:1—7 forms an introduction to the whole book in its present form. The fact that the 'motto' of 1:7 is echoed near the end of the instructions (9:10), in the body of the sentences (15:33) and near the end of the book (31:30) is probably no accident. Although at first sight the acrostic poem about the capable wife may seem an odd way to end the book, on closer inspection it does seem to be placed where it is deliberately. One probable reason for the use of the acrostic form in the Hebrew Bible is to convey the idea of completeness – so, the poem completes the book of Proverbs. Some features of the poem suggest that it is meant to provoke echoes of Proverbs 1—9. In those chapters there are several female figures: mother, bride, wife, the loose woman, the adulteress, and the personified figures of Wisdom and Folly. Unlike the loose woman, the adulteress and Folly, who are wayward and ignorant (5:6; 7:11; 9:13) the capable wife is reliable (31:11–12) and wise (31:26). Like Wisdom she is a teacher (31:26/8:14) and 'far more precious than jewels' (31:10/ 3:15; 8:11). Therefore, like Wisdom (1:28; 3:13; 4:22; 8:17, 35) she is worth finding (31:10). Above all, like Wisdom (1:7; 9:10), the source of her virtues is 'the fear of the LORD' (31:30).

From what has been said above, it is clear that the formation of the book of Proverbs was a complex and, no doubt, lengthy process. Collections of material were made, and these were then combined in several stages until the whole book as we have it was gathered together and given the introduction and conclusion provided by Proverbs 1:1—7 and 31:10–31. This probably happened in the post-exilic period, but there are so many uncertainties about the formation of this book that one cannot be sure of this.

THE ARRANGEMENT OF THE SENTENCES

The general impression gained on reading through Proverbs 10:1—22:16 and 25:1—29:27 is that the ordering of the sentences is haphazard. For instance, it is hard to understand why, although about half the proverbs in ch. 10 concern the righteous and the wicked (some occurring in small groups of two or more), these are interspersed with others on quite different subjects for no apparent reason. Despite extensive studies no one has produced a widely accepted explanation of any principles underlying the arrangement of the material. Three main possible principles of ordering have been explored.

- *Thematic* Sayings are put into groups dealing with the similar subjects or themes. For example, there is a group of proverbs about the fool in Proverbs 26:1–12 (except v. 2), followed by a group about the lazy person (26:13–16).
- *Verbal* Adjacent sayings use the same or similar words. This, of course, will tend to happen if they deal with similar subjects, but the use of similar words need not mean similarity of subject. For example, every verse in Proverbs 15:33—16:7 contains the name of Yahweh.
- *Paranomasia* This means an affinity of sound, which can occur in a number of ways. For, example, in Proverbs 11:9–12 each sentence begins with the same letter of the Hebrew alphabet (*bet*).

The fact is that these kinds of links never group together more than a handful of sentences.

> **Digging deeper:**
> **THE ARRANGEMENT OF THE SENTENCES**
>
> Read through Proverbs 10, noting the sentences that are about the righteous and the wicked. Then see if you can think of any reasons why the other sentences that are interspersed with them are placed where they are. Consult some commentaries to see whether they make any suggestions.

AMENEMOPE AND PROVERBS 22:17—24:22

As we have seen, the (reconstructed) title in Proverbs 22:17a and the title in Proverbs 24:23a mark out a distinct section within the book of Proverbs. This section is also marked out by its literary features. The basic unit is not the two-part wisdom sentence but a four-part sentence (or quatrain). Moreover, the form is that of the instruction and not the simple statement.

These stylistic features are shared with the *Instruction of Amenemope*. However, more striking, and more significant, are the similarities of content. These are set out in 'The *Instruction of Amenemope*: Parallels with the Book of Proverbs' on p. 106. Comparison with *Amenemope* has given scholars a probable answer to a problem in the Hebrew text of Proverbs 22:20. This says, 'Have I not written for you "three

THE *INSTRUCTION OF AMENEMOPE*: PARALLELS WITH THE BOOK OF PROVERBS

Proverbs 22:24: Make no friends with those given to anger, and do not associate with hotheads.
Amenemope 11:13–14: Do not befriend the heated man, nor approach him for conversation.
Proverbs 22:28: Do not remove the ancient landmark that your ancestors set up.
Amenemope 7:12–13: Do not move the markers on the borders of the fields, nor shift the position of the measuring-cord.
Proverbs 22:29: Do you see those who are skilful in their work? They will serve kings; they will not serve common people.
Amenemope 27:16–17: The scribe who is skilled in his office, he is found worthy to be a courtier.
Proverbs 23:1–2: When you sit down to eat with a ruler, observe carefully what is before you, and put a knife to your throat if you have a big appetite.
Amenemope 13–18: Do not eat in the presence of an official and then set your mouth before [him]; if you are sated content yourself with your saliva. Look at the bowl that is before you, and let it serve your needs.
Proverbs 23:4–5: Do not wear yourself out to get rich: be wise enough to desist. When your eyes alight upon it, it is gone; for suddenly it takes wings to itself, flying like an eagle toward heaven.
Amenemope 9:14–16; 10:4–5: Do not strain to seek increase, what you have, let it suffice you. If riches come to you by theft ... They make themselves wings like geese, and fly away to the sky.
Proverbs 23:6–7: Do not eat the bread of the stingy; do not desire their delicacies; for like hair in the throat, so are they.
Amenemope 14:5–7: Do not covet a poor man's goods, nor hunger for his bread; a poor man's goods are a block in the throat, it makes the gullet vomit.

The quotations from *Amenemope* are from the translation by Miriam Lichtheim, in Hallo and Younger (1997, pp. 115–122).

days ago" (*shilshom*) in admonitions and knowledge?' A slight emendation of the text gives the reading, 'Have I not written for you "thirty" (*sheloshim*) (sayings) of admonition and knowledge?' The conclusion of *Amenemope* begins, 'Look to these thirty chapters, they inform, they educate.' The book is indeed divided into 30 short chapters. A number of scholars (e.g. McKane) have indeed found 30 sayings in this section of Proverbs following the introduction in 22:17–21 – though they do not always agree on the details of the division. These analyses have not found universal acceptance.

The parallels with *Amenemope* are quite marked in Proverbs 22:22—23:11. Six of the ten sayings that McKane identifies in this section of Proverbs have close parallels in the Egyptian work. The intriguing, and unanswerable, question is why the similarities do not continue in the remaining 20 sayings. Although most scholars think that the degree of similarity between Proverbs 22:17—23:11 and *Amenemope* indicates a direct dependence of the Hebrew compiler on the Egyptian work, others are not convinced of this. They argue that the compiler might be drawing on a general knowledge of common Egyptian proverbs. However, in that case it is surprising that a group of

Think about
PARALLELS WITH *AMENEMOPE*

How striking do you find the parallels between *Amenemope* and Proverbs set out in the 'The *Instruction of Amenemope*: Parallels with the Book of Proverbs' box? What do you think about the possible explanations for them?

sayings with close parallels in *Amenemope* should all appear close together in this section of Proverbs.

WOMAN WISDOM IN THE BOOK OF PROVERBS

One of the striking features of the book of Proverbs is the number of female figures in the book and the significant role that some of them play. There are the references to the mother as teacher (Prov. 1:8; 6:20), including the queen who teaches her son about the behaviour and duties of a king (31:1–9). As well as the capable wife of the acrostic poem (31:10–31) there is the 'wife of one's youth' (5:18–19). In contrast to these positive female icons there are the 'loose woman' (2:16–19; 5:3–6; 6:24–29; 7:1–27) and Folly (9:13–18). However, the main female figure is Wisdom herself.

Wisdom first appears personified as a woman in Proverbs 1:20–33. She is depicted as crying out in the public places of the city, addressing the 'simple ones'. In a first-person speech she warns of disaster for those who have not paid any heed to her words, and promises security to those who pay heed. The poem in praise of wisdom in 3:13–20 uses both anthropomorphic and personal language, so that it too seems to be presenting wisdom as a female figure. This is equally the case in 4:5–9. The picture of wisdom as the generous hostess in 9:1–6 clearly stands in contrast to both the 'loose woman' and Folly.

The most developed presentation of personified wisdom is found in Proverbs 8. In 8:1–20 Wisdom speaks in the kind of way that she does in 1:20–33.

Although 8:22–31 picks up on the theme of wisdom and creation mentioned in 3:19–20, it goes beyond anything found in the other passages in which wisdom is personified. The primordial nature of Wisdom as the product of Yahweh's first act of creation is emphasized in vv. 22–26. From v. 27 onwards the emphasis is on Wisdom's presence alongside Yahweh in creation. But is Wisdom depicted as simply *present*, or as *active* during the process of creation? The answer depends on the translation of one Hebrew word in v. 30 (*'amon*). Among the many suggested translations there are three main proposals.

- The word may be derived from a verb meaning 'trustworthy'. This has led to it being translated as 'confidant', or even 'darling'.
- The word may come from a verb meaning 'to nurse'. This has led to the translation 'nurseling/little child'.
- A commonly suggested emendation of the word (based on the assumption that it is a word borrowed from Akkadian) is *'omman*, meaning 'expert, craftsman'.

Although the third suggestion would open up the possibility of Wisdom playing an active role in creation, the context does not demand this. It simply speaks of Wisdom being 'beside' Yahweh and 'before' him as he carried out his creative acts. There has been much debate about whether or not Wisdom is simply a personification or an hypostasis, an entity separate from Yahweh. The third suggestion might open up this possibility. However, even then v. 22 makes Wisdom subordinate to Yahweh as a created entity. In the light of the uncertainty about the meaning of *'amon* it seems best to see Wisdom in Proverbs 8:22–31 as a vividly portrayed personification of an attribute of Yahweh rather than as an hypostasis.

**Digging deeper:
PROVERBS 8:20**

The following commentaries present different views of the meaning of this verse. Read what they say and draw your own conclusion.

M. V. Fox *Proverbs 1–9*, 2000.
W. McKane *Proverbs: New Approach*, 1970.
R. E. Murphy *Proverbs*, 1998.
R. N. Whybray *Proverbs*, 1994.

A number of attempts have been made to trace the origins of the picture of personified Wisdom and her relation to the created world. One quite popular view (propounded by Kayatz) sees the prototype in Maat, the Egyptian goddess of 'order/truth/justice'. Maat is an hypostasis, embodying the divine order that is imminent in the world. However, Maat was never a popular and well-known deity and, in the extant texts, is never depicted giving a speech like those of Woman Wisdom in Proverbs. Fox questions whether the scattered references to Maat in Egyptian texts provide a likely background to the figure of Wisdom in Proverbs 8.

B. Lang rejects Maat as the prototype for Wisdom, and suggests instead that it is to be found in a Canaanite goddess. However, no Canaanite wisdom goddess is known. Moreover Woman Wisdom bears little resemblance to any of the known Canaanite goddesses. She is not sexually aggressive nor does she represent the realm of fertility. Her gifts are not the fruit of the womb and the field, but justice and righteousness, which lead to wealth (8:19–21).

Knox drew attention to aretalogies – compositions in praise of gods – in which the Egyptian goddess Isis speaks in first-person terms, and noted some similarities to Proverbs 8. However, these only became popular in the late third century BC, too late to be relevant as a prototype for Proverbs 8.

Just as plausible as these suggestions is the supposition that the fact that the word for 'wisdom' in Hebrew is a feminine noun meant that when personified wisdom was naturally depicted as a woman. Personification is quite a common literary technique, especially in poetry. C. Camp has argued that several roles of human women (as opposed to goddesses) were woven into the picture of Woman Wisdom in Proverbs.

The evaluation of the personification of wisdom as a woman in Proverbs 1—9 has evoked a wide spectrum of responses from feminist scholars. Some (e.g. Brenner, Newsom) argue that although the 'voice' of wisdom is female it conveys a male, patriarchal ideology. A. O. Bellis has responded to this with particular reference to Proverbs 7, which she argues expresses genuinely feminine concerns within the context of the writer's society. Camp and K. A. Farmer are among those who are generally positive about the female personification of wisdom. Farmer gives three reasons for this.

- It provides a positive reflection on women's role as a source of wisdom and instruction.
- It provides an alternative and less exclusively masculine way of speaking about God.
- Wisdom ways of thinking encourage women (and others whose experiences vary from the 'norm' in their society) to value their own experience and observations of reality and to use them to test traditional formulations of truth.

Think about
WISDOM AS FEMININE

Read the sections of Proverbs in which wisdom is personified as a woman. Then consider how you respond to Farmer's reasons for regarding this personification positively from a feminist perspective.

PROVERBS AND THEOLOGY

The fact that there is almost no mention of Israel's cult or of her salvation-history tradition in the book of Proverbs has led writers on Old Testament theology to ignore or even denigrate it until fairly recently. Its supposed 'foreign' origins have not helped. This can be seen in what were probably the two most influential works on the subject in the twentieth century, those by W. Eichrodt (published in German in 1933–1939) and G. von Rad (published in German 1957–1960). Eichrodt's theology centres on the covenant relationship between God and Israel. He devotes only a few pages ('The Wisdom of God' in vol. 2, pp. 80–92) to the wisdom literature, concentrating on Proverbs 8:22–31. In his first volume, on 'The Theology of Israel's Historical Traditions' Von Rad has a section on 'Israel before Yahweh', dealing with Israel's response to Yahweh's dealing with her in her history. Subsections on Proverbs 10—31 (pp. 418–441), Proverbs 1—9 and Job (pp. 441–453) and Ecclesiastes (453–459) fit in awkwardly here since there is no response to Israel's historical experiences of Yahweh in these books. In 1970 Von Rad published a seminal work, *Wisdom in Israel*, which marked the growing interest of scholars in taking more account of the wisdom literature in their theological thinking about the Old Testament. Two more recent books in which this has been attempted are the works by Clements and Perdue. Here we will consider briefly a few topics that have been the subject of some discussion.

THE FEAR OF YAHWEH

The idea of 'fearing God/Yahweh' is found throughout the Hebrew Bible. It is very likely that the phrase had its origin in the sense of religious awe when confronted with the Numinous. It is used in this sense in the account of the exodus and covenant making at Sinai (Exod. 14:10, 31; 20:18–20). At Sinai, awe and reverence for Yahweh lead to the commitment to obey him. So, the account of that experience in Deuteronomy ends with two statements about what the 'fear of Yahweh' means.

So now, O Israel, what does the LORD your God require of you? Only to fear the LORD your God, to walk in all his ways, to love him, to serve the LORD your God with all your heart and with all your soul, and to keep the commandments of the LORD your God and his decrees that I am commanding you today, for your own well-being. (Deut. 10:12–13)

You shall fear the LORD your God; him alone you shall worship; to him you shall hold fast, and by his name you shall swear. (Deut. 10:20)

So, 'fearing Yahweh' came to mean having a loyalty to, and love for, Yahweh that is shown in obedience to his commandments. As a result it is given as the motivation for such practical matters as how one treats people who are deaf or blind or elderly (Lev. 19:14, 32). It is the practical aspect of the fear of the Lord meaning 'to walk in his ways . . . for your own well-being' that predominates in Proverbs. However, there is no reason to assume that in Proverbs the concept has become purely moral in content and lost the connotation of religious awe and devotion.

The importance of this concept for the book of Proverbs is indicated by the placing of the 'motto' immediately after the prologue to the book.

The fear of the LORD is the beginning of knowledge;
fools despise wisdom and instruction. (Prov. 1:7)

As we have seen, echoes of this run like a linking thread through the book:

The fear of the LORD is the beginning of wisdom,
and the knowledge of the Holy One is insight. (Prov. 9:10)

The fear of the LORD is instruction in wisdom,
and humility goes before honour. (Prov. 15:33)

Charm is deceitful, and beauty is vain, but a woman who fears the LORD is to be praised. (Prov. 31:3)

The variants in these verses are instructive. First, in Proverbs 9:10 and 15:33 'wisdom' is used to replace 'knowledge', so confirming the link of 'wisdom' with 'the fear of the Lord' implied in 1:7b. Second, in 15:33 'instruction in wisdom' replaces 'the beginning of wisdom'. This supports the usual translation of the other verses against the suggestion that the word translated 'beginning' might be translated as 'the best part'. It also indicates that the sense of 'the beginning' is 'first principle' or 'basis' rather than an initial stage that gets left behind. Both 9:10b and 15:33b suggest a relational meaning for 'the fear of the Lord' (cf. Prov. 2:5). The 'knowledge' of God is understood in relational terms in the Hebrew Bible (e.g. Hos. 4:1; 6:6). Proverbs 15:33 particularly specifies an attitude of humility towards Yahweh (cf. Prov. 22:4). Finally, the designation of the capable wife as 'a woman who fears the Lord' shows that 'fearing the Lord' has to do with human life and behaviour in general, and is not just a matter of cultic observances. In a way that is reminiscent of the promise of 'well-being' in Deuteronomy 10:13, Proverbs links the fear of Yahweh with gaining 'life' (Proverbs 3:7–8; 10:27; 14:27; 19:23; 22:4). The content of these proverbs shows that what is in mind is 'quality of life' now, in our physical existence. The moral aspect of fearing Yahweh is summed up in Proverbs 8:13.

The fear of the LORD is hatred of evil.
Pride and arrogance and the way of evil
and perverted speech I hate.

Proverbs 3:7, 16:6 and 23:17 express
similar sentiments. For the sages, 'the fear
of Yahweh' had both an inward aspect of
one's relationship to Yahweh and an
outward aspect of one's conduct in life.

Digging deeper:
THE FEAR OF THE LORD

Using a concordance, find all the proverbs that
speak of 'the fear of the Lord'. Do they fall into
any distinct groups according to their content?
In the light of them, evaluate what has been
said in the text about the meaning of 'the fear
of the Lord' in the book of Proverbs.

McKane, among others, argued for an 'old
wisdom' that was practical and secular,
which was later subject to 'theological
reorientation' to Yahwism by the linking of
wisdom with Yahweh and the creation of
'Yahweh proverbs'. As we have seen, the
idea that wisdom, either outside or inside
Israel, was ever 'secular' in our modern
sense is now widely questioned. There is
therefore no good reason to regard all the
references to 'the fear of Yahweh' as late
additions to Israel's corpus of wisdom
literature.

WISDOM AND CREATION

In the Hebrew Bible, God is revealed in
several different ways. The most direct
ways are in the Torah (Law) revealed at
Sinai and in the 'word of the Lord' spoken
by the prophets. However, there are also
God's acts in the history of Israel. None of
these was clear and free of problems. The
law was not comprehensive and needed
adaptation (note the differences between
the laws about freeing slaves in Exodus
21:2–11 and Deuteronomy 15:12–18).
Recognizing true from false prophets was a
frequent problem, with no easy answer
(the guidelines given in Deut. 13:1–5;
18:20–22 do not solve all the possible
problems). It took special insight to see
and understand the hand of God at work
in the complexities and contingencies of
history. At first sight there is no obvious
source of divine revelation in the wisdom
literature. The human teacher is obvious,
but there is no appeal to divine authority,
no reference to the Torah or claim to speak
in the name of Yahweh. There is, though,
the call to 'find', 'get' or 'heed' Wisdom.
Scholars have come to recognize that this
points to the created order as a source of
divine revelation.

Proverbs 3:19–20 links wisdom with
creation, and this is expanded upon in
8:22–36. In 8:22–30 the cosmos is depicted
as a well-ordered structure designed and
executed by Yahweh. Wisdom seems to
embody the principles of order. In 8:31
Wisdom is depicted as playing (this is a
common meaning of the Hebrew word
often translated 'rejoice' here) in the
created world, and in particular,
delighting in human beings. Here Wisdom
seems to be the mediator between the
Creator and the creatures, especially
humans. It is not surprising, therefore, that
8:32–36 is a call to listen to Wisdom
because 'whoever finds me [Wisdom] finds
life and obtains favour from the LORD'.
Some scholars think that this theme of
Wisdom as the order enshrined in creation
continues in 9:1–6. They suggest that the
'house' of 9:1 is the cosmos. The 'seven
pillars' might be the seven planets of

antiquity (the five visible planets plus the sun and moon). However, this is only one possible understanding of an enigmatic verse.

Proverbs 3:19–20 and 8:22–36 provide the basis for understanding the enterprise of the sages in ancient Israel. By careful observation of the patterns that can be discerned in life, seen through the lens of 'the fear of the Lord', and reflection on experience in the light of 'the knowledge of the Holy One', it is possible to gain insight into divine wisdom. As a source of revelation this is no more, or less, problematic than discerning Yahweh's hand in the events of history, separating true prophecies from false ones, or rightly interpreting and applying the Torah.

One reason why Proverbs has suffered from theological neglect in the past is that it has been seen as a pragmatic 'handbook of morals' that tended to divorce behaviour from spirituality. However, a proper understanding of what it means by 'the fear of the Lord' and its 'creation theology' points the way to a spirituality that leads to an integrated life. Proverbs is free from those dichotomies that often characterize religious life and institutions. Here injustice of various kinds and exploitation of other people is dealt with as forcefully as drunkenness and sexual immorality. The worlds of politics and business are as much the spheres in which to live out 'the fear of the Lord' as is the home.

REWARD AND RETRIBUTION

Scholars have often seen in Proverbs an assumption of a more or less mechanical association between an action and its outcome, the so-called 'deed–consequence nexus'. There are some proverbs that seem to support this.

> The wicked earn no real gain,
> but those who sow righteousness get a
> true reward. (Prov. 11:18)

> Whoever sows injustice will reap
> calamity. (Prov. 22:8a)

However, there are at least three features of the material in the book of Proverbs that suggest the sages had a rather more nuanced view than is sometimes attributed to them, as Van Leeuwen, among other recent scholars, has stressed. The first is the point made above about the inherent limitations of proverbs, and the indications of this in those proverbs which seem to contradict each other (Prov. 26:4–5) or at least stand in tension with one another (10:15; 11:4).

Second, there are proverbs that reflect the complexity of real life by recognizing the opposite of what is presented as the norm in the book. Poverty can be the result of injustice (13:23) and not laziness (10:4). Injustice can lead to wealth (16:8). Indeed, several of the 'better than' sayings reflect the injustices and inequalities of life, which leave the righteous at a disadvantage (e.g. 15:16).

Finally, there are proverbs that recognize the limitations of human wisdom and understanding and the unfathomable nature of divine wisdom. For example,

> The human mind may devise many plans,
> but it is the purpose of the LORD that
> will be established. (Prov. 19:21)

> All our steps are ordered by the LORD,
> how then can we understand our own
> ways? (Prov. 20:24)

No wisdom, no understanding, no
counsel,
can avail against the LORD. (Prov. 21:30)

The horse is made ready for the day of
battle,
but the victory belongs to the LORD.
(Prov. 21:31)

The last of these proverbs stands in tension
with Proverbs 21:18, which attributes
success in war to taking advice and wise
counsel.

The general note of confidence in the book
of Proverbs is an expression of the sages'
faith in the divine ordering of creation.
This makes for a measure of predictability
in life. R. Van Leeuwen suggests that there
is a pedagogical reason for the
predominance of proverbs setting out the
'norm' – namely the need to establish the
'basic rules' of life as the framework within
which to deal with the exceptions.
However, the sages were not naïve, and
accepted that things can turn out
differently from what one expects. In part,
at least, this is because Yahweh's wisdom
transcends human wisdom.

WISDOM AFTER PROVERBS

The personification of Wisdom in Proverbs
1—9 was the start of a development that
continued in later Judaism and had an
important influence on early Christian
theology. The first stage of this
development is found in Ben Sirach 24, a
hymn of self-praise uttered by Wisdom. She
is once more associated with creation (v. 3),

I came forth from the mouth of the Most
High,
and covered the earth like a mist.

It is clearly stated that she is God's
creature (v. 9, 'he created me'). She was
specifically ordered to dwell in Israel (vv.
8–12), where she flourished (vv. 13–17).
The hymn ends with an invitation (vv. 19–
22), which echoes those in Proverbs.
However, Ben Sirach then makes a
comment that explicitly identifies Wisdom
with the Torah (v. 23),

All this is the book of the covenant of the
Most High God,
the law that Moses commanded us
as an inheritance for the congregations
of Jacob.

Ben Sirach was writing in Hebrew in
Palestine in the early second century BC.
Towards the end of that century an
Alexandrian Jew writing in Greek
produced a book that has become known
as the Wisdom of Solomon. He goes
beyond Proverbs and Ben Sirach in
making Wisdom an active participant in
the creation of the cosmos. She was 'an
associate in [God's] works . . . the active
cause of all things . . . fashioner of what
exists' (Wis. 8:4–6). To Wisdom he
attributes divine qualities (holy, all-
powerful, overseeing all, 7:23). She
pervades all things (7:24) and is 'a breath
of the power of God, and a pure emanation
of the glory of the Almighty' (7:25). Later
Wisdom is identified with the pillars of
cloud and fire that accompanied Israel in
the wilderness (10:17). In the story in
Exodus these are symbols of God's
presence. The author of the Wisdom of
Solomon seems to have gone beyond
personification to make Wisdom an
hypostasis.

There are echoes of Proverbs, the thought
of Ben Sirach and the Wisdom of Solomon

in John 1:1–14, where John speaks of the pre-existent Word (*Logos* in Greek). This Word was with God before all things, was the agent in creation and became 'flesh' to dwell among humans and reveal God to them. Here John is combining ideas about Wisdom from the Jewish tradition with Greek, especially Stoic, thought about the Divine Logos that pervades creation. There are strong echoes of the language of Wisdom 7:24–26 in Hebrews 1:2–3. There are also echoes of language about Wisdom in Colossians 1:15–17. It is clear that the development of Jewish thought about Wisdom provided the early Christians with language to talk about God being revealed in a human being, Jesus of Nazareth.

FURTHER READING

Items marked * are considered suitable as first ports of call, while others are more complex, or relate to specific issues.

COMMENTARIES

The book of Proverbs has been rather neglected by commentators writing in English until quite recently. Although now quite dated, Toy's commentary is a classic of its time and its frequent references to the early translations from Hebrew are still useful. Kidner's brief commentary is also somewhat dated but has helpful exegetical comments on the text. McKane's commentary was an important contribution to the study of the book of Proverbs because of its in-depth analysis of non-Israelite wisdom literature. It is also valuable for its study of the language of the book. Like other volumes in the DSB series, Aitken's has a devotional slant. Whybray's commentary is perhaps the

most accessible of the welcome batch of more recent commentaries on this book.

K. T. Aitken *Proverbs*. DSB. Edinburgh: St Andrew Press, 1986.

M. V. Fox *Proverbs 1–9*. AB. New York, NY: Doubleday, 2000.

* D. Kidner *Proverbs*. TOTC. London: IVP, 1964.

W. McKane *Proverbs: A New Approach*. OTL. London: SCM, 1970.

R. E. Murphy *Proverbs*. WBC. Nashville, TN: Thomas Nelson, 1998.

* L. G. Perdue *Proverbs*. Interpretation. Louisville, KY: Westminster John Knox Press, 2000.

C. H. Toy *The Book of Proverbs*. ICC. Edinburgh: T. & T. Clark, 1899.

* R. N. Whybray *Proverbs*. NCB. London: Marshall Pickering, 1994.

OTHER BOOKS AND ARTICLES

A. O. Bellis 'The Gender and Motives of the Wisdom Teacher in Proverbs 7', in A. Brenner and C. Fontaine (eds.) *Wisdom and Psalms*. A Feminist Companion to the Bible (2nd Series), Sheffield: Sheffield Academic Press, 1998; pp. 79–91.

A. Brenner 'Proverbs 1–9: An F Voice?', in A. Brenner and F. van Dijk-Hemmes (eds.) *On Gendering Texts*. Leiden: Brill, 1993; pp. 113–130.

C. Camp *Wisdom and the Feminine in the Book of Proverbs*. Sheffield: Almond Press, 1985.

* J. L. Crenshaw *Old Testament Wisdom: An Introduction*. Louisville, KY: Westminster John Knox Press, 1998 (rev. edn).

R. E. Clements *Wisdom in Theology*. Carlisle: Paternoster, 1992.

R. E. Clements 'Wisdom and Old Testament Theology', in J. Day, R. P.

Gordon and H. G. M. Williamson *Wisdom in Ancient Israel*. Cambridge: CUP, 1995; pp. 269–286.

J. Day, R. P. Gordon and H. G. M. Williamson *Wisdom in Ancient Israel*. Cambridge: CUP, 1995.

W. Eichrodt *Theology of the Old Testament*. London: SCM, 1961/1967; 2 vols.

*K. A. Farmer 'The Wisdom Books', in S. L. McKenzie and M. P. Graham (eds.) *The Hebrew Bible Today: An Introduction to Critical Issues*. Louisville, KY: Westminster John Knox Press, 1998; pp. 129–151.

J. M. Hadley 'Wisdom and the Goddess', in J. Day, R. P. Gordon and H. G. M. Williamson *Wisdom in Ancient Israel*. Cambridge: CUP, 1995; pp. 234–243.

W. W. Hallo and K. L. Younger Jnr (eds.) *The Context of Scripture*, Leiden: Brill, 1997; vol. 1.

C. Kayatz *Studien zu Proverbien 1–9*. WMANT 22. Neukirchen-Vluyn: Neukirchener Verlag, 1966.

W. L. Knox 'The Divine Wisdom', *JTS* 38 (1937), 230–237.

B. Lang *Wisdom and the Book of Proverbs: An Israelite Goddess Redefined*. New York, NY: Pilgrim Press, 1986.

* J. D. Martin *Proverbs*. OT Guides. Sheffield: Sheffield Academic Press, 1995.

R. E. Murphy *Wisdom Literature*. FOTL 13. Grand Rapids, MI: Eerdmans, 1981.

R. E. Murphy 'The Personification of Wisdom', in J. Day, R. P. Gordon and H. G. M. Williamson *Wisdom in Ancient Israel*. Cambridge: CUP, 1995; pp. 222–233.

* R. E. Murphy *The Tree of Life*. Grand Rapids, MI: Eerdmans, 1996 (2nd edn).

C. A. Newsom 'Woman and the Discourse of Patriarchal Wisdom: A Study of Proverbs 1–9', in P. L. Day (ed.), *Gender and Difference*. Minneapolis, MN: Fortress, 1989; pp. 142–160.

* L. G. Perdue *Wisdom and Creation: The Theology of Wisdom Literature*. Nashville, TN: Abingdon, 1994.

R. Van Leeuwen 'Wealth and Poverty: System and Contradiction in Proverbs', *Hebrew Studies* 33 (1992), 25–36.

G. von Rad *Old Testament Theology*. Edinburgh: Oliver & Boyd, 1962, 1965; 2 vols.

G. von Rad *Wisdom in Israel*. London: SCM, 1972.

R. N. Whybray *Wisdom in Proverbs*. London: SCM, 1965.

R. N. Whybray *The Book of Proverbs: A Survey of Modern Study*. Leiden: Brill, 1995.

R. N. Whybray *The Composition of the Book of Proverbs*. Sheffield: JSOT Press, 1995.

Chapter 5

JOB

THE STRUCTURE OF THE BOOK OF JOB

The structure of the book of Job in the form we have it is fairly clear. To begin with there is an obvious distinction between the bulk of the book, which is written in Hebrew poetry, and the prose prologue and epilogue. The prose sections tell the story of Job. The poetry consists of speeches, and there are three main groups of them. The largest consists of three rounds of speeches, which form a discussion between Job and his three friends Eliphaz, Bildad and Zophar. There are clear introductions to each speech, 'Then X answered...' Following these speeches there are four by a character called Elihu. Finally the speeches are rounded off by two speeches by Yahweh, to each of which Job makes a short response. This is set out in more detail in the table 'Structure of the Book of Job' on p. 118.

Consideration of this structure raises some questions. The third round of speeches between Job and his friends appears to be truncated. Bildad's speech is short and there is no speech by Zophar. Was this the original plan, or has something happened to it? The poem concerning wisdom seems to be something of an intrusion. Why is it there? As we shall see, consideration of the content of the book strengthens these questions and introduces others.

A BRIEF OVERVIEW

THE PROLOGUE

The story of Job seems to be set outside Israel, and indeed in early times before Israel existed (see p. 123). Job is introduced as a genuine God-fearing man of considerable wealth. The reader is then taken 'behind the scenes' into the heavenly council to hear a conversation between the Lord and the Satan (i.e. 'the Accuser/Adversary'; 'Satan' here is a title, not a name), whose job seems to be to report on the failings of human beings. The Lord holds up Job as a glowing example of a 'blameless and upright man, who fears God'. In reply the Satan questions Job's motivation. He suggests that Job fears God only because of the material blessings this brings, and suggests that he should be put to the test

---

STRUCTURE OF THE BOOK OF JOB

Prologue: The Testing of Job (1:1—2:13)
1. The integrity of Job (1:1–5)
2. The first test (1:6–22)
   a. A heavenly gathering (1:6–12)
   b. Job is struck by disasters (1:13–19)
   c. Job's reaction (1:20–22)
3. The second test (2:1–10)
   a. A heavenly gathering (2:1–6)
   b. Job is struck by illness (2:7–8)
   c. Job's response (2:9–10)
4. The arrival of Job's friends (2:11–13)

The Speeches of Job and His Friends (3:1—31:40)
1. Job curses the day he was born (3:1–26)
2. First round of speeches (4:1—14:22)
   a. Eliphaz (4:1—5:7)
   b. Job (6:1—7:21)
   c. Bildad (8:1–22)
   d. Job (9:1—10:22)
   e. Zophar (11:1–20)
   f. Job (12:1—14:22)
3. Second round of speeches (15:1—21:34)
   a. Eliphaz (15:1–35)
   b. Job (16:1—17:16)
   c. Bildad (18:1–21)
   d. Job (19:1–29)
   e. Zophar (20:1–29)
   f. Job (21:1–34)

4. Third round of speeches (22:1—26:14)
   a. Eliphaz (22:1–30)
   b. Job (23:1—24:25)
   c. Bildad (25:1–6)
   d. Job (26:1—27:23)
5. A poem concerning wisdom (28:1–28)
6. Job's final speech (29:1—31:40)
   a. Job describes his previous situation (29:1–25)
   b. Job describes his present humiliation (30:1–31)
   c. Job challenges God with a declaration of innocence (31:1–40)

Elihu's Speeches (32:1—37:24)
1. Introduction (32:1–5)
2. First speech (32:6—33:33)
3. Second speech (34:1–37)
4. Third speech (35:1–16)
5. Fourth speech (36:1—37:24)

Yahweh's Speeches to Job (38:1—42:6)
1. First round (38:1—40:5)
   a. Yahweh's speech (38:1—40:2)
   b. Job's reply (40:3–5)
2. Second round (40:6—42:6)
   a. Yahweh's speech (40:6—41:34)
   b. Job's reply (42:1–6)

Epilogue: The Vindication of Job (42:7–17)
1. Yahweh's verdict (42:7–8)
2. Job prays for his friends (42:9)
3. Job's restoration (42:10–17)

---

on this point. The Lord responds by allowing the Satan to take away Job's possessions. We then read how, all in one day, Job hears of four disasters that deprive him of his animals, servants and children. They are brought about by an alternation of human (Sabeans and Chaldeans) and natural (fire and wind) causes. His response is summed up in the phrase, 'the LORD gave, and the LORD has taken away; blessed be the name of the LORD'. At a second meeting of the heavenly council the Lord again commends Job and the Satan again

questions his motivation. He is authorized to strike his person, but not to take his life. Job is struck down with a loathsome and painful disease. However, he refuses to listen to his wife and curse God and so gain a speedy death. Three of his friends come to mourn with him and sit with him in silence for seven days and nights.

In the prologue the author establishes that Job is innocent of moral fault. His suffering is *not* a punishment for his sins. By doing this he is asserting that there is a problem of innocent suffering.

THE SPEECHES OF JOB AND HIS FRIENDS

Job ends the silence with a lament in which he curses the day of his birth. He expresses the wish that he had died at birth. Death seems preferable to his present misery.

This provokes a response from his friends. Each asserts in his own way that God is just and so rewards the righteous and punishes the wicked. It therefore follows, in their view, that suffering is evidence of wrongdoing, and that the remedy is confession of sin and repentance. In the initial round of speeches each supports this belief in a different way. Eliphaz describes a mystical experience that came to him at night (Job 4:12–21). The essence of the revelation he receives, that no human can claim to be righteous before God, does not really speak directly to Job's complaint, since it applies to his friends too. However, the point seems to be that God will see through any false human righteousness including, by implication, Job's. Bildad rests his argument on the traditional teaching of former generations (8:8–10), and implies that what has happened to Job must be due to his sin and that of his children. Zophar has a cut-and-dried theology, which he applies rigidly. God's wisdom is unlimited and Job has no right to challenge it (11:7–9). His suffering must be evidence of God's displeasure (11:10–11). Indeed God is probably letting him off lightly (11:6)! If Job will confess and repent he will be restored (11:13–20).

Job is incensed by the words of his friends. He calls upon them (6:28–30) and God (10:1–7; 13:13–18) to recognize his innocence. He charges his friends with being liars who misrepresent God (13:4–7). Job's claim is not that he is utterly sinless, but that he has done nothing to deserve the degree of suffering that has been visited upon him (7:16–21). His friends address only Job. In his speeches, Job alternates between addressing them and addressing God. Besides asserting his innocence, he expresses the desire to be able to plead his case before God directly. Yet the court is rigged – Job has to appeal for justice to his accuser (9:15)! Moreover, God's power and wisdom are too great for any human to be able to stand up to him (9:2–4; 16–21). Job gets to the point of charging God with injustice – heedlessly destroying both the blameless and the wicked (9:22). He longs for a mediator who can stand between him and God in court, but there is not one (9:32–33). Despite all this, Job still wants his day in court with God to prove his innocence (13:1–3). He calls on God to give him respite from his sufferings so that they can meet on more equal terms (13:20–23). This round of speeches ends with Job lamenting that while a tree that has been cut down to a stump can sprout again, death is the end for humans (14:7–12). He wishes that Sheol, the abode of the dead, could be a place of temporary respite for him (14:13–17), but knows that this is a vain hope (14:18–22).

Digging deeper:
JOB 14

Andersen is one of the few recent commentators to argue that in Job 14 there is a clear expression of belief in resurrection from the dead. He reaches this conclusion by arguing that Job is not using 'western logic', which follows a step-by-step linear discourse. Instead, he argues, Job states his real opinion in vv. 14–17, in the middle of the speech, and flanks it with contrasting opinions, which he rejects. Most other commentators take vv. 14–17 to be 'a flight of optimism' (Habel), or 'an impossible dream' (Clines), which Job finds he cannot sustain. Read these contrasting views for yourself in the commentaries by Andersen (1976), Clines (1989) and Habel (1985).

There is no real engagement in argument in the speeches. Job and his friends tend to speak past each other rather than genuinely dialogue with each other. As the second and third rounds proceed there is little advance in the arguments, simply an increase in the vehemence of the rhetoric. This can be seen in Eliphaz's speeches. The tone of the first is fairly gentle and persuasive. In the second he chides Job in quite strong words for his foolish talk (15:2–6) and arrogance (15:7–16). By the third speech he has lost his patience and openly accuses Job of 'great wickedness' (22:5) and calls on him to humble himself before God and to 'remove unrighteousness from your tents' (22:23).

In his reply to Zophar's second speech, Job rejects the claim that people get their just deserts in this life. He asserts that all too often the wicked do prosper and enjoy life. His friends are misrepresenting reality (Job 21). He continues to assert his innocence and plead for a meeting with God. A strange tension arises in him. He regards God as his enemy, trying to destroy him (16:6–14). Yet he finds himself appealing to God against God! He expresses the confidence that, although his earthly friends have rejected him, he has a 'witness in heaven' who will argue his case with God (16:18–22). It is hard to see who this 'witness' is other than God, and the echo in v. 18 of Genesis 4:10, where God hears Abel's blood calling out to him, supports this. There is a similar appeal to God in Job 17:3.

There are some major textual difficulties in the famous and much debated passage, 19:23–29. Here Job expresses the belief that he does have a 'Redeemer' or 'Vindicator' who will eventually vindicate him and punish those who maligned him. Again, this figure seems to be God. The Hebrew word translated 'Redeemer' is *go'el*. As we mentioned before (p. 55), this is a legal term and denotes the person (usually a close relative) who had the duty to stand up for someone and secure their rights or avenge their death. This is quite an intimate term to use of God. Debate rages over whether Job is expecting this vindication before or after his death and, if it is after death, whether he has resurrection in mind. In the light of vv. 23–24, with its wish that an enduring record be made of his words, it does seem that he is expecting death to come before he is vindicated. However, the Hebrew of v. 26 is too problematic to conclude more than that he expects to be conscious of his vindication even if it does come after death.

Digging deeper:
JOB 19:23–29

Most people's knowledge of this passage is based on the libretto of Handel's great oratorio, *The Messiah*. The libretto makes it a clear statement of faith in future deliverance. However, as noted in the overview, the meaning of the Hebrew text is far from clear. Study this passage with the help of two or three commentaries so that you get a grasp of what the problems are in the passage and the different ways in which it might be understood. You will then be in a position to draw your own conclusion as to its likely meaning.

Some scholars think that the description of God's power in Job 26:5–14 would be a suitable continuation of Bildad's short speech in 25:1–6, and that the description of the fate of the wicked in 27:7–10, 13–23 would be more appropriate on Zophar's lips than Job's. We will discuss this issue later. The poem on the inability of humans to search out God's wisdom (ch. 28) forms an interlude before Job's final speech. In this he recollects his former happiness and laments his present state. He then concludes with a defiant speech in which he challenges God by calling down on himself a series of curses if he has committed certain specified crimes (ch. 31).

ELIHU'S SPEECHES

Instead of God responding to Job's challenge, another character appears, Elihu. In a short prose introduction (Job 32:1–6) he is identified as a young man who has been angered both by Job's complaints against God and his friends' inability to respond effectively to his arguments. Having held back in deference to his elders, he now speaks out. After a lengthy, rather bombastic self-introduction he eventually responds to Job by arguing that God uses suffering to warn people and turn them away from sin (33:14–18) and as a means of disciplining people so that they will turn to God for forgiveness and be deterred from further wickedness (33:19–33). This is not a totally new perspective – Eliphaz touched on it in his first speech (5:17–18) – but Elihu develops it a length. Elihu returns to it in his fourth and final speech (36:8–16). In his second and third speeches, Elihu says little that has not been said already by Job's three friends. There is no response to these speeches by either Job or his friends.

The most impressive part of Elihu's speeches is the concluding description of God's mighty works of creation and the appropriate human response to them (36:24—37:24). The poetic style of these speeches is rather pedestrian in comparison with the brilliant poetry of the preceding chapters.

GOD'S SPEECHES AND JOB'S RESPONSES

At last God does speak to Job, out of a storm. In the Hebrew Bible, appearances of God are usually accompanied by imagery reminiscent of storm, volcano and earthquake. God's initial words are a rebuke. Job lacks knowledge and his arguments obscure the truth. God then challenges Job with a series of questions, which draws attention to the wonders of nature that Job cannot explain or control. These fall into four main sections: the creation of the world (Job 38:4–11), the wonders of the heavens (38:12–21), the weather (38:22–38), and finally a series of wild creatures (38:39—39:30). These questions are expressed in brilliant poetry. At the end God calls for a response from Job (40:1–2). All he can say is that he is unworthy of making a reply. He has said too much already and will not say any more (40:3–5).

God begins a second speech by throwing out another challenge to Job. Why has Job accused God of ruling the world unjustly in order to justify himself? Does Job have the power and ability to rule the universe justly? God then calls on Job to consider two marvellous creatures, which are described in some detail: Behemoth (40:15–24) and Leviathan (41:1–34). This speech ends without any words of challenge or rebuke. Job is moved to confess the greatness of God's power and that he has spoken foolishly of things which he did not understand (42:1–3). His understanding of these things has not increased, but he declares that he does now have a deeper knowledge of God (42:4–5). The meaning of Job 42:6 is not clear. The literal sense is, 'I despise (or dissolve) and repent upon dust and ashes.' If the first verb is taken in the sense of 'despise', an object has to be supplied from the context, and the most likely ones are 'myself' or 'my (foolish) words'. There is no great difference between these. 'I repent' must be taken here in the sense (which it often has), 'I change my mind'. Job is not doing here what his friends have demanded all along, admitting his sinfulness and repenting of it. He is admitting that his previous understanding of God was deficient. The whole response is a self-humbling in the face of his new, deeper experience of God.

Digging deeper:
JOB 42:6

The understanding of this verse depends on deciding:

- what it is that Job despises.
- what the word translated 'repent' means here.
- what the preposition in the phrase 'upon/concerning/in dust and ashes' means.
- what the phrase itself means, once the meaning of the preposition is decided.

Consult the larger commentaries for discussions of the possibilities.

THE EPILOGUE

The prose epilogue begins with God telling Eliphaz that he is angry with him and the other two friends because, 'you have not spoken of me what is right, as my servant Job has' (Job 42:7). He then commands them to offer a sacrifice for themselves and to ask Job to pray for them. When they did this, and Job prayed for them, God accepted Job's prayer (42:8–9). Job is then restored, receiving twice the blessings he had had before. He died in happy and fulfilled old age.

THE COMPOSITION OF THE BOOK OF JOB

THE PROSE STORY

The obvious distinction between the prose prologue and epilogue and the poetic speeches in the book raises questions about the literary relationship between these two parts of the book. Were they written by the same author? If not, which was written first, the prose story or the poetic speeches? A few scholars (e.g. W. B. Stevenson) have argued that the prologue and epilogue were later additions to the speeches. However, the speeches need some prologue to make them fully intelligible. Most scholars are persuaded by the argument that if the present prologue is not the original one, it is hard to understand why that original one should have been replaced by one that surely cannot be any more relevant to the speeches than the original. The story in the prologue needs some kind of satisfying conclusion, and this is not provided within the speeches but in the epilogue. As it now stands, the epilogue presupposes both the speeches (in general terms) and the prologue. There are a number of echoes of the prologue in the epilogue. The verdict of God on Job (Job 42:7) echoes what has been said in the prologue about Job not sinning by what he said (1:22; 2:10). Job's intercession for his friends (42:8–9) corresponds to his earlier intercession for his children (1:5). The sympathy and comfort shown by his relatives (42:11) corresponds to his friends coming to console and comfort him in the prologue (2:11).

Most scholars conclude that the prologue and epilogue together preserve an old story about Job. Ezekiel 14:12–20 refers to Noah, Daniel and Job as three exemplary righteous men. The Daniel mentioned here is not the hero of the biblical book of Daniel (who would have been a contemporary of the prophet Ezekiel, and whose name is spelt differently in Hebrew, *daniyyel* instead of *dani'el* as in Ezekiel) but is probably a wise and good Phoenician king of the distant past who is mentioned in the texts found at Ugarit. This suggestion is supported by the fact that Ezekiel refers to him again in a poem about the king of the Phoenician city of Tyre (Ezek. 28:3). It seems likely that all three figures are regarded as 'patriarchs' from the distant past. Certainly the lifestyle depicted for Job has similarities with that of the patriarchs in the book of Genesis. Like them his wealth is measured in terms of his animals and servants. As head of his household he offers sacrifices himself, without the need of a priest. He lives to an age commensurate with that of the patriarchs.

Did the author of the poetic speeches simply take over an existing prose narrative, replacing whatever originally stood between the present prologue and epilogue, or did he rewrite the story?

Those who argue against a rewriting point to apparent differences between the poetry and prose. It is argued that in the prose Job is presented as a man of exemplary patience, but in the speeches he is quite different. The difference is not in fact that great. In the prologue Job refuses his wife's urging to curse God and die. However, he does not curse God in the poetic speeches either, even in his most vehement complaints against God. It is said that Job 19:17 refers to Job's sons as living, whereas they are killed in the prologue. However, the Hebrew is literally 'the children of my womb'. In Job 3:10, where the Hebrew is literally 'my womb', it clearly means 'my mother's womb'; hence Job 19:17 could well be a reference to Job's siblings ('children of my mother's womb'), not his children. In any case, Job 8:4 and 29:5 imply that Job's children are dead, so if there is any inconsistency, it is internal to the poetry.

Emphasis is sometimes put on the fact that, with the exception of Job 12:9, the name Yahweh is not used of God in the poetry. The presence of Yahweh in this verse may be a copyist's error due to the echo of Isaiah 41:20b. In the speeches of Job and his friends God is usually referred to as El, Eloah or Shaddai, with Elohim being used rarely. In the prose God is usually referred to as Yahweh, though also sometimes as Elohim. However, in the prose Yahweh is found on Job's lips only once (Job 1:21), so the difference from the poetry is not that great. Moreover, in the introductions to God's speeches and Job's responses the name Yahweh is used (Job 38:1; 40:1, 3, 6; 42:1). There seems to be a consistency here in the use of Yahweh when speaking of the intimacy of the relationship between God and Job. Many

scholars find an apparent theological tension between the epilogue and the speeches. We will discuss this issue later. On the whole it seems most likely that the author of the speeches retold an old story as the setting for them.

A few scholars have tried to discern different sources or stages of development within the prologue and epilogue (e.g. G. Fohrer, who argues for no less than five), but these arguments have not found wide acceptance.

THE THIRD ROUND OF SPEECHES

We have seen that there are grounds for suggesting that the text of the third round of speeches might now be in some confusion. Bildad's speech is short and Job's reply contains some sections that might sound better on the lips of his friends. There is also an unexpected heading in the middle of it (Job 27:1) as well as at the beginning (26:1). However, despite various attempts to reconstruct this round of speeches (see the examples in the box 'Proposed Reconstructions of the Third Round of Speeches' on p. 125; Snaith lists over 20 attempts) none has found wide acceptance. Also, a Targum of Job (an Aramaic paraphrase) found at Qumran (11QTgJob) reflects the text of these chapters in the form that we have it. The scroll of the Targum dates from the first century AD, but the language of the Targum suggests that it was produced in the second century BC. So, if the text did fall into disarray, it did so fairly early in the history of the book, and there seems little likelihood of being able to reconstruct it with any confidence. Faced with this conclusion, many scholars do their best to make sense of the text as it stands.

PROPOSED RECONSTRUCTIONS OF THE THIRD ROUND OF SPEECHES

Dhorme (*Le Livre de Job*, 1926)

Eliphaz	22:1–30
Job	23:1—24:17 + 24:25
Bildad	25:1–6 + 26:5–14
Job	26:1–4 + 27:2–12
Zophar	24:18–24 + 27:13–23

Stevenson (*The Poem of Job*, 1947)

Eliphaz	22:1–30
Job	23:1—24:25
Bildad	25:1–6 + 26:5–14
Job	26:2–4 + 27:2–6, 11–12, 22
Zophar	27:7–10, 13–21, 23

Gordis (*The Book of God and Man*, 1965)

Eliphaz	22:1–30
Job	23:1—24:25
Bildad	25:1–6 + 26:5–14
Job	26:1–4 + 27:1–12
Zophar	27:13–23

Habel (*The Book of Job*, 1985)

Eliphaz	22:1–30
Job	23:1–17
Bildad	25:1–6 + 26:5–14
Job	26:1–4 + 27:1–12
Zophar	24:1–25 + 27:13–23

Some scholars do argue for the integrity of the text as it stands. They see the petering out of the friends' speeches as deliberate. It is an indication of their inability to respond convincingly to Job's vehement assertion of his innocence and the inadequacy of their theology (e.g. Andersen, Good). The description of the fate of the wicked in Job 27:7–23 is taken as an ironic warning to the friends to beware that what they have said about this does not happen to them because of their false accusations against Job. A particular example of this kind of approach is Janzen's treatment of these chapters. He takes 24:18–20 as Job's quotation of his friends' views, followed by his own refutation of them in 24:21–24. Bildad's speech (25:1–6) is cut short by a sarcastic reply from Job (26:1–4) followed by Job's mimicking of what Bildad intended to say (26:5–14). Job then utters an oath of innocence (27:1–6) and a curse against his enemies (27:7–12). Finally, he sarcastically makes Zophar's speech for him (27:13–23). Job's pre-empting of his friends' speeches is a sign both of the bankruptcy of their arguments (they have nothing new to say) and of Job's unwillingness to continue in dialogue with them.

Digging deeper:
THE THIRD ROUND OF SPEECHES

Study the proposed reconstructions of the third round of speeches that are listed in the box 'Proposed Reconstructions of the Third Round of Speeches'. Then read Job 24—27 in the light of the summary of Janzen's interpretation given in the subsection 'The third round of speeches' (or read Janzen's commentary itself). What conclusion do you come to concerning whether or not these chapters need 'reconstruction'? If they do need it, which of the proposals is most convincing?

JOB 28

There is a widespread view that this beautiful poem about wisdom does not really belong in the rounds of speeches between Job and his friends (Good and Janzen, however, try to interpret it as part of Job's speech). Its calm tone does not fit well with the frenzied tone of Job's closing speeches. That it is spoken by Job is an assumption based on the heading at Job 27:1. However, there is a fresh heading at 29:1 which separates it from what follows. In the poem God is referred to as Elohim (27:23) and Adonai (v. 28) rather than one of the three words that characterize the speeches. Most scholars conclude that this was originally an independent poem. Because the poetry is of the same high quality as the speeches, and because what it says about the unsearchableness of divine wisdom is in harmony with the divine speeches it is quite probable that the poem is by the author of the speeches. When and why it was added is a matter of debate. Maybe it was added simply to preserve it. However, if seen as a comment by an 'outsider' on the debate between Job and his friends, it comes at a not unsuitable place. It expresses the viewpoint that humans lack the ability to understand the divine wisdom and that the appropriate response to this fact is to reverence God and avoid evil. This prepares the way for the divine speeches and, placed where it is, it provides a dramatic interlude between the main rounds of speeches and Job's final speech.

ELIHU'S SPEECHES

There are four reasons for questioning whether Elihu's speeches were originally part of the book.

- *Style* Most scholars find the poetry of these speeches inferior to that of the rest of the book. It is pedestrian and repetitious.
- *Language* It is argued that there is a higher proportion of Aramaisms in these speeches than in the others, which may be an indication of a later date for this part of Job.
- *Structure* Elihu appears abruptly at a point where God might be expected to appear and, at the end of his speeches, disappears never to be mentioned again. He claims to have the answer to the problem, which Job's friends could not supply, yet in the epilogue he is not mentioned, whether for praise or blame.
- *Theology* As we have seen, the content of these speeches adds little to what has already been said, though there is a greater emphasis on the educative role of suffering. The reader who knows the prologue can see that this is no more relevant to Job's problem than the rest of what Job's friends have said. So what is the point of what Elihu says as far as the message of the book is concerned?

**Think about
SUFFERING AS 'EDUCATIVE'**

The idea that one way of approaching suffering positively is to see it as having an 'educative' role is quite common in religious and philosophical discussions of suffering. It is expressed in various ways in the New Testament, e.g. Romans 5:1–5; Hebrews 12:5–11; James 1:2–4. How do you respond to this idea?

The validity of each of these reasons for rejecting the speeches as an original part of the book has been called in question. There is no reason why an author should always write in the same style and, in particular, it has been argued (e.g. by Dhorme and Habel) that the pedestrian style of the poetry of Elihu's speeches is intended as part of the characterization of him by the author. Similarly, the Aramaisms may be intended to give his speech a distinct 'accent' different from that of Job and his friends (as Andersen argues). The structural reason is probably the strongest, but it is not conclusive. Both Andersen and Habel argue that Elihu is not really a protagonist in the argument between Job and his friends but is an adjudicator. In this his role is parallel to Yahweh's. He provides the human evaluation of the debate. Yahweh provides the divine appraisal. It is because of his different role that Elihu does not get a mention in the epilogue, any more than the Satan does. Also, some scholars see Elihu's speeches as having a structural role in the book. They provide a dramatic interlude, which builds tension as the reader waits for God to appear. On the theological front, Elihu's admission that Job's friends had not provided an answer to his arguments, and his failure to provide anything more convincing, emphasizes the intractability of the problem of suffering.

Faced with these competing arguments, most scholars conclude that the speeches probably are a secondary addition to the book. A few are disposed to see them as added by the original author to a second (or later) edition of his work.

Digging deeper:
ELIHU'S SPEECHES

The view that Elihu fulfils the role of an 'adjudicator' or 'arbitrator' rather than being a protagonist in the debate is argued for by Andersen (1976, pp. 49–52) and Habel (1985, pp. 443–447) in their commentaries. Read these arguments for yourself and see whether you find them convincing.

YAHWEH'S SPEECHES

A number of scholars (e.g. Rowley) have questioned whether Yahweh's second speech was part of the original book. There are two reasons for this. First, they argue, the second speech adds little to the first and, after Job's submission, it seems unnecessary, even harsh, for God to go on questioning him. Second, it is argued that its poetic style is inferior to that of the first speech. Those who remove the second speech usually add Job 42:1–6 to 40:3–5 to form Job's response to Yahweh's speech.

Both of these reasons rest on quite subjective judgements, and there are many scholars who reject them. It is possible to argue that the speeches are in fact complementary. The first emphasizes Yahweh's wise ordering of the world, whereas the second emphasizes his power, as demonstrated by two of his creatures. Also, there is a progression from a consideration of creatures that are largely independent of humans to creatures that are dangerous to them. There are scholars (e.g. Dhorme, Eaton, Gordis) who disagree with the view that the poetry of the second speech is inferior to that of the first. Most scholars do accept that both divine speeches were an original part of the book.

THE FORMATION OF THE BOOK

Given the disagreements about which parts of the present book might have been later additions to an original composition, it is not surprising that scholars have proposed a wide range of theories concerning the likely process by which the book reached its present form (see the examples in the box 'The Formation of the Book of Job' on p. 128). Some scholars have continued to argue for the essential unity of the book (e.g. Andersen,

Whybray, both somewhat tentatively). Some older commentators tended to discount certain sections of the book, which they regarded as later additions when expounding its main message. More recent commentators (e.g. Clines, Good, Habel, Janzen, Rodd, Whybray) seek to interpret it as a literary whole in the form in which we now have it, arguing that, however it reached that form, the final editor(s) must have seen a main theme running through it.

THE FORMATION OF THE BOOK OF JOB

Some theories regarding the stages of development

The numbers refer to proposed successive stages in the book's development.

Studer (*Das Buch Hiob*, 1881)
1. 29:1—30:31 + 3:3—27:6 + 31:1–40
2. 28:1–28
3. 38:1—39:30
4. 32:1—37:24
5. 1:1—3:2
6. 26:7–23 + 40:1—42:17

Dhorme (*Le Livre de Job*, 1926)
1. 1:1—27:23 + 29:1—31:40
2. 28:1–28 + 38:1—42:17
3. 32:1—37:24

Snaith (*The Book of Job: Its Origin and Purpose*, 1968)
1. 1:1—2:10 + 3:1–26 + 29:1—42:6 + 42:10–17
2. 2:11–13 + 4:1—28:28 + 42:7–9
3. 32:1—37:24

Perdue (*Wisdom in Revolt: Metaphorical Theology in the Book of Job*, 1991)
1. 1:1—2:13 + 42:7–17
2. 3:1—27:23 + 29:1—31:40 + 38:1—42:6
3. 32:1—37:24
4. 28:1–28

THE TEXT AND LANGUAGE OF THE BOOK OF JOB

The Hebrew text of Job seems to have suffered significant corruption during its transmission. There are places where it is rather obscure and others where it makes little sense. Scholars have therefore resorted to emending the text rather more than they have in any other book of the Hebrew Bible. The Old Greek translation of Job was in circulation by about 100 BC. It is about one-sixth shorter than the current Hebrew text, the Massoretic Text (MT) (see the box 'Omissions in the Old Greek Text' on p. 129), despite having some lengthy additions at Job 2:9 (a speech by Job's wife) and Job 42:17 (background information on the characters in the story), and is a fairly free translation in places. In producing his Greek text, Origen supplemented the Old Greek text with sections from Theodotion's translation. The Aramaic Targum of Job found at Qumran (11QTgJob) has been dated to the second century BC on linguistic grounds. It consists of one large roll, 27 large fragments and a number of smaller fragments. These contain portions of Job 17—42. It generally agrees with the MT, but sometimes is closer to the Old Greek. As we have noted already, it agrees with the MT of Job 24—27. The Syriac Peshitta of Job was translated directly from the Hebrew and gives help with some difficult words and passages.

The language of Job causes as many problems as the text. There are about 100 words that are not found anywhere else. This is not all that surprising in such a lengthy piece of Hebrew poetry.

OMISSIONS IN THE OLD GREEK TEXT

The following list of the number of lines of text omitted in each section of Job is taken from the commentary by Driver and Gray.

Chs 1—2	I
Chs 7—14	23–29
Chs 15—21	59
Chs 22—31	124
Chs 32—37	114
Chs 38—42:6	43
Chs 42:7–17	3

Many of the lines omitted are recurring lines or repeat things said earlier in the speeches. This suggests deliberate abridging of the speeches by the Greek translator.

The use of synonyms in the parallelism that marks such poetry encourages the use of rare words, which simply have not survived in other Hebrew literature. The meaning of some of these can be deduced from the use of words from the same root in other Semitic languages. The discovery of the Canaanite texts at Ugarit has provided useful new evidence in this regard.

Sometimes the author uses a common Aramaic word as the synonym for a Hebrew word in poetic parallelism. In addition, there are other types of Aramaisms in Job, both in the form of words and in some idioms. There are also a significant number of words that are best understood by reference to Arabic. The epilogue and prologue of the book are written in good classical Hebrew, comparable to that of the narratives of Genesis and the books of Samuel.

THE DATE AND AUTHORSHIP OF THE BOOK OF JOB

The fact that the story of Job seems to have a setting similar to that of the stories of the Hebrew patriarchs led the Talmud to ascribe the book to Moses. Other rabbinical sources suggest a wide range of dates from patriarchal times to the time of Ezra. Most modern scholars argue for a date somewhere between the seventh and third centuries BC. This uncertainty in dating reflects the lack of clear evidence on which to make a decision. The dating of the Aramaic Targum of Job found at Qumran to the second century BC and a probable reference to the book of Job in the Wisdom of Jesus Ben Sirach 49:9 (written in the early second century, the reference is in the Hebrew and Syriac texts, but not the Greek) makes a date any later than 200 BC unlikely. The following are some of the more common arguments used in dating the book.

- The number of Aramaisms in the book might point to a date well into the Persian period when Aramaic was increasingly the language used by the Jews. However, as we shall see, some scholars argue that the Aramaisms are more evidence of *where* the book was written rather than *when*.

- Attempts are made to place the book within developments in theology evidenced in other biblical books. For example, in Job 'the Satan' is the title of an office, as it is in Zechariah 3:1–2. In 1 Chronicles 21:1, which is usually dated to the third or fourth century BC, it is a name. This is used to argue for a date no later than 300 BC. The issue of individual responsibility before God, which is found in the preaching of

Jeremiah (Jer. 31:29–24) and Ezekiel (Ezek. 18, 33), is seen by some scholars as an important background to the book of Job, so placing it later than these prophets. However, in both those books the issue is the fairness, or otherwise, of children suffering for the sins of their parents. There is no hint of this in Job. Others argue that the assumption of monotheism in Job points to a date later than the prophecies of Isaiah 40—55 (usually dated *c.* 550 BC) in which the issue of Yahweh being the one and only true God is still a live one.

- Another line of approach concerns supposed allusion or quotations in Job from other books in the Hebrew Bible. Here are some typical examples:

Compare: . . . who made the Bear and Orion,
the Pleiades and the chambers of the south. (Job 9:9)

With: The one who made the Pleiades and Orion,
and turns deep darkness into the morning. (Amos 5:8a)

Compare: Who among all these does not know
that the hand of the LORD has done this? (Job 12:9)

With: So that all may see and know, all may consider and understand,
that the hand of the LORD has done this. (Isa. 41:20)

Compare: My companions are treacherous
like a torrent-bed,
like freshets that pass away. (Job 6:15)

With: Truly, you are to me like a deceitful brook,
like waters that fail. (Jer. 15:18)

It is the possible allusions to the words of Jeremiah and Isaiah 40—55 in particular that lead some scholars to favour a fifth- or sixth-century date for Job. The difficulty with this kind of argument is that it rests on two questionable assumptions: that the allusion is genuine, and that the author of Job is dependent on the other writer (rather than vice versa, or that both are drawing on a common source).

- It is argued by some scholars that the books of Job and Ecclesiastes both reflect a 'crisis' in Jewish wisdom thought, a questioning of traditional ideas about divine justice and retribution. They therefore date Job at about the same time as Ecclesiastes (*c.* 300 BC). However, the postulation of a specific 'crisis' is pure hypothesis. The issue of divine justice and retribution is one that surfaces at a number of times and places in Hebrew literature, such as Genesis 18:22–32, the 'confessions' of Jeremiah (e.g. Jer. 12:1–5), Habakkuk, and some of the psalms of lament (e.g. Pss 37; 73).

The fact is that there are no firm grounds on which to date the book of Job with any certainty. Most scholars seem to settle for a date in the fourth or fifth century BC.

Discussion of the book's authorship has been related to the discussion of the peculiarities of Job's language and the possible location of 'the land of Uz' in which the story is set. Lamentations 4:21 identifies Uz with Edom and Genesis 36:28 links it with 'Seir in the land of Edom'.

Jeremiah 25:20 mentions Uz separately from Edom but locates it in the south with Philistia. On the other hand Genesis 10:23 and 22:21 link Uz with Aram, suggesting a location to the north of Israel. In Job 1:3 Job is said to be 'the greatest of all the people of the east'. Here 'the east' no doubt means to the east of the river Jordan. In the light of this diverse evidence some scholars have located Uz in or near Edom to the south-east of Israel, which would allow for contact with the Arabic language. The appendix to the LXX translation of the book makes Job an Edomite king and says that his home was on the border of Edom and Arabia. However, others have located it in the Hauran, to the north-east of Israel, where there would be contact with Aramaic, and possibly Arabic.

In the twelfth century AD the Jewish scholar Ibn Ezra expressed the view that, given the peculiarities of its language, Job had probably been translated into Hebrew from another language. Since then scholars have occasionally argued that it was translated from either Arabic or Aramaic. In modern times Guillaume has argued that the book was originally written in Arabic by an author living in a Jewish colony in Arabia, whereas Tur-Sinai has argued for an Aramaic original. Gordis has argued strongly against the suggestion that translation from another language is the best explanation of the peculiarities of Job's language. First, he argues that, while difficulties in the original text may lead to mistranslations, translators usually produce a smooth translation in the language into which they are translating a book. Second, he suggests that many of the apparent Arabisms and Aramaisms in Job may be the result of the author using rare Hebrew words, which have not survived in any other Hebrew book, but which share a common Semitic root with words that have survived in the other languages. Gordis does, however, argue that the concentration of Aramaisms in Job, and especially the use of Aramaic words as synonyms for Hebrew words in poetic parallelism, shows that the author had a good knowledge of Aramaic. Hartley suggests that either the author wrote in a dialect of Hebrew that was closer to Aramaic than the classical Hebrew used in most of the Bible, or that he may have been multilingual.

It is clear that, as with the question of the date of the book, there is very little in the way of firm evidence to enable us to come to any confident conclusions about its author.

ANCIENT LITERATURE COMPARABLE TO JOB

Although nothing quite like the book of Job has been found in ancient non-Israelite literature, there are some texts that have some similarity in their literary form and/or the themes with which they deal.

A Sumerian poem called *Lamentations of a Man to His God*, which dates from *c.* 2000 BC, begins with a short exhortation to praise and lament to one's god. It then introduces a man who, despite his good life, was overwhelmed by sufferings. His lamentations are quoted at some length. He complains about the lying words of his friends and asks why he should be treated as the wicked are. He asks why his god neglects him and does nothing to help him, indeed seems to heap more trouble on him. In his weeping and lamenting he is supported by both family and professional mourning women. The bitterness and volume of the lamentation seem at least as important as the brief confession of sin in leading his god to have pity on him and restore him. The man's complaints have some similarities to Job's, but the overall teaching of the poem is more in line with that of Job's friends.

The Babylonian text *I will Praise the Lord of Wisdom* (*c.* 1300 BC) is a hymn of thanksgiving to Marduk following recovery from illness. In it a ruler recollects his suffering, which is described in some gruesome detail, and records the lament he made at the time. He complained of being forsaken by the gods, rejected by his family and friends, thrown down from his position of social eminence, and exhausted by his disease. Although he had lived piously he suffered like the ungodly. It seemed to him that the gods had capriciously reversed the values, despising the good and favouring the wicked. When he sought a word from Marduk there was no answer, the diviners could tell him nothing. Eventually he had dreams that indicated that Marduk's wrath was appeased and that he would deliver him. Gradually, he was restored. He then went in procession to Marduk's temple, declaring himself an example of Marduk's mercy for all who transgressed the requirements of the temple. The main similarity to Job is in the sufferer's sense of injustice and of the incomprehensibility of the ways of the gods.

Both of these texts are monologues. One that is closer to Job in form is *The Babylonian Theodicy* (*c.* 1000 BC). It is an acrostic poem of 27 stanzas of 11 lines each. In each stanza all the lines begin with the same cuneiform sign. The text is a dialogue between a sufferer and his friend or, possibly, friends. It expresses the difference between the reality of suffering and the traditional pious teaching on the subject. The sufferer relates his own troubles to his friend, who tries to restrain his bitterness and complaints, recommending prayer and just conduct. The sufferer cites examples of injustice in life and society from which he deduces that those who neglect god prosper and that the pious are made destitute. His friend declares this to be blasphemy and argues that one has to accept that the ways of god are hard to grasp. He is forced to concede that the gods gave humans a lying nature, and to this extent they are responsible for the ills of society. The sufferer then utters an appeal for pity from his friend and mercy from his guardian spirits. He affirms that the sun-god, the god of justice, is shepherd of the peoples. This ending is echoed by the sentence produced by the acrostic. In this the author of the work declares that he is one who reverences the god and the king. Like Job, this work recognizes the inadequacy of a simplistic teaching about rewards and retribution in the face of the reality of suffering. It gives no solution to the resulting dilemma, but advocates continuing to live a pious life nonetheless.

As its name indicates, the Babylonian *Dialogue of Pessimism* (*c.* 1300 BC) also uses the dialogue format, in this case a discussion between a man and his servant. Its content is discussed in the chapter on Ecclesiastes/Qoheleth. It has little in common with Job.

An Egyptian poem, *The Dispute over Suicide* (*c.* 2100), is a dialogue between a man and his soul. The subject is the man's desire to commit suicide. Two of the themes developed in it are reminiscent of Job: the fact that the wicked seem to flourish while the just perish and the man's longing for death in the face of the injustices of life.

The Protests of the Eloquent Peasant is a story in prose within which nine semi-poetic speeches by a peasant are reported. They are all made to the chief steward by a peasant who has been wronged by one of the chief steward's vassals. They are all pleas for justice. The man's ordeal is prolonged by the Pharaoh, who delights in the peasant's eloquence. In the end he is rewarded by being given a position of honour and the goods of his oppressor. There are similarities to Job in the form of the work, but it does not call the justice of the gods into question.

There is no reason to suppose any direct dependence between Job and these Sumerian, Babylonian and Egyptian works. What they show is that the issues dealt with in Job are perennial ones, which writers have dealt with in a variety of different ways. One work from outside the wider culture of the ancient Near East with which Job has been compared is the Greek drama *Prometheus Bound* by Aeschylus (*c.* 460 BC). The play begins with Prometheus being punished by Zeus by being pinned to the mountains at the end of the world. The body of the play consists of a series of dialogues between Prometheus and various visitors. In them he speaks of the good he has done humans for which he is, in his view, being unjustly punished by Zeus, against whom he utters defiance. However, he also expresses the belief that one day Zeus will want reconciliation with him. The last visitor is Hermes, a messenger from Zeus, who demands from Prometheus a secret that he possesses concerning the ultimate downfall of Zeus. Prometheus refuses to give it, and the play ends with him depicting the shattering descent of Zeus and calling on heaven and earth to witness the wrong he suffers.

A different kind of parallel with Job is found in some Egyptian wisdom writings. The *Onomasticon of Amenope* lists all that the Creator (Ptah) made in heaven and on earth and in some places coincides with the order of the natural phenomena listed in Job 38—39. In *The Satirical Letter of Hori* (*c.* 1580–1080 BC) an official seems to adopt the teacher's method of closely questioning a pupil as a means of deflating a scribe who has written to him. Again there is a parallel, this time in form rather than content (the official's questions concern geography), with Job 38—39.

THE BOOK OF JOB AS LITERATURE

Apart from the major division between poetry and prose, form critics are able to discern within Job a considerable variety of different literary forms, such as: lament (Job 3), proverb (5:2), hymnic material (5:9–16), parables (8:11–19), disputation (ch. 21), wisdom poem (ch. 28), the oath of innocence (ch. 31). This diversity of material within the book contributes to the problem that scholars have had in attempting to classify it on the basis of literary genre. As we have seen, there is no other work quite like it within the body of ancient Near Eastern literature that has survived. Various suggestions have been made: an answered lament, a tragedy, a black comedy, a drama, a court trial, a parody, a wisdom dispute. The problem of classifying it led Pope to conclude that it is *sui generis*, defying any one classification. Most scholars simply describe it in general terms as 'wisdom literature'. This is based on the themes that recur in it (suffering, rewards and punishment, creation, wisdom in various forms) and its dialogue form.

A number of literary techniques are deployed in Job, besides those commonly encountered in Hebrew poetry. One example is the repetition of words as a thread through a passage. This may be a straightforward repetition, such as the word 'place' in ch. 28. However it may involve word play, as in Job 3:9, 16, 20. In this case the 'light' of v. 9 is the physical light of day. In v. 16 the word has the double meaning of 'daylight' and 'life'. Finally, in v. 20 it is used as a synonym for 'life'.

Another example is the use of irony. This is used in more than one way. Verbal irony is common. In his speech in ch. 7, Job speaks of his 'emptiness' (v. 3), 'no return' from Sheol (v. 10), 'anguish' (v. 11) and of things that 'terrify' him (v. 14). Eliphaz takes up these words in his description of the anguish experienced by the wicked in 15:20–35. This adds some point to what he says in v. 6, 'your own mouth condemns you'. There is also dramatic irony. In 22:26–30 Eliphaz promises Job that if he repents and is reconciled to God, he will even become an intercessor who could deliver others from the wrath of God. How ironic it is then when, in the epilogue, Eliphaz and his two friends are condemned by God, Job is vindicated and Eliphaz is told to ask Job to intercede for them! A third form of irony is when phrases from elsewhere in the Hebrew Bible are used in an ironic sense, as Psalm 8:4 seems to be in Job 7:17–18.

> What are human beings that you are
>   mindful of them,
> mortals that you care for them? (Ps. 8:4)

> What are human beings, that you make
>   so much of them,

that you set your mind on them,
visit them every morning
test them every moment? (Job 7:17–18)

The prevalence of irony in Job is what has led Dell, among others, to argue that Job is a parody that expresses scepticism towards the ideas of traditional wisdom.

Recent literary studies of Job have shifted the focus from interest in the different parts of the book, their possible origins and how they were brought together to form the present book, to an interest in the book in its present form. As a result they have highlighted the literary unity of the book. Habel's study is a good example of this.

He finds a number of key words that appear in both the prose 'frame' and the poetic dialogues and serve to provide continuity between them. One such word is 'blameless'. Job is introduced to the reader as 'blameless' (Job 1:1), a fact that God confirms (v. 8) in the heavenly council. Bildad implies that he must be guilty of wrongdoing because 'God will not reject a blameless person' (8:20). In response Job affirms that he is 'blameless' (9:21–22). The related Hebrew noun is used by Job's wife when she says (translating the Hebrew literalistically): 'Do you hold fast [NRSV "still persist in"] your blamelessness [NRSV "integrity"]? Curse God, and die' (2:9). Eliphaz counsels Job to take hope from 'the blamelessness ["integrity"] of your ways' (4:6). In his speech, which effectively ends the dialogue, Job echoes his wife's words when he utters an oath (a form of curse on himself, not God) and says, 'until I die I will not put away my blamelessness [NRSV "integrity"] from me. I hold fast

my righteousness and will not let it go' (27:5–6).

He argues that the distinction between 'narrative' and 'dialogue' is usually overdrawn, with the dialogue seen as a static interlude in the plot of the story, which is given in the narrative of the prologue and epilogue. In his view the speeches are an integral part of the plot. The narrative statement in 3:1 links the prologue with the speeches. It reports that Job is going to curse the day of his birth. That curse is itself a type of action, a 'speech act'. It compels his friends to end their silence, and so provokes the dialogue. At 27:1 the author signals a new stage in the plot when the introduction of the speech changes from, 'Then X answered' to, 'Job again took up his discourse and said'. This introduces another curse, which balances that in ch. 3. Job's 'discourse' in chs 29—31 ends with a self-imprecation intended to provoke a confrontation with God, just as the curse in ch. 3 provoked one with his friends. Habel argues that the appearance of Elihu is not an intrusive addition by an inept editor. In 9:33 Job complained that, 'there is no umpire [*mokiah*] between us'. Elihu picks this up in 32:12 (which Habel translates as, 'But behold there is no arbiter [*mokiah*] for Job') with the implication that he is going to play that role. He therefore calls on Job to present his legal case in court (33:5) because he will not terrify Job, as Job has complained God would (9:34). Elihu's speeches provide the human verdict on Job. This is followed by the dramatic appearance of God, which leads to Job's final words (42:6) and his restoration. So, Habel sees the speeches as part of a complex plot that includes the whole book.

Habel points out an 'envelope structure' (often called an *inclusio*) in the description of Job in 1:1 as someone who 'feared God and turned away from evil' and the closing lines of Job 28:28 (translating the Hebrew literalistically): 'Truly, the fear of the Lord, that is wisdom; and to turn away [NRSV "depart from"] from evil is understanding'. Habel argues that this indicates that ch. 28 is not a later addition to the book, but was intended by the author to be the end of the dialogue between Job and his friends.

Think about
WORDS AS 'SPEECH ACTS'

The modern study of language has put some emphasis on the way in which a verbal statement can be a type of action. Take, for example, the following kinds of statements: commands, promises, reprimands, words of forgiveness. Does this provide some support for Habel's suggestion that the 'plot' of Job is carried forward by speeches rather than by the kind of actions we normally expect in the plot of a story?

THE EPILOGUE

As has already been noted, many scholars see an apparent theological tension between the epilogue and the rest of the book. The opening verses of the prologue might seem to imply the conventional doctrine of rewards and punishments. Job is presented as both 'blameless and upright, one who feared God and turned away from evil' and as 'the greatest of all the people of the east'. The reader might assume that there is a direct connection between his great piety and his great wealth and social standing. However, the assumption that there always *must* be such a link is shattered once God accepts the Satan's challenge to test Job. The dialogue then explores the implications of this shattering of the link. In Job 42:7–9 God condemns Job's friends for defending the position that there *must* be a link between piety and prosperity. Yet what follows, Job's restoration, seems to re-establish the link and so contradict the main thrust of the book's message.

A small number of scholars (e.g. Buttenwieser) have explained the apparent contradiction by suggesting that the epilogue is an addition to the book by a later, and inept, editor. Some others (e.g. Pope) have argued that the restoration of Job was an essential part of the old folk tale of Job and that the author of the dialogues simply could not discard it when he took the tale over as the frame for them. Many scholars have not found either of these arguments satisfying. It seems unlikely that the book ever existed without an epilogue that gave some kind of 'closure' to the narrative contained in the prologue. As we have noted when discussing the composition of the book, there is good reason to believe that the author of the dialogues retold the old folk tale and did not simply take over an existing form of it. That being so, and given the willingness to shatter the traditional doctrine of rewards and punishments in the prologue, why should the author reinstate it in the epilogue? Is that what is really happening?

Clines argues that the epilogue does not contradict the rest of the book, but 'deconstructs it'. A contradiction is an open clash between two philosophies, which may result in one replacing the other. This is what happens in the prologue when God allows the Satan to test Job. Clines defines 'deconstruction' as undermining the philosophy that a text asserts. 'Undermining' is something that goes on under the surface. Clines argues that this is the case in the epilogue because there is no open contradiction of the message of the rest of the book; however, such a contradiction is implied by the restoration of Job's possessions and children. This deconstruction leaves the reader uncertain about the message of the book.

A 'deconstructive' reading of the epilogue is open to question on at least two grounds. First, as we have noted, many scholars have seen an apparent contradiction (and some regard it as a real one) between the epilogue and the rest of the book. The problem is not simply an implication that lies beneath the surface of the text. Second, recent studies of the process of reading have emphasized that books are usually designed to be read in a 'linear' way, from beginning to end. Therefore the reader is meant to understand the text at a particular point in the light of what has gone before. Quite a lot of commentators have adopted this principle (without invoking any explicit theory of the process of reading) and sought to understand the epilogue in a way that does not contradict what has gone before.

Rowley argues that, in the light of the breaking of the link between righteousness and prosperity, Job's restoration must be understood to be due not to his righteousness but to the fact that the test is ended. He sees this as demanded by the artistry of the book. There needs to be some fitting conclusion to the test, and anything other than the restoration of Job would be intolerable to the reader. A number of scholars argue along similar lines (e.g. Andersen, Eaton, Habel).

Both Crenshaw and Perdue see in the epilogue not so much the restoration of Job as the restoration of God's reputation, or the 'redemption of God' as Perdue puts it. God's acceptance of the Satan's 'wager' and the resultant affliction of Job at least raises questions about God's concern for Job, which need addressing. These are answered, to at least some extent, by God's treatment of Job in the epilogue.

In all these interpretations of the epilogue the scholars stress that God acts freely, not under the constraint of any inevitable linking of piety and prosperity, such as asserted by Job's friends. Janzen develops this point at more length than most others. He stresses that God's actions in the epilogue must be seen as arising out of God's freedom. This freedom is the lesson to be learned from the dialogues and their climax in the divine speeches. God is not bound to act according to any strict law of reward and punishment. He can, and does, act gratuitously towards his servants. In fact, Janzen points out, the theme of gratuitous action runs through the epilogue. The giving of the names of Job's daughters, but not his sons, breaks with the expected conventions of Hebrew narrative. Moreover, Job acts gratuitously in giving his daughters inheritance rights, something that Hebrew law required only when there were no male heirs. So, far from the epilogue reinstating the law of rewards and punishments, its theme is free acts of grace.

Think about
PIETY AND PROSPERITY

The idea that there should be a strong link between piety and prosperity, or goodness and prosperity, is quite common both in popular thought (e.g. the proverb 'Honesty is the best policy' quoted earlier) and some forms of religion (e.g. the so-called 'health, wealth and prosperity gospel') today. Doesn't this make the book of Job a book of continuing relevance for today ?

THE MESSAGE OF THE BOOK OF JOB

The book of Job has probably prompted a wider diversity of interpretations than any other book in the Hebrew Bible. It is not only biblical scholars and theologians who have been fascinated by it. It has captured the imagination of artists, dramatists, poets, philosophers and psychoanalysts. All we can do here is provide a survey of some, hopefully fairly representative, interpretations.

GROUNDS FOR COURAGE IN THE FACE OF THE MYSTERY OF SUFFERING

Gordis sees the issue of the operation of the divine law of justice in the life of the individual as the central concern of the book of Job. In ancient Israel there developed a conventional doctrine of God rewarding the righteous and punishing the wicked. This was applied to communal groups and to the nation as a whole. Even on this corporate level it was problematic, but it became more and more problematic as the fate of the individual became increasingly the centre of concern, as it does in the preaching of Jeremiah and Ezekiel. Job's friends expound and apply the conventional doctrine. The major contribution of Job's speeches to the issue is the fact that, confronted with the dilemma of the suffering of the righteous in an immoral world created by a just God, Job refuses to give up his idea of what is right and just.

Gordis argues that the author of Job expresses his own positive views on the problem in the speeches of Elihu and Yahweh. Elihu stresses the role of suffering as a form of moral discipline. It can be a spur to higher ethical attainment. While this is a valid point, says Gordis, it is not the principal answer to the problem. In the vivid and joyful descriptions of the wonders of nature in Yahweh's speeches the poet expresses his belief in pattern and order in creation, even though humans cannot fully fathom it. Similarly, humans can believe that there is rationality and justice in the moral realm even though they cannot comprehend it fully. In Gordis' view the message of the book is that the analogy of the natural order gives the believer in God grounds for facing the mystery of suffering with a courage based on faith in the essential righteousness of God.

SUFFERING CAN DEEPEN OUR KNOWLEDGE OF GOD

Rowley points out that the reason given for Job's suffering in the prologue is clearly one that cannot be generalized to other cases, and in any case it is not explained to Job himself. He argues, therefore, that the purpose of the book cannot be to offer an explanation of innocent suffering, or indeed of suffering in general. In his view the book is not concerned with theology (seeking rational answers) but religion (personal encounter with God). Job saw his suffering as evidence of isolation from

God. This false theology caused his existential problem. He did not realize that innocent suffering is not proof of isolation from God. In the divine speeches Yahweh reminds Job of the mysteries of nature that go beyond his comprehension, and suffering is one of these. The supremely important thing for Job is that God came to him in his suffering, showing him that he was not isolated from God. In his closing words Job repents of the folly of his previous words, which arose from his failure to realize the corollary of his innocence. The message of the book is that though humans must suffer in the dark, their very suffering may be an enrichment of their experience if in it they know the presence of God.

VALUING GOD'S PRESENCE FOR ITS OWN SAKE

For Crenshaw the divine speeches fail to provide any answers to the problem of innocent suffering and divine injustice. The first speech teaches Job that he cannot rule the universe and that it can survive without him, or humans in general. The creatures referred to are all ones which have little or no contact with humans. In the second speech God rebukes Job for trying to justify himself at God's expense, in that Job's vindication could come about only if God pleaded guilty to the charge of perverting justice. By ignoring the very issue that led Job to confront his Maker, God taught Job that he was wrong to assume that the universe operates according to a principle of rationality. With the demise of that principle, the need for personal vindication disappears, since God's anger and favour cannot be directly correlated with human vice or virtue. Job's final words show that the loss of the principle of rationality might be

accompanied by a significant gain, the ability to cherish God's presence for its own sake, the very issue that the Satan raised in the prologue.

THE 'REDEMPTION OF GOD'

Perdue seeks to understand the book of Job through understanding the metaphors, both explicit and implicit, which the writer uses of God, humanity and the world. The dramatic climax of the book is the appearance of Yahweh and his speeches from the whirlwind. Here Perdue sees the metaphor of the Storm God coming to do battle. Initially it is a battle of words with Job, a human rebel. In the series of questions that make up the first speech, Yahweh challenges Job to a war of words. The purpose of this, as of the second speech, is to convince Job that only Yahweh, not any ordinary mortal, has the knowledge and power to rule the cosmos. In this speech there is an implicit deconstruction of the metaphor of humans as kings in God's creation. The only 'creature' Yahweh is said to bring to birth (probably acting as midwife, not parent) and nurture is Yam (the sea, Job 38:8–11). All the animals described, apart from the horse, are wild creatures that live in regions uninhabited and uncontrolled by humans. In God's world humans are not the centre of the universe and retributive justice is not mentioned. Job is struck dumb by this speech. His vision of a just world administered by human kings has collapsed.

In the second speech the controlling metaphor is the Creator's battle with the chaos monsters. Yahweh begins by defending his own justice, arguing that Job's innocence does not necessarily imply divine guilt. Job has challenged the righteous rule of God. Yahweh now challenges Job. If he wishes to rule the cosmos he must defeat the awesome chaos monsters, Behemoth and Leviathan. The fact is that no one on earth can overcome these monsters (41:33–34). Perdue sees in these speeches the message that the cosmos is orderly, but that the powers of chaos are mighty and must be defeated on a regular basis if Yahweh's edicts are to order the world in justice. In his second speech Job acknowledges and praises Yahweh's sovereignty. What he rejects in 42:6 is his lamentation and rebellious words, which sought to subvert the order of creation.

In the epilogue the theological stance of Job's friends, with their emphasis on retribution and uncontested divine sovereignty, is rejected as false. Job's stance of questioning divine justice and demanding that God hear the pleas of victims as he rules the universe, is affirmed as right. In the light of what has gone before in the divine speeches the restoration of Job is not a reward for his perfect piety, but the vindication of God, who acts to set things right. In this sense God is redeemed. The message of the book is that the world is God's kingdom, subject to his royal decree. However, there is an ever-recurrent battle with evil. Humans are not kings in God's world but God's 'slaves' (Perdue's translation of the word usually translated 'servant' in Job 42:8). But they are slaves called to join in the battle with evil, even by calling the Creator to act justly.

A CHALLENGE TO HUMAN SELF-UNDERSTANDING

Whereas Perdue uses metaphors as the way into interpreting Job, Janzen uses irony as the key. As he puts it, ironic statements 'mean something else than what they seem to say, a something else which undercuts their apparent meaning'. This undercutting opens the possibility of 'reconstruction', of building a new meaning in place of the old one. In this way irony invites 'morally active engagement' by the reader in affirming a new meaning. Janzen regards the questions in the divine speeches as not just rhetorical (statements presented as questions) but as ironic. As such they are not a rebuff to Job's presumption but a challenge and invitation to change his theology. What this change involves, argues Janzen, is indicated by Job 42:6, which he translates as, 'Therefore I recant and change my mind concerning dust and ashes'. The phrase 'dust and ashes' occurs in the Hebrew Bible in only three places: Genesis 18:27; Job 30:19; 42:6. In both Genesis 18:27 and Job 30:19 it expresses the speaker's sense of creaturely status. Janzen argues against those who see God's questions, both by their tone and content, as emphasizing the insignificance of Job, and so of humans. Humans are not excluded from the list of creatures, they are present as the creature whom God addresses with questions about the rest of creation. Understood as ironic, the rhetorical questions (Who are you? Where were you? Are you able?) face Job with the challenge of how he will understand himself: solely as a creature, or as a creature who will take up the divine image through engagement with the world, even though it remains partly mysterious to him. Janzen sees Job as accepting that challenge in his second response to God.

READER-RESPONSE

Although Janzen does give his own understanding of the meaning of the book of Job, he does not claim that it is the only possible meaning. He argues that ironic statements can be either 'stable' or 'unstable'. Stable ironies are those in which the writer uses irony to subvert one position and replace it by another, which the writer regards as firm and unsubvertable. Unstable ironies are those in which the subversion does not lead to any firm position. Janzen regards the ironies in the divine speeches as unstable and leaving the reader with the challenge of 'morally active engagement' to decide the meaning of the speeches, and the whole book, in their own context. This is one way of opening the door to what is called 'reader-response criticism'. This approach is based on the premise that, to a greater or lesser extent, it is the reader of a text who gives it a meaning. Most reader-response approaches are 'ideological' in the sense that they make use of a specific ideological position as the 'spectacles' through which the text is read. In the introduction to his commentary on Job, Clines gives brief 'readings' of the book from different ideological positions: feminist, vegetarian, materialist and Christian.

FEMINIST READINGS OF JOB

Job's wife is, understandably, a figure of particular interest to feminist readers of the book. Pardes sees her as prefiguring, and to some extent generating, the impatience of the dialogues. She challenges Job's adherence to a model of 'perfect' devotion to a 'perfect' God when the reality of the situation, in which she has shared his losses, looks very different. His angry reply may indicate that she has expressed something that was not so far from his own mind. Although he refuses to 'curse God and die', when the dialogue begins he does utter a curse (on the day of

his birth) and the wish that he had never been born. His wife helps him to begin the questioning that leads him to a new understanding of God. However, her words are too challenging for the writer to mention her again in the epilogue. Pardes sees significance in the fact that in the epilogue Job's daughters, but not his sons, are named. Their names, Jemima (Bright Day or Dove), Keziah (Cassia, a perfume) and Keren-happuch (Horn of Antimony, a cosmetic used to beautify the eyes), indicate that Job has discovered a new world of beauty and fragrance, of feminine grace. Job expresses his respect for his daughters by what in those days was a very unusual act, giving them inheritance rights. Pardes sees in this an indication that in his surrender to God Job has given up the male compulsion to control.

Van Wolde gives a somewhat similar reading of the role of Job's wife in the story. However, she argues that the meaning of what Job's wife says is ambiguous. Her translation of Job 2:9 is:

> His wife said to him,
> 'Are you persisting in your piety?
> Bless God/say good-bye to God and die.'

She points out that the first part of what Job's wife says is a repetition of God's words about Job in 2:3, 'Job still persisted in his piety.' The second part echoes what the Satan said in Job 1:11 and 2:5b, 'See if he will not say good-bye to your face.' So, Job's wife quotes both God and the Satan and uses the Hebrew verb *barak* which can mean both 'bless' (as in Job 1:10, 21) and 'curse' (as in Job 1:5, 11, 2:5). Does she mean that Job should 'say good-bye to [or curse]' God, and so provoke his own death, or that he should bless God and die with the blessing on his lips, perhaps by taking his own life? Given this ambiguity, does Job's response mean that he does not want to curse God, or that he does not want to bless him? Either way, his wife makes Job begin to reflect on his situation and confront for the first time his own death, so that he begins to ask questions. Van Wolde sees this reflection indicated by the fact that the straightforward statement and blessing of 1:21 ('YHWH has given and YHWH has taken away. Blessed be the name of YHWH') is now replaced by a question ('If we accept good from the deity why should we not then accept evil?'). Note also that the name YHWH has been replaced by 'the deity' (the translations are those of Van Wolde). So, it is his wife's question which starts Job on the process of questioning, which leads to the change and deepening of his relationship to God.

A LIBERATION THEOLOGY READING

Gutiérrez approaches the book of Job as a liberation theologian. For him the central question of the book is, 'How are we to talk about God?', and in particular how we are to do this in the situation of the suffering of the innocent in Latin America. In his view the prologue, epilogue and Job's initial lament raise the question, 'Can humans have a disinterested faith in God?' The author of the book believes this is possible and uses Job as his mouthpiece. Gutiérrez argues that the book combines the language of prophecy (seen in the dialogue and Elihu's speeches) and of contemplation (found in the divine speeches and Job's responses). In the end Job discovers that the language of prophecy (which expresses the justice demanded by God's love) must be supplemented by the language of contemplation and worship (which expresses the gratuitousness of God's love).

The problems of suffering and divine justice do underlie the book, but its main purpose is to show that if thinking about God is reduced to thinking about God's justice, God is reduced to an idol. Unless we accept the mysteriousness of God – a God who acts freely and gratuitously, and so is free to express the gratuitousness of his love – we distort the nature of justice. The divine speeches show that God's unbounded and unmerited love reaches out to the whole creation. The key to the book is Job's second response to God. He does not repent of what he has said. Through his experience of suffering he has acquired a moving understanding of the suffering of others. This has made him abandon the morality of rewards and punishments. What he repudiates is his lamentation and dejection. He realizes that he has regarded God as a prisoner of a particular way of understanding justice, and he now rejects that outlook. Justice alone does not have the final say. It is grace that gives full meaning to justice. It is belief in God's unmerited love that leads to a 'preferential option' for the poor (they do not deserve that privileged position in and of themselves) and to solidarity with those who suffer poverty, oppression and exploitation.

> ### Think about
> ### THE MESSAGE OF JOB
>
> How far are the different 'messages' found in the book by the various scholars whose views are summarized compatible with one another? Take any one of them as 'the' message and then see which others can be taken as complementary to it and which might contradict it.

FURTHER READING

Items marked * are considered suitable as first ports of call, while others are more complex, or relate to specific issues.

COMMENTARIES

Many commentaries have been written on this fascinating and enigmatic book. Clines' commentary includes an exhaustive bibliography of the literature on Job. The volumes by Rodd and Whybray each provide a good overview of the book, Whybray's being somewhat more technical. Andersen and Rowley each provide fairly brief commentaries. Rowley is notable for his concise, balanced judgements on scholarly debates. The translation and reprinting of Dhorme's large commentary is an indication that it is a 'classic' on this book. The commentary by Driver and Gray is particularly strong on the text and language of Job. However, with regard to the language, account now has to be taken of the comparative material from Ugarit, and this is a strength of Pope's commentary. Gordis' large work is the result of a lifetime's study of the book and includes many useful specialist studies as well as a detailed commentary. Clines, Habel and Janzen represent the new trend to more literary approaches to the book

* F. I. Andersen *Job*. TOTC. London: IVP, 1976.

M. Buttenwieser *The Book of Job*. London: Hodder & Stoughton, 1922.

D. J. A. Clines *Job 1–20*. WBC. Dallas, TX: Word Books, 1989.

E. Dhorme *A Commentary on the Book of Job*. London: Nelson, 1967 (a translation by H. Knight of the French edn of 1926).

S. R. Driver and G. B. Gray *Job*. ICC. Edinburgh: T. & T. Clark, 1921.

J. C. L. Gibson *Job*. DSB. Edinburgh: St Andrews Press, 1985.

R. Gordis *The Book of Job*. New York, NY: Jewish Theological Seminary of America, 1978.

N. C. Habel *The Book of Job*. OTL. London: SCM, 1985.

J. E. Hartley *The Book of Job*. NICOT. Grand Rapids, MI: Eerdmans, 1988.

J. G. Janzen *Job*. Interpretation. Atlanta, GA: John Knox Press, 1985.

M. H. Pope *Job*. AB. Garden City, NY: Doubleday, 1973 (3rd edn).

* C. S. Rodd *The Book of Job*. EC. London: Epworth Press, 1990.

* H. H. Rowley *Job*. NCB. London: Nelson, 1970.

N. H. Tur-Sinai *The Book of Job: A New Commentary*. Jerusalem: Kiryath-Sepher, 1957.

* N. Whybray *Job*. Sheffield: Sheffield Academic Press, 1998.

OTHER BOOKS AND ARTICLES

D. J. Clines 'Deconstructing the Book of Job', in D. J. Clines *What Does Eve Do to Help?*, JSOTSup 94, Sheffield: JSOT Press, 1990; pp. 10–123.

* J. L. Crenshaw *Old Testament Wisdom: An Introduction*. Louisville, KY: Westminster John Knox Press, 1998 (rev. edn).

K. J. Dell *The Book of Job as Sceptical Literature*. BZAW 197. Berlin and New York: W. de Gruyter, 1991.

* J. H. Eaton *Job*. OT Guides. Sheffield: JSOT Press, 1985.

G. Fohrer *Introduction to the Old Testament*. London: SPCK, 1970.

E. M. Good *In Turns of Tempest*. Stanford, CA: Stanford University Press, 1990.

R. Gordis *The Book of God and Man: A Study of Job*. Chicago: University of Chicago Press, 1965.

A. Guillaume *Studies in the Book of Job with a New Translation*. Leiden: Brill, 1968.

G. Gutiérrez *On Job: God-Talk and the Suffering of the Innocent*. Maryknoll, NY: Orbis, 1988.

N. C. Habel 'The Narrative Art of Job: Applying the Principles of Robert Alter', *JSOT* 27 (1983), 101–111.

W. G. Lambert *Babylonian Wisdom Literature*. Oxford: OUP, 1960.

R. E. Murphy *Wisdom Literature*. FOTL 13. Grand Rapids, MI: Eerdmans, 1981.

* R. E. Murphy *The Tree of Life*. Grand Rapids, MI: Eerdmans, 1996 (2nd edn).

I. Pardes 'Conclusion', in I. Pardes (ed.), *Countertraditions in the Bible: A Feminist Approach*. Cambridge, MA: Harvard University Press, 1992; pp. 144–156.

L. G. Perdue *Wisdom in Revolt*. Sheffield: Sheffield Academic Press, 1991.

* L. G. Perdue *Wisdom and Creation: The Theology of Wisdom Literature*. Nashville, TN: Abingdon Press, 1994.

J. B. Pritchard *Ancient Near Eastern Texts Relating to the Old Testament*. Princeton, NJ: Princeton University Press, 1969 (3rd edn).

H. H. Rowley 'The Book of Job and Its Meaning', in H. H. Rowley *From Moses to Qumran*. London: Lutterworth Press, 1963; pp. 141–183.

N. H. Snaith *The Book of Job: Its Origin and Purpose*. London: SCM, 1968.

W. B. Stevenson *The Poem of Job*. Oxford: OUP, 1947.

G. L. Studer *Das Buch Hiob*, Bremen: M. Heinsius, 1881.

E. van Wolde *Mr and Mrs Job*. London: SCM, 1997.

Chapter 6

ECCLESIASTES

WHO WAS QOHELETH?

In this chapter 'Ecclesiastes' will be used to refer to the biblical book and 'Qoheleth' to refer to the person whose teaching is preserved in the book. Like much of Ecclesiastes, the Hebrew word that is used to designate the person whose 'words' are recorded in the book (*qoheleth*, Eccl. 1:1) is something of a puzzle. Grammatically the word is feminine in gender; however, it is always used in the book with a masculine form of the verb. Also, in 12:8, and probably also 7:27, the word is preceded by the definite article, so that the reference is to *the* Qoheleth. This suggests that Qoheleth is a title rather than a name.

Qoheleth seems to be derived from the verb *qahal*, meaning 'to assemble, gather'. By its form it belongs to a small group of words that denote particular functions or professions. Some of them came also to be used as titles of such functionaries. On this basis Qoheleth means something like 'assembler'. What did 'the Assembler' assemble? In the light of Ecclesiastes 12:9 one might conclude that it was proverbs. However, in all its uses in the Hebrew Bible the verb *qahal* refers to gathering people together. This is why, when the Hebrew Bible was translated into Greek, Qoheleth was translated as *ekklesiastes*, a word meaning someone who was a member of a public assembly. When the related noun *ekklesia* ('public assembly') became the word used to denote 'church', Qoheleth came to be understood as 'the preacher'. This is the translation used in older English versions of the Bible. Modern versions usually change this to the more neutral title, 'the teacher'. In Ecclesiastes 12:9 we are told that, among his activities, Qoheleth did teach people. Whom he taught, and in what context, is a matter of guesswork. The contents of the book suggest to some scholars that his main audience was the better-off young men who had time to spare for study and discussion. It may be that he ran his own school but, as we have seen, there is no clear evidence of such institutions in Israel or Judah until Ben Sirach's school in the early second century BC.

The opening verse of the book describes Qoheleth as 'the son of David, king in Jerusalem'. Taken at face value this seems to identify Qoheleth with Solomon, and that is how it has been understood

Digging deeper:
THE MEANING OF QOHELETH

Use a concordance, Bible dictionary (such as *NIDOTTE*) and a Hebrew–English lexicon to study the use of the verb *qahal* and related words in the Hebrew Bible. On the basis of this information, draw your own conclusion as to the likely meaning of the name or title Qoheleth.

traditionally. However, since at least the time of Martin Luther, there have been those who have realized that this identification is problematic on the evidence of the book itself. First of all, why would Solomon use a 'pen name'? It is a lot easier to understand why someone might identify himself with Solomon as a literary device. The reason for adopting this device is explained in Ecclesiastes 2:12, 'for what can the one do who comes after the king? Only what has already been done.' The implication is that if a king cannot find meaning and purpose in life, who can? So, by adopting the 'persona' of a king the writer can explore major possible sources of meaning. In fact any attempt at identification with Solomon ends after the first two chapters, when it has served its purpose in enabling the author to present his search for meaning from the vantage point of someone who has the time, money and power to explore a wide range of possibilities.

Even in these chapters there are indications that the writer is not the historical Solomon. Translated literally, Ecclesiastes 1:12 says: 'I, Qoheleth, was king over Jerusalem.' Since, according to 1 Kings, Solomon died 'in office', it is strange to find him speaking as if alive but no longer king. Then, in Ecclesiastes 1:16a, the writer says: 'I said to myself, "I have acquired great wisdom, surpassing all who were over Jerusalem before me."' The only Israelite king who ruled in Jerusalem before Solomon was his father David. It is unlikely that Solomon would compare himself with the earlier Jebusite kings of the city. These two verses do make sense as part of a literary device in which the writer is assuming the position of a king of Solomon's stature but is not too concerned about pretending to be the historical Solomon. Later in the book there are rather critical observations about kings and government that seem far more likely to have come from an ordinary person who has experienced the failings of rulers than from a king (Eccl. 4:1; 5:8–9; 8:2–5; 10:5–7, 20).

On this internal evidence alone it is understandable that the great majority of scholars since the nineteenth century have concluded that Qoheleth is not Solomon, but adopts a Solomonic role in order to explore different possible avenues as

Think about
ROLE PLAY AND REFLECTION ON LIFE

If you wanted to write a reflection on the meaning of life today, what roles might you adopt as an aid to helping yourself and your readers to explore by imagination possible avenues as sources of meaning? A prime minister? A pop-music idol? A famous sports-person? A movie star? A wealthy business tycoon? Is there today any one figure who could provide a way into as wide a range of avenues as Solomon did?

sources of meaning in life in the opening chapters of the book. As we shall see, there are also other reasons for concluding that the book does not come from Solomon of the tenth century BC.

THE TEXT AND LANGUAGE OF ECCLESIASTES

The text of Ecclesiastes seems to have been well preserved. The problems encountered in understanding it arise from the unusual language, form and message of the book rather than any problem in the transmission of the text. A few fragments of the Hebrew text of the book were found at Qumran. They support the Massoretic Text.

The LXX contains a translation of the book into Greek that is very literal. In a handful of instances it seems to bear witness to a variant form of the Hebrew text that gives a better sense than the Massoretic Text. The Latin Vulgate is a freer translation of the Hebrew than is the LXX. The Syriac Peshitta generally agrees with the Massoretic Text. The Aramaic Targum is not a translation but an interpretative paraphrase, which makes Qoheleth into a consistently orthodox thinker.

Since at least the seventeenth century, scholars have regarded the type of Hebrew in which Ecclesiastes is written as evidence against Solomonic authorship. The language is distinctly different in vocabulary, grammar and syntax from the 'classical Hebrew' in which most of the biblical books are written. It is more like the Hebrew of those books which were clearly written in the post-exilic period, such as Ezra, Nehemiah and Chronicles.

Moreover, even more than these books, it has similarities with the later Mishnaic Hebrew used by the early rabbis. A number of explanations have been put forward to explain the peculiarities of Ecclesiastes' Hebrew.

One of the features of 'late' or 'post-biblical' Hebrew is that it is influenced by the vocabulary and grammatical forms of Aramaic. Aramaic is a Semitic language closely related to, but distinct from, Hebrew. It became the common language of the Persian Empire. It eventually replaced Hebrew as the common language of the Jews themselves. The influence of Aramaic is so marked in Ecclesiastes that some scholars (e.g. Torrey; Ginsberg, 1950) have argued that the book as we now have it is a translation of an original Aramaic work. This argument has been subjected to detailed criticism (e.g. by Gordis and Whitley) and seems now not to have any scholarly support. Some of the argument is detailed and technical, but Gordis makes a couple of more general points. The first is that an important part of the argument in favour of the book being a translation is the claim that some of the difficulties in the book can be explained as 'mistranslations'. Gordis argues that some of these explanations do not stand up to close examination. He then suggests that the whole argument is misconceived. A translator may misunderstand, and so mistranslate, a text but will usually express the result in clear, native language. He points to the fact that difficulties in the Hebrew text of certain biblical books 'disappear' in the smooth English of most translations. Gordis also points out that Aramaisms occur in an inconsistent way in Qoheleth, and argues that this is less likely to be the result of translation than of an author who is familiar with two closely related languages and moves more or less unconsciously between them.

In 1952 Dahood argued that Ecclesiastes was written by a Jew who was influenced by the Phoenician language, and must therefore have lived in one of the Phoenician cities. This theory has also been critically examined by Gordis and, especially, Whitley. It has found very little support among scholars.

There now seems to be a general consensus, which agrees with Gordis' conclusion that the peculiarities of the language are primarily the result of the author being someone who was very familiar with Aramaic and, as a result, readily slipped into using Aramaic words and usage. Whybray suggests that another reason for some of the obscurity of the language may be that the author was trying to express complex and abstract ideas that are not easily expressed in classical Hebrew prose. The reason for this is that the classical prose has few conjunctions and tends to avoid the use of subordinate clauses. This makes it difficult to express the kind of qualifications and subtleties that are common in Qoheleth's reflections.

WHEN AND WHERE DID QOHELETH LIVE?

As mentioned above, Dahood suggested that Qoheleth lived in Phoenicia, but this opinion has found very little support. In the nineteenth century in particular some scholars argued that Qoheleth lived and wrote in Alexandria in Egypt. In part this was because of the Greek influence they saw in the book (a point to be discussed later). However, in support of this contention they also pointed to the references to the king as someone with whom Qoheleth's students might come into personal contact (especially Eccl. 8:2–4) and a possible allusion to maritime trading (Eccl. 11:1–2). None of this has been found conclusive. The references to the king may simply be based on traditional sayings, and in any case 'king' could mean 'local ruler', whatever his official status – provincial governor in the case of Jerusalem after the exile. Also, there were international seaports in Palestine as well as Egypt.

What little evidence there is in the book points to Jerusalem as its place of origin. There are references to local conditions such as the rain (Eccl. 11:3; 12:2), the changes of the wind (1:6; 11:4), the use of wells and cisterns for water storage (12:6) and the almond tree (12:5), which are, in fact, not compatible with an Egyptian setting for the book but are characteristic of Judea. Most significantly there are the references to the temple and sacrifice (5:1; 9:2). These seem to assume that Qoheleth's students had ready access to the Jerusalem temple.

The conclusion that the language is best explained if Qoheleth was well-acquainted with Aramaic and that it has many of the features of Mishnaic Hebrew points to a date well into the post-exilic period. It is generally agreed that Ben Sirach shows acquaintance with Ecclesiastes (the evidence is listed by Barton and summarized by Gordis, 1968). Ben Sirach's work is usually dated no later than 180 BC. Also, fragments of Ecclesiastes have been found at Qumran, and are dated c. 150 BC, suggesting that the book was fairly well-known by then. Moreover, Ecclesiastes shows no knowledge of the turbulence of the 160s in Palestine when the persecution of the Jews by Antiochus IV Epiphanes led to the Maccabean Revolt. All this suggests that the book cannot be dated much later than 200 BC.

Digging deeper:
ECCLESIASTES AND BEN SIRACH

Study the evidence listed by Barton and/or Gordis as showing that Ben Sirach was acquainted with Ecclesiastes. How convincing do you find it?

In the nineteenth century some scholars claimed to find numerous Graecisms in the book. These might point to a date well after Alexander the Great's conquest of the Persian Empire in 334–331, to allow time for the spread of the influence of the Greek language in Palestine. However, careful examination of the claimed Graecisms by various scholars showed that they all have analogies in Hebrew or related Semitic languages (Barton, and Gordis, 1968, provide useful summaries).

Fredericks argues that many of the features in Qoheleth's language that are thought to point to a late date have precedents in biblical Hebrew. He concludes that the language should not be dated later than the exilic period, and could be earlier. Schoors has argued that Fredericks' case is flawed because he considers each linguistic feature in isolation. It is the cumulative evidence of the combination of features in the book that suggests a late post-exilic date. Most scholars still think that the

language suggests a third-century or, at the earliest, a late fourth-century, date for the book. For many this is supported by finding evidence of the influence of Hellenistic Greek thought in the book. This will be discussed below.

THE MAN AND THE BOOK

Since at least the nineteenth century there has been a debate about how much of the book of Ecclesiastes is the original words of the man known as Qoheleth. There are two features of the book that provoke this question, both of which were noted by, and a cause of concern for, some of the early rabbis. First, there are contradictory statements within the book. A glaring example is provided by Ecclesiastes 8:12–14. In vv. 12–13 it is said that the wicked will not prosper in the long run and that all will be well for those who fear God. The next verse says exactly the opposite. There are several other contradictory statements that are well separated from one another (e.g. Eccl. 3:17; 9:1–2). Second, some of the statements in Ecclesiastes seem to contradict what is said in other biblical books (e.g. 8:14).

In the second half of the nineteenth century it became common for scholars to deal with this problem by suggesting that the original words of Qoheleth were often disturbingly critical of the thinking in the mainstream 'wisdom tradition'. As a result his words were edited by others of less critical views who made additions and insertions to soften what he had said and make it more 'orthodox'. An extreme example of this was the commentary by D. Siegfried, published in German in 1898, which postulated nine different editors with varying theological views. They were responsible for more than half of the material in the book as we have it (Barton gives a summary of Siegfried's analysis). If Qoheleth's words were really so objectionable, and hard to make sound 'orthodox', one is left wondering why they were not simply suppressed!

There have always been those who have argued for other explanations of the apparently contradictory viewpoints in the book. More recently some of these have regained favour as it has become clear that theories of multiple editors have not proved satisfactory. One possibility is that the book is an anthology of independent pieces from different times in Qoheleth's life and that the variations in attitude and mood reflect different life experiences and stages of life. This raises the question of who made the anthology. Was it Qoheleth himself, or one of his students? In the introduction and conclusion of the book there is clear evidence of some editorial activity. Also, is there any discernible order in the arrangement of the material? As we shall see, there are very different opinions about this.

Another possibility is that Qoheleth is quoting traditional teaching and then commenting on it, sometimes even seeking to refute it. In his day authors did not use the device of quotation marks to indicate quoted material. The readers were left to recognize it for themselves. A possible example of this technique of 'quotation and comment' is in Ecclesiastes 4:5–6.

> Fools fold their hands, and consume
> their own flesh.
> Better is a handful with quiet than two
> handfuls with toil and a chasing
> after wind.

The sentiment of v. 5 has its parallel in Proverbs 6:10–11; 24:33–34. The traditional response to this proverb would probably be some words in praise of hard work (e.g. Prov. 13:4; 21:5). Qoheleth, however, contends that it is best to be satisfied with the results of only a moderate amount of effort. That these are his words is suggested by the characteristic phrase 'a chasing after wind' and his comments elsewhere about the futility of excessive toil (e.g. 1:3; 2:18f.). A variant on this view is that in the book Qoheleth is carrying on a dialogue with a real or imagined opponent. The problem with this view is that there is only limited agreement in identifying the 'quotations' and 'responses'. Also, in some cases it is argued that the 'quotations' are used to summarize or support Qoheleth's own view.

Loader takes a somewhat similar view when he argues that the apparent contradictions consist of a 'pole' and a 'contra-pole', which are held in tension. He argues that one side of each apparent contradiction is a viewpoint that is characteristic of 'conventional wisdom'. The other side is then Qoheleth's response. On this basis he concludes that there are no real contradictions in Qoheleth's own thought. Critics have argued that not all of Loader's 'opposites' are truly polar, and that his 'pole versus contra-pole' schema often produces forced interpretations.

Finally, another possible explanation of the apparent contradictions is that they arise from the dialectical character of Qoheleth's thought. He sees reality as complex. It is not possible to do justice to its complexity either by emphasizing only one side of it, or by charting some 'middle way' between two extremes. The apparent

Digging deeper:
QUOTATIONS IN ECCLESIASTES

Whybray (1981) suggests that a saying (specifically, a two-part sentence) is probably a quotation if it is:

1. a self-contained saying;
2. very similar in form to sayings in Proverbs 10—29;
3. consistent with the ideas expressed in Proverbs but standing in tension with Qoheleth's main ideas;
4. lacking in 'late' linguistic features.

Using these criteria he identifies what he regards as eight 'clear examples' of quotations: Ecclesiastes 2:14a; 4:5; 4:6 (omitting, 'and a chasing after wind'); 7:5; 7;6a (omitting, 'this also is vanity') ; 9:17; 10:2; 10:12.

Fox (1999) accepts that he may be right in identifying these as quotations. However, in his view, unless the quoter 'distances' himself from a quotation it becomes his own. He argues that, if Qoheleth had wanted to, he could have made the quotations clear. They could have been made explicit by saying: 'The sages say ... but I say ...' There are also a variety of less explicit ways of indicating quotations:

1. by the mention of another person beside the main speaker in the immediate context in such a way that the reader associates the saying with that person;
2. by a reference to 'mouth' or 'words' or something else that indicates speech;
3. by a shift in grammatical number and person, such as, 'They say ...'

In his view identifying 'quotations' can too readily become a way of avoiding facing up to difficulties in the text.

Study the 'quotations' identified by Whybray and then make your own assessment of Fox's critique in the light of them.

contradictions have simply to be accepted because the whole truth lies beyond the comprehension of the human mind. As a result Qoheleth's writing is marked by what is described by the German phrase, *Zwar-aber Aussage*. This may be translated into English as the 'granted, but on the other hand, statement'. Several scholars have tried to analyse the book in these terms. The trouble is that the 'buts' do not usually follow on directly from the 'granted'. Thus, he says that, because of oppression, the dead are more fortunate than the living (Eccl. 4:2), but only much later says that it is better to be alive because the living have hope and know that they will die, but the dead know nothing (9:4–5). A possible explanation of this is that the book is a loose anthology of sayings.

Despite the seeming contradictions, there are words (e.g. 'wisdom', 'time/season', 'profit'), phrases (e.g. 'under the sun', 'vanity of vanities') and themes (e.g. the value of wisdom, the proper attitude to work, the inevitability of death, the enjoyment of life) that run through the book and give a sense of unity to it. For this reason most recent scholars are generally agreed that the bulk of the book comes from one person but, as this survey has

A ZWAR-ABER AUSSAGE ANALYSIS	
From: H. W. Hertzberg, 1963	
Zwar	**Aber**
1:16	1:17–18
2:3–10	2:11
2:13–14a	3:14bf.
3:11a	3:11b
3:17	3:18f.
4:13–16a	4:16b
7:11–12	7:7 (transposed)
8:12b–13	8:14–15
9:4b	9:5
9:16a	9:16b
9:17–18a	9:18b—10:1
10:2–3	10:5–7

shown, there is no agreement on the best way to explain the rather enigmatic nature of the book.

LITERARY STRUCTURE

The fact that the book lacks a clearly structured argument has not stopped scholars from searching for a literary structure. There is a limited measure of agreement about such a structure. It is generally agreed that Ecclesiastes 1:1–3 and 12:8–14 form a prologue and epilogue that frame the body of the book, which is substantially Qoheleth's own words. The prologue and epilogue, and possibly a few additions in the body of the text, are commonly seen as the work of an editor, or editors. In 1:1–2, 7:27 and 12:8–14 Qoheleth is spoken of in the third person (some English translations obscure this) and so it is natural to see these as written by someone else. Within this framework, the first and last sections (1:4–11 and 12:1–7) have a distinctive semi-poetic style. They have probably been placed where

they are to form an appropriate introduction and conclusion to Qoheleth's thoughts. The style and subject matter of 1:12—2:26, where Qoheleth takes on a 'Solomonic persona', makes this a distinct section. It also introduces many of the topics that are discussed in following material. If these observations are accepted, the main issue in discerning a literary structure in the book concerns the arrangement of the material in 3:1—11:10.

Some scholars have divided the book into major sections according to the subject matter or themes that they see being dominant in these sections. Ginsberg (1955) divides the book into four main sections, apart from the title and epilogue, as shown in 'Ginsberg's Structure of Ecclesiastes'.

GINSBERG'S STRUCTURE OF ECCLESIASTES		
Title	1:1	
A	1:2—2:26	Theme: 'All is zero (*hevel*)'.
B	3:1—4:3	Theme: 'All happenings are foreordained, but never foreseeable'.
A'	4:4—6:9	Theme: 'All is zero (*hevel*)'.
B'	6:10—12:8	Theme: 'All happenings are foreordained, but never foreseeable'.
Ep.	12:9–14	

According to Ginsberg the two themes of A and B are linked together by Ecclesiastes 3:9–13. The initial question of 1:3 is repeated in 3:9 and is given the answer that people gain nothing from their toil because God has ordained it that way. In A' and B' Ginsberg sees a resumption of the themes of A and B respectively, and a drawing out of the consequences that follow from them. The main criticism of this analysis is that much of the material does not fit into the proposed themes. Ginsberg himself admits this, describing some sections as 'digressions' (e.g. 5:1–9; 9:17—10:19), for which he gives no explanation.

Other scholars have based their structural analysis on the discerning of a combination of literary devices and thematic sections. Rousseau finds the structure known as the chiasm in the framework of the book.

ROUSSEAU'S STRUCTURE OF ECCLESIASTES

A	Title	1:1
B	Theme	1:2–3
C	Prologue	1:4–11
C'	Epilogue	12:1–7
B'	Theme	12:8
A'	Redactional note	12:9–14

As can be seen in 'Rousseau's Structure of Ecclesiastes', in a chiasm the second half of the structure parallels the first, but is a mirror image of it. Here one might question how far A and A' do really correspond to one another. Within this framework Rousseau divides the material into seven 'cycles'. Each of these ends with an exhortation to enjoy life.

Earlier scholars had recognized the recurrent refrain about enjoying life (Eccl. 2:24–26; 3:12–13, 22; 5:18–20; 8:15; 9:7–10; 11:7–10) but had not been able to discern how it might function as a structural marker. It is questionable whether Rousseau has really succeeded since three of his sections (4, 5 and 7 in 'Rousseau's

---

ROUSSEAU'S CYCLES

A	1.	Solomon's confession (1:12—2:26).
B	2.	The sage cannot know God's design in general (3:1–13).
	3.	The sage cannot know what follows death (3:14–22).
C	4.	Various deceptions and exhortations (4:1—5:20).
	5.	Various deceptions and exhortations (6:1—8:15).
B'	6.	Wisdom's ineffectiveness (8:16—9:10).
C'	7.	Deceptions and exhortations (9:11—11:10).

Cycles') have the same very vague title rather than a genuine theme. Within each cycle Rousseau argues that the material is often arranged on the principle of 'parallelism' produced by repeated themes, phrases or words. Thus within the first cycle he sees two parallel halves.

> Wisdom is deceptive (1:12–18) – Wealth is deceptive (2:1–11)
> Wisdom is deceptive (2:12–17) – Wealth is deceptive (2:18–23)

He is more successful in finding what seem to be genuine patterns at this lower level than at the overall structural level.

Perhaps the two very different analyses of the book by Wright and Crenshaw provide examples of the two extremes to which scholars have gone with regard to the structure of the book. Wright sees Ecclesiastes 1:4–11 and 11:7—12:7 as stressing the two main themes of the book: the profitlessness of toil and the invitation to enjoy life. Within the body of the book he looks for purely literary markers as a guide to its structure. He uses the repeated phrases '[this also/all is vanity and] a

WRIGHT'S ANALYSIS

Prologue (1:1–3)
Theme 1: toil is profitless (1:4–11)
I. Qoheleth's investigation of life (1:12—6:9)
    Double introduction (1:12–15, 16–18)
    Study of pleasure-seeking (2:1–11)
    Study of wisdom and folly (2:12–17)
    Study of the fruits of toil (2:18—6:9)
II. Qoheleth's conclusions (6:10—11:6)
    Introduction (6:10–12)
    A. Man cannot find out what is good for him
        to do
        Critique of traditional wisdom
        On the day of prosperity and adversity
        (7:1–14)
        On justice and wickedness (7:15–24)
        On women and folly (7:25–29)
        On the wise man and the king (8:1–17)
    B. Man does not know what will come after
        him
        He knows he will die: the dead know
            nothing (9:1–6)
        There is no knowledge in Sheol (9:7–10)
        Man does not know his time (9:11–12)
        Man does not know what will happen
        (9:13—10:15)
        He does not know what evil will come
        (10:16—11:2)
        He does not know what good will come
        (11:3–6)
Theme 2: exhortation to enjoyment (11:7—12:8)
Epilogue (12:9–14)

chasing after wind' as the concluding refrain of six subsections in what he takes to be the first half of the book: 1:12—6:9. In the second half he finds four subsections in 7:1—8:17 marked by the phrase 'not find out', and six in 9:1—11:6 marked by 'do not know'. A number of criticisms have been made of this analysis. Wright is not entirely consistent in his use of the 'marker' phrases. For example, he ignores the occurrence of the 'marker phrase' in 4:4 and in 1:14 the phrase occurs in the middle of a subsection, not at its end. Then there is the question why he has chosen these three phrases when there are also other phrases which Qoheleth repeats (e.g. 'under the sun'). Finally, some of the subsections lack any real thematic coherence (e.g. 2:18—6:9; 10:16—11:2). In a subsequent study Wright applied numerology to support his analysis. This rests on the fact that in Hebrew the characters of the alphabet are used as numerals as well as being letters. Wright points out that the numerical value of the phrase 'vanity of vanities all is vanity' in Hebrew is 216, which is the number of verses in 1:1—12:8. Also, the word 'vanity' (numerical value 37) occurs three times in 1:2, giving the number 111 (3 x 37). There are 111 verses in 1:1—6:9, vindicating, in his view, a clear break after 6:9. He makes other, more complex, numerological observations. The problem is the number of seemingly arbitrary assumptions he has to make to find numerical patterns that fit his proposed structure. Moreover, there is the point that the current verse divisions of the book were fixed in the medieval period, and we do not know whether the original editor of the book would have thought in terms of the same verses, if he thought in terms of verses at all.

Crenshaw is one of the several commentators who have given up looking for an overall structure and simply divided the book into what seem to them to be coherent subsections. Comparison of his analysis with that of others (e.g. Schoors; Whybray, 1989) shows that there is considerable agreement, but not unanimity, about the subsections.

CRENSHAW'S ANALYSIS

1:1	The Superscription
1:2–3	Motto and Thematic Statement
1:4–11	Nothing New Under the Sun
1:12—2:26	The Royal Experiment
3:1–15	A Time for Everything
3:16—4:3	The Tears of the Oppressed
4:4–6	Proverbial Insights about Toil and Its Opposite
4:7–12	The Advantages of Companionship
4:13–16	The Fickle Crowd
5:1–9	Religious Obligations
5:10—6:9	The Disappointments of Wealth
6:10–12	A Transitional Unit
7:1–14	A Collection of Proverbs
7:15–22	On Moderation
7:23–29	Seeking and Finding
8:1–9	Rulers and Subjects
8:10–17	The Mystery of Divine Activity
9:1–10	The Shadow of Death
9:11–12	Time and Chance
9:13–18	Wasted Wisdom
10:1–20	A Collection of Proverbs on Wisdom and Folly
11:1–6	The Element of Risk
11:7—12:7	Youth and Old Age
12:8	Thematic Statement (*inclusio*)
12:9–14	The Epilogue(s)

Besides the superscription and epilogues (Eccl. 12:9–11, 12–14), Crenshaw regards the following as editorial glosses: Ecclesiastes 2:26a; 3:17a; 8:12–13; 11:9b; and possibly 5:19 and 7:26b.

Digging deeper:
THE STRUCTURE OF ECCLESIASTES

Read through Ecclesiastes 6:10—11:6, comparing Wright's analysis of this section of the book with Crenshaw's. Which do you find more convincing?

A BRIEF OVERVIEW

The section divisions used here are similar to, but not identical with, those proposed by Crenshaw.

ECCLESIASTES 1:1–3

The 'superscription' (v. 1) has been discussed on p. 145, and the 'motto' (v. 2) and 'theme' (v. 3) are discussed in some detail on pp. 163–4.

ECCLESIASTES 1:4–11

This piece of rhythmic prose refers to the earth, sun, wind and waters. There may be an echo here of the four basic 'elements' of the cosmos according to Greek thought: earth, fire, air and water. Qoheleth's concern, however, is not with the structure of the cosmos but with the meaninglessness of it. Apart from the passing of time, nothing else changes, and humans have no ability to bring about real change or progress. Any appearance of progress is simply the result of the past being forgotten.

ECCLESIASTES 1:12—2:26

In this 'royal testament' Qoheleth adopts the role of King Solomon (1:12) in order to explore different possible sources of meaning in life. As he often does, he begins by summarizing his 'experiment' and conclusions (1:13–18) before describing them in detail. In turn he describes his pursuit of physical pleasure and possessions (2:1–11), wisdom (2:12–17) and constructive work (2:18–23). He concludes that each of these is only 'vanity'. All that remains is to enjoy what good things God does give, however ephemeral and inadequate this joy may be.

ECCLESIASTES 3:1–15

In the ancient Near East it was a mark of wisdom to know the 'proper time' for things. The poem in vv. 1–8 asserts that everything has its 'proper time'. In the reflection that follows Qoheleth asserts that this time is set by God and the knowledge of God's purposes is beyond human understanding. Events, therefore, lie outside human control. All humans can do is enjoy the pleasures that come as a gift from God.

ECCLESIASTES 3:16—4:3

The theme of this section is injustice, considered in general (3:16–22) and through a specific example (4:1–3). Faced with injustice in the world, Qoheleth finds little comfort in the idea of divine retribution, because humans and animals seem to share the same fate in death. Only the pursuit of enjoyment, where this is possible, can bring some consolation.

ECCLESIASTES 4:4–16

Here Qoheleth declares that three desires that often motivate people are 'vanity': the desire to succeed in competition with others (vv. 4–6); the desire for riches (vv. 7–8) and the desire for political power and fame (4:13–16). It is not clear how the section on the value of companionship (vv. 9–12) relates to its context. The link may simply be the 'catch word' 'second/ another', which occurs in vv. 8, 10, 15 (this is not clear in English translations).

ECCLESIASTES 5:1–7

This section contains sayings that concern speech in the context of the cult. In particular they deal with sacrifice (v. 1), prayer (vv. 2–3) and vows (vv. 4–7). It amounts to a commendation of moderation in piety rather than enthusiasm that might lead to rash words.

ECCLESIASTES 5:8–9

This brief section is an ironic comment on the oppression that arises because government officials are more concerned with keeping their jobs than with justice. The meaning of v. 9 is unclear – compare various English translations of it.

ECCLESIASTES 5:10—6:9

The theme of wealth unites this section. Through reflections on life, proverbs and stories, Qoheleth argues that the gaining and use of wealth are vanity. In the middle of the section Qoheleth once again comments that there is some amelioration to be found in the enjoyment of whatever good things God may give.

ECCLESIASTES 6:10–12

Qoheleth repeats one of his basic themes. Events have been preordained and humans cannot change them. Because they cannot know the outcome of events, the meaning of them is hidden from humans.

ECCLESIASTES 7:1–14

This collection of sayings is united by word repetition, not logic. In Hebrew, six of the sayings begin with the word *tov* ('good/ better', vv. 1, 2, 3, 5, 8, 11) and in one it is the second word (v. 14). This word occurs 11 times in all in these verses. Other common words are 'wise/wisdom' (six times), 'heart' (five times) and 'fool' (four times). There are also some plays on Hebrew words that sound alike. The section ends with the by now characteristic advice: to enjoy what one can in life since the real meaning of events is hidden from humans.

ECCLESIASTES 7:15–24

Again Qoheleth counsels moderation. He cautions against both excess of wickedness and folly and excess of wisdom and righteousness. This is based on his own observation of life. He advises the person who 'fears God' to take the middle way between extremes (v. 18). The opening 'all this' of vv. 23–24 could refer either to what goes before, or what follows. Maybe it is a deliberate 'bridging' reflection, stressing the inaccessibility of true wisdom.

ECCLESIASTES 7:25–29

This section is held together by the repeated use of three words: 'seek', 'find' and 'sum of all things'. In it Qoheleth expresses his view of humanity as a whole. There are differing interpretations of what that view is – see the 'Interpretation of Ecclesiastes 7:25–29' box.

ECCLESIASTES 8:1–9

Qoheleth now gives advice concerning behaviour before the king. This suggests that at least some of his 'students' were, or were likely to become, young courtiers. Like other wise men, he gives advice so that they might get on in the world. His characteristic view of life comes to the fore in vv. 6b–9 where he says that no one has the power or knowledge to act correctly in every situation.

ECCLESIASTES 8:10–17

Qoheleth returns to consideration of the problem of reward and punishment. He quotes the orthodox view (vv. 12–13) but surrounds it by observations that show that at best it oversimplifies reality. Retribution does sometimes overtake the wicked, but often only after a long delay. This encourages wrongdoers. All too often the righteous and the wicked seem to be treated alike. Once again he commends taking what enjoyment one can out of life. It is not possible to understand God's justice since no human can understand what God is doing in this world.

Digging deeper:
THE INTERPRETATION OF ECCLESIASTES 7:25–29

Many commentators understand Qoheleth to be saying that women are more bitter than death (v. 26) and that he has found no woman, and only the occasional man, who is virtuous (v. 28). Moreover, although God created all humans 'straightforward/upright' all have gone wrong (v. 29).

Other commentators argue that in v. 26 Qoheleth is not speaking of *all* women but of a particular type of woman, such as the adulteress or prostitute who is contrasted with the virtuous woman in the book of Proverbs. The *Living Bible* version makes this explicit by rendering the verse as, 'A prostitute is more bitter than death'. Some then follow this by arguing that in v. 28b Qoheleth quotes a popular proverb, the truth of which he denies. This is what he is referring to as what 'he has not found' in v. 28a. Support for this interpretation of vv. 27–28 is found in the statement of v. 29, which makes no distinction between men and women.

The first interpretation is argued for by Longman (1998, pp. 201–207) and the second by Murphy (1992, pp. 75–78). Read their arguments and draw your own conclusion.

ECCLESIASTES 9:1–10

This section is among the most pessimistic in the whole book, though the ideas expressed in it have already been expressed earlier in the book. Death, says Qoheleth, comes to everyone and it is the definitive end. Neither righteousness nor religiosity saves anyone from it. However, death is worse than life. Therefore he commands his students to enjoy life while they can, in every way they can and with as much vigour as they possess.

ECCLESIASTES 9:11–12

These verses make the point that success can never be taken for granted. Humans are always subject to the time and chance, which may bring unexpected calamity.

ECCLESIASTES 9:13–16

Qoheleth uses an anecdote once again to point out the limitations of wisdom. The advice of a wise man does have a positive short-term effect. However, because he lacks wealth and status he and his deed are soon forgotten. This section prepares the way for the collection of proverbs about wisdom and folly that follows it.

ECCLESIASTES 9:17—10:15

This collection of proverbs is loosely held together by the subject of wisdom and folly. Embedded in it is an illustrative anecdote (10:5–7). The statement in 10:1b seems to sum up the general theme of 9:17—10:4, that a little of a bad thing (folly) can spoil quite a lot of a good thing (wisdom). The following anecdote illustrates this by making the point that the mistake of putting a fool in an influential position can cause social upheaval. If there is any common thread in 10:8–11, and commentators dispute over this, it seems to be the unfairness of life because of unpredictable happenings. The proverbs in 10:12–15 denigrate fools, especially the way they (mis)use words. Here, as in some other places, we can see that, despite his strictures about the limitations of human wisdom, Qoheleth does see value in it because of its relative superiority when compared with folly.

ECCLESIASTES 10:16–20

These proverbs are loosely connected by their concern with order in society. The king should be the guardian of this (vv. 16–17), but it also depends on the behaviour of the citizens. Qoheleth commends diligence (v. 18), the enjoyment of life (v. 19) and respect for those in power (v. 20).

ECCLESIASTES 11:1–6

According to 11:3 life is a mixture of inevitability (v. 3a) and randomness (v. 3b). Hidden behind this lies the activity of God (v. 5). In the light of these observations we might be tempted to fatalism and inactivity (v. 4). However, this section begins and ends (vv. 1, 6) with the counsel to get on with life, taking the risks this involves, but also taking due precautions against disaster (v. 2).

ECCLESIASTES 11:7—12:7

The theme of this section is youth, old age and death. Youth, says Qoheleth, is the time to enjoy life, before the faculties become impaired (12:1). Yet in the enjoyment he counsels youths to remember that death is inevitable (11:8b), humans are answerable to God (11:9c), and youth is transient (11:10, here *hevel* probably has this temporal meaning). There is general agreement that 12:2–5 depicts the failing of the human faculties with advancing age, though detailed understandings of the passage differ – see the 'Old House of Ecclesiastes 12:2–6' box. The imagery in v. 6 is evocative of death, but its details are unclear. It may be that the 'bowl' is the bowl of an oil lamp (the same word has this sense in Zech. 4:2–3) holding oil and a wick, and that it is suspended by the chord. The snapping of the chord would then lead to the destruction of the lamp and extinguishing of its light. The 'wheel' is probably the pulley that would be used to raise the 'pitcher' from a well or cistern. The destruction of both would make the water, often a symbol for life, unavailable.

ECCLESIASTES 12:8

Some take this as the concluding verse of the previous section, but it also acts as the conclusion to Qoheleth's words, corresponding to the 'motto' of 1:2 and forming an *inclusio* with it, framing his words.

ECCLESIASTES 12:9–14

The epilogue contains some information about Qoheleth (vv. 9–10), a brief evaluation of his work (vv. 11–12) and a final admonition to the reader to 'fear God and keep his commandments' (vv. 13–14).

Digging deeper:
THE OLD HOUSE OF ECCLESIASTES 12:2–6

Commentators have taken three main approaches to this description of the house.

1. It has been argued that these verses are to be taken on the literal level as describing the events surrounding a funeral.

2. Others see in these verses the depiction of a house and household facing a devastating storm. This is then understood as a metaphor for the body and its physical decline with the advance of old age.

3. From the Targum onwards some have treated these verses as an allegory of old age, finding connections between aspects of the image of the house and specific bodily parts.

One weakness of the literal approach is that it does not seem to account adequately for the storm imagery of v. 2. The metaphorical approach has been criticized for not taking account of seemingly obvious allegorical references, such as to the teeth and eyes in v. 3b. The problem with the allegorical approach is that while some of the connections made seem plausible (such as v. 3b) others seem forced, e.g. there has been considerable disagreement about the identification of the 'house guards' and 'strong men' of v. 3a.

For helpful discussions of this passage see the articles on it by Sawyer and Fox, and then decide how you think it should be interpreted.

The significance of this epilogue for a 'canonical interpretation' of the book is discussed later.

LITERARY FORMS

As we have seen, the distinction between Hebrew poetry and prose is sometimes not clear. Comparison of different English translations will show that the translators do not always agree over what is prose and what is poetry in Ecclesiastes. Some sections, such as 7:1–12, clearly have the same poetic form as the sentences in the book of Proverbs. Others have poetic qualities, which are more (e.g. 1:4–11) or less (e.g. 12:2–7) evident. Then there are sections that few would deny are clearly prose (e.g. 4:13–16, 6:1–6).

One of the striking features of the book is the variety of material in it. There are two collections of sentence proverbs (7:1–12; 10:1–20), as well as other proverbs scattered elsewhere in the book. These include the same types of sentence as occur in Proverbs: antithetical (7:4), synonymous (10:18) and progressive (10:3). Qoheleth seems to have liked 'better than' proverbs (4:1–16; 6:9; 7:1–10; 9:17). He also uses another form of saying that occurs in Proverbs: the admonition. This consists of a command or exhortation combined with a motive for heeding it (e.g. 5:2, 4; 7:9; 9:7). Qoheleth sometimes expands on the motive-clause, making it the point of departure for further reflections (e.g. 8:2f.).

Qoheleth makes use of the 'moral tale', a story that he claims is based on his own experience or observation and from which he draws a moral. There are straightforward examples in 4:13–16 and 9:13–16. The 'royal testament' in 1:12–2:26 is more complex since it is not the basis for a simple moral point but for a series of reflections on the meaning of life.

On a number of occasions Qoheleth records his reflections on something he has observed (7:15–18) or on some aspect of life (9:1–10).

The two poetic or semi-poetic pieces in 1:4–11 and 12:1–7 have already been mentioned. Commentators differ over whether the imagery in 12:1–7 is to be taken literally (describing the decay of an old house) or allegorically (with the 'house' being the human body). Some who take it literally see it as a parable about the need to take heed of human mortality.

LITERARY GENRE

Does Ecclesiastes fit into any known genre of ancient Near Eastern literature? There is no general consensus about a positive answer to this question, but parallels have been found between Qoheleth and various ancient Near Eastern texts or groups of texts. We will survey these briefly.

The Egyptian 'Instructions' have been discussed in relation to the book of Proverbs. A few of them (e.g. *The Instruction of Merikare*, *The Instruction of Amenemhet*) are first-person speeches put into the mouths of long-dead rulers and contain admonitions based on their reflections on life. This gives them a formal similarity to the 'Solomonic speech' in Ecclesiastes.

Another Egyptian genre to which people sometimes appeal are the 'Songs of the Harper'. These were songs sung to entertain guests at feasts. They tended to question the belief in the afterlife and to emphasize enjoyment of life in the present. A particularly striking example, dating

---

A HARPER'S SONG FROM THE TOMB OF KING INTEF

He is happy, this good prince! Death is a kindly fate.
A generation passes, another stays, since the time of the ancestors.
The gods who were before rest in their tombs,
Blessed nobles too are buried in their tombs.
[Yet] those who built tombs, their places are gone, what has become of them?
I have heard the words of Imhotep and Hardedef, whose sayings are recited whole.
What of their places?
Their walls have crumbled, their places are gone, as though they had never been!
None comes from there, to tell of their state, to tell of their needs, to calm our hearts,
Until we go where they have gone!
Hence rejoice in your heart!
Forgetfulness profits you, follow your heart as long as you live!
Put myrrh on your head, dress in fine linen, anoint yourself with oils fit for a god.
Heap up your joys, let your heart not sink!
Follow your heart and your happiness, do your things on earth as your heart commands!
When there comes to you that day of mourning,
The Weary-hearted [Osiris] hears not their mourning, wailing saves no man from the pit!

Refrain: Make holiday, do not weary of it!
          Lo, none is allowed to take his goods with him,
          Lo, none who departs comes back again!

Translation by Miriam Lichtheim in Hallo and Younger (1997, pp. 48–49).

---

from about 2100 BC, was found in a royal tomb. It is written in the first person, is sceptical about the future life, and emphasizes the celebration of the present life. The parallels with Ecclesiastes are more in content than form.

Think about
ECCLESIASTES AND THE HARPER'S SONG

Read the Harper's Song from the tomb of King Intef and then read Ecclesiastes 1:4, 11; 3:22; 11:9–10. How striking, or otherwise, do you find the similarities? Do they really show a similar outlook on life and death?

From the Old Kingdom down to the Hellenistic period, 'grave biographies' were inscribed on the walls of Egyptian tombs. These are presented as posthumous first-person speeches by the deceased. They normally contained three features: an autobiographical narrative, ethical maxims, and exhortations addressed to visitors to the tomb. The exhortations often call on the visitors both to reflect on their mortality and also to enjoy life. From the time of the New Kingdom onward a pessimistic tone begins to appear in some of the biographies. This includes doubt about the efficacy of mortuary religion, anxiety about death and the state of the dead, and increased emphasis on the sovereignty and freedom of the gods, even to the point of questioning their administration of retributive justice. The parallels of these later autobiographies with Ecclesiastes are obvious.

The Mesopotamian text known as *The Dialogue of Pessimism* dates from about 1200 BC. It is a dialogue between a nobleman and his wise slave, both speaking in the first person. The nobleman announces that he intends to follow a particular course of action, which his slave supports with a proverbial reply. The nobleman then abruptly changes his mind, whereupon the slave again supports his decision by using proverbial observations about the possible disastrous consequences of the originally intended action. In the end the wise slave concludes that reality is without meaning and that the only proper response to this is suicide. The formal literary similarities to Ecclesiastes are the use of first-person speech and the use of wisdom sayings to support opposite positions.

Longman has appealed to a group of Mesopotamian texts which he calls 'fictional Akkadian autobiographies'. These have a three-part structure. There is an introduction with a first-person identification of the speaker, who is a long-dead ruler. The second section is a narration of personal exceptional achievements by the ruler. The nature of the third section varies. In three cases this consists of wisdom admonitions, instructions on how to behave. Longman sees a parallel to these latter texts in the structure of the body of Ecclesiastes: autobiographical introduction (1:12), autobiographical narrative (1:13—6:9), and wisdom admonitions (6:10—12:7). He stresses that the parallel is solely one of

form, and not of content. It is difficult to see why he extends the autobiographical narrative beyond 2:26 or, if he does so, why he ends it at 6:9. There are some brief autobiographical references after this point.

One conclusion to be drawn from this survey is that the 'fictional royal autobiography' expressed as a first-person speech was a well-known literary device expressed in various genres in the ancient Near East. So, the use of it by Qoheleth has its precedents. It is not clear that Ecclesiastes fits into any one of these genres, though the 'fictional Akkadian autobiography' is a possibility.

INFLUENCES ON ECCLESIASTES

Scholars have quite often tried to explain the differences between Ecclesiastes and the other books in the Hebrew Bible by invoking foreign influence on Qoheleth's thought. In the nineteenth century in particular, though still sometimes today, scholars claimed to find evidence of dependence on a wide range of Greek philosophies, including Aristotelianism, Stoicism and Epicureanism, not to mention even earlier Greek writers. The fact that the proposed parallels in thought, and sometimes phraseology, come from many different periods and a wide range of writers throws doubt on the whole hypothesis. One scholar was forced to suggest that Qoheleth lived in Alexandria and was an avid reader in its great library! We have already seen that it is unlikely that Qoheleth wrote in that city. If Qoheleth wrote in Jerusalem in the third century, as seems probable, a close acquaintance with a wide range of Greek writers seems unlikely. Recent scholars who have postulated strong Greek influence (e.g. Whitley) have dated the book in the mid-second century. Most modern scholars accept that there is some Greek influence on the book, but see this as the result of Qoheleth being affected by the general impact of Hellenistic culture on him. As a teacher and intellectual he may have been more open to this than most of his Jewish compatriots in Jerusalem.

There have also been suggestions that Qoheleth was influenced significantly by Egyptian thought. Parallels have been suggested between his thought and phraseology and Egyptian literature from almost every period. Whitley, among others, has shown that most of the supposed parallels are imprecise and can be matched by parallels from other ancient Near Eastern and Greek literature. Moreover, it is unlikely that Qoheleth could have mastered not only the Egyptian spoken in his day, but the very different earlier forms of the language and the difficult hieroglyphic script in which it was written. Of course, throughout Israel's history there was cultural contact with Egypt, and so Qoheleth would have had a general acquaintance with Egyptian thought.

Following the publication of the Old Babylonian version of the *Epic of Gilgamesh* in 1902 it was widely held that Eccl. 9:7–9 was directly based on a passage from this epic (Old Babylonian Version, Tablet X iii 6–14). Most scholars now think that the similarities have been over-pressed (Brown is an exception) and that they are no greater than those to be found in a variety of texts, Egyptian, Greek and Mesopotamian, which deal with the same ideas.

EXTRACT FROM THE *GILGAMESH* EPIC, OLD BABYLONIAN VERSION

When the gods created mankind
They appointed death for mankind,
Kept eternal life in their own hands.
So, Gilgamesh, let your stomach be full,
Day and night enjoy yourself in every way,
Every day arrange for pleasures,
Day and night, dance and play,
Wear fresh clothes,
Keep your head washed, bathe in water,
Appreciate the child who holds your hand,
Let your wife enjoy herself in your lap.
This is the work . . . [tablet damaged]

Tablet X, lines 3–14, translated by Stephanie Dalley (1991, p. 150).

The general conclusion to be drawn from this seems to be that Qoheleth grapples with some of the 'big issues' of life, which are the concern of thoughtful people in all cultures. Moreover, he lived and wrote at a time when Hellenistic culture was encouraging a coming together of the previously independent cultures of the eastern Mediterranean world. As a result it is not surprising that similarities of theme and ideas can be found between Ecclesiastes and a wide range of literature.

QOHELETH: PESSIMIST, SCEPTIC OR 'PREACHER OF JOY'?

Undoubtedly the best-known verse in Ecclesiastes is 1:2 in its traditional translation, 'Vanity of vanities, says the Preacher, vanity of vanities! All is vanity.' This is repeated in 12:8, and running through the first half of the book are the phrases, 'All is vanity and a chasing after wind' (1:14; 2:11, 17) or its variant, 'This also is vanity and a chasing after wind' (2:26; 4:4, 16; 6:9). Clearly, a major issue in seeking to understand Qoheleth's theology is understanding what he means by 'vanity'. Unfortunately, the Hebrew word he uses (*hevel*) has a wide range of possible meanings. The commonest that have been appealed to in relation to Qoheleth are:

- 'vanity' in the sense of meaninglessness, futility;
- 'absurdity' in the sense of that which is unreasonable or irrational;
- 'absurdity' in the sense of what is incomprehensible and mysterious;
- 'ephemerality', that which passes quickly.

The 'motto' of 1:2 is followed immediately by the 'theme' of 1:3: 'What do people gain from all the toil at which they toil under the sun?'A key word here is the Hebrew word translated as 'gain' (*yitron*). The two statements need to be interpreted in the light of each other. Each is in its own way 'universal' in scope. The repetition 'vanity of vanities' in 1:2 is a Hebrew way of expressing a superlative 'completely/utterly vain', and this is followed by saying 'all is vanity', so that nothing is excluded. The phrases 'all the toil' and 'under the sun', give 1:3 a similarly all-inclusive sense.

The range of interpretation of these verses is represented by Crenshaw and Perdue. Crenshaw takes *hevel* in the sense 'absurd' or 'futile' and sees in 1:2 a totally negative assessment of life. He takes *yitron* to mean 'advantage' and so understands 1:3, in the light of 1:2, to be saying that humans can gain nothing by all their toil. The

conclusion is a very pessimistic outlook on life.

Perdue points out that the literal meaning of *hevel* is 'breath', which leads to the metaphorical sense of ephemerality. He argues that this is the major connotation of the word in its occurrences in Qoheleth. For example, he translates 6:12 as, 'For who knows what is good for one while living the few days of one's brief [*hevel*] life, for he [God] has made them like a shadow' (cf. 3:19; 7:15; 9:9; 11:8). Perdue then points out that the verb translated 'striving/chasing after' in 1:14 and its parallels can mean either 'to pasture' or 'to desire', depending on the root from which it is derived. He takes it as 'to desire'. The word for 'wind' is often used in the sense of 'spirit', including that which animates living beings. So, he translates the whole phrase as, 'all is breath quickly passing and a desire to retain life's animating spirit'. He questions the usual translation of *yitron* as 'gain'. The meaning of the word is uncertain, since it only occurs in Qoheleth (1:3; 2:11, 13; 3:9; 5:8, 15; 7:12; 10:10, 11). Perdue argues for the meaning 'endurance, continuation', and translates 1:3 as, 'What continues to endure from the labour at which one toils during life?' He therefore concludes that rather than seeing life and its activities as meaningless, Qoheleth primarily laments its brevity.

These two different understandings of 1:2–3 lead to different understandings of the seven passages running through the book that advocate the enjoyment of life. Crenshaw sees them as encouraging pleasures in a rather hollow attempt to salvage something out of the meaninglessness of life. On the basis of Perdue's understanding these passages can be seen in a more positive light. Whybray (1982) points out that the passages form a series in which there is a steady increase in emphasis and that the last of them (11:9—12:7) has a key position at the end of the book. A common feature of these passages is the statement that all enjoyment comes as a gift from God. The exhortations to accept enjoyment of life as a gift from God can be seen as implicitly affirming that, despite its brevity, life does have some positive qualities because God has not abandoned his creatures to a life of sheer despair.

Digging deeper:
THE MEANING OF *HEVEL* IN ECCLESIASTES

The following scholars argue for different meanings of *hevel* in Ecclesiastes. Read what they have to say, and decide which you think makes the most convincing case.

Fox (1999, pp. 27–42), argues for the meaning 'absurd'.
Longman (1998, pp. 61–65), argues for the meaning 'meaningless'.
Perdue (1994, pp. 206–208), argues for the meaning 'ephemeral'.

THEOLOGICAL THEMES

Because scholars have tended to stress the differences between Ecclesiastes and other parts of the Hebrew Bible, and because they have looked for 'foreign' influence on his thinking, the fact that there is considerable continuity between his thought and that found in the rest of the Bible has often been neglected. Like the rest of the biblical wisdom literature, Ecclesiastes makes no mention of the Israelite salvation-historical traditions or of Israel as Yahweh's covenant people. In Qoheleth's case this is understandable in the light of his concern to understand life as it is experienced by individual men and women as members of the human race. Nevertheless, there are strong continuities with the rest of the Bible, which suggests that he is taking a lot of traditional biblical beliefs for granted. There are a number of places where Qoheleth seems to be making use of, or alluding to, earlier Hebrew literature. He shares with his fellow-Jews the firm belief that there is one God, the Creator of all (3:11), who is transcendent (5:2) and sovereign over all (3:14; 6:10). Both humans and animals were created from the dust (3:20) and are animated by breath (3:19). The world was created good (3:11). However, through their own fault, human nature has become corrupted (7:29; 8:9). As a result the world is now full of evil, hardship, frustration and injustice (2:11; 3:16; 4:1, 3). Humans, like the animals, must die and return to the dust (3:19–20; 12:7). Beyond death lies the shadowy, joyless, state of Sheol (9:5–6). Yet, while it lasts, life is a gift from God to be enjoyed to the full, because that is what God intends (2:24; 3:13; 5:19; 9:7–10; 11:7–10). Qoheleth takes it for granted that humans should worship God (5:1).

Ecclesiastes is not the only biblical book that stands in tension with other parts of the Hebrew Bible. There is greater recognition now than there used to be of the diversity of thought that there is in the Hebrew Bible. There are, for example, passages in Genesis, Job, the Psalms, and Jeremiah that question God's justice in dealings with humans in terms not very

ECCLESIASTES AND HEBREW LITERATURE

Genesis 3:19	You are dust, and to dust you shall return.
Ecclesiastes 12:7	The dust returns to the earth as it was.
Deuteronomy 4:2	You must neither add anything to what I command you nor take anything away from it.
Deuteronomy 12:32	You must diligently observe everything that I command you; do not add to it or take anything from it.
Ecclesiastes 3:14	I know that whatever God does endures for ever; nothing can be added to it, nor anything taken away from it.
Deuteronomy 23:21–22	If you make a vow to the LORD your God, do not postpone fulfilling it; for the LORD your God will surely require it of you, and you would incur guilt. But if you refrain from vowing, you will not incur guilt.
Ecclesiastes 5:4–5	When you make a vow to God, do not delay fulfilling it; for he has no pleasure in fools. Fulfil what you vow. It is better that you should not vow than that you should vow and not fulfil it.
I Samuel 15:22	Surely, to obey is better than sacrifice.
Ecclesiastes 5:1	To draw near to listen is better than the sacrifice offered by fools.
I Kings 8:46	For there is no one who does not sin.
Ecclesiastes 7:20	Surely there is no one on earth so righteous as to do good without ever sinning.

dissimilar from those found in Ecclesiastes. Qoheleth may stand out as a more radical voice than others, but he still stands within the Hebrew tradition, which he subjects to his searching questioning.

GOD

In the Hebrew Bible in general there is a tension in the understanding of God. On the one hand God is transcendent, wholly other than humans, and his ways and thoughts are beyond human understanding. On the other hand this God enters into a covenant relationship with Israel, makes himself known through the prophets, can be met with in worship and seeks a love relationship with people. In Ecclesiastes it is the transcendence and otherness of God that are stressed. 'God is in heaven, and you upon earth' (5:2). Humans 'cannot find out what God has

done from the beginning to the end' (3:11; see also 8:16–17; 11:5). Ecclesiastes 6:10 is generally understood as a statement about the inability of humans to change what God has decreed.

The comment in 9:11 that 'time and chance happen to them all' has often been taken as an expression of a notion similar to the Greek doctrine of an impersonal fate controlling the lives of human beings. However, the word rendered as 'chance' here is a very rare Hebrew word and there is no reason to suppose that it means more than 'what happens'. Since in Ecclesiastes the 'time' when things happen is under God's control, the same is presumably true of 'what happens'. There are no grounds for reading into 9:11 a doctrine of impersonal fate independent of God, or the idea that God is an impersonal force.

The aspect of life in which the inability to understand God's ways seems most problematic to Qoheleth is the fate of the wicked and the righteous. Qoheleth is very aware of injustice and oppression (3:16; 4:1–3). Is God concerned about this? Does he do anything to put it right? The statement in 9:2 that 'the same fate comes to all, to the righteous and the wicked' refers to death rather than to what people experience in life. However, both 7:15 and 8:14 assert that the righteous may suffer the fate deserved by the wicked, and vice versa. Although they do not say that this is *always* the case, the implication is that divine justice is not to be seen obviously at work in life. Standing in tension with this are passages in the book which state that God *will* distinguish between the righteous and the wicked and reward them according to what they deserve. The most obvious examples are 3:16–17 and 8:10–13. In view of Qoheleth's understanding of Sheol (9:10) this action of God must happen in this life. What are we to make of this tension? In the past the tension has often been explained as the result of these verses being intrusions by an 'orthodox' editor, a 'solution' that is less readily adopted today. Some scholars suggest that these are statements of the 'orthodox' view, which Qoheleth then refutes. However, what follows is more a questioning of what has been asserted, in the light of experience, than a 'refutation' of it. Maybe what is being reflected is a genuine tension in Qoheleth's own thought.

In a few passages (3:14; 5:7; 7:18; 8:12–13) Qoheleth speaks of the 'fear of God'. In 8:12–13 those who fear God are contrasted with sinners who 'do evil'. In 3:14 fearing God is the response to recognition of God as Creator and to the unknowability of his purposes. The Hebrew of the first part of 5:7 is very obscure, and it is not clear whether this verse is to be taken as the conclusion of 5:1–6 or as standing alone. If it is the conclusion of the section, then the fear of God is related to not speaking in

---

Think about
MEANING AND MEANINGLESSNESS IN LIFE

Fox (1999, pp. 138–141) suggests (quoting Viktor Frankl) that life can be made meaningful in three ways.

1. Through what we give to it by our creative works.
2. By what we take from it in terms of our experience.
3. Through our response to what we cannot change.

In his view Qoheleth seeks meaning in only the second and third ways, ignoring the first.

Fox also suggests that for Qoheleth meaningfulness requires that an action or quality produces an appropriate consequence. To be appropriate a consequence must:

1. be immediate (8:10–11);
2. apply to the individual who did the action or embodies the quality (2:16, 18);
3. be publicly visible (8:11);
4. occur consistently (6:1–2; 8:14);
5. not be lost with the passing of time (4:15–16).

How far do you agree with this understanding of 'meaning'? What kind of understanding of God does it imply? How far is this consistent with the full biblical understanding of God?

ways that might anger God. There are some problems in interpreting 7:15–18, but here, too, the fear of God is related to avoiding self-destructive behaviour. So, in three of these four passages the fear of God is the motivation for behaviour. What is not clear is whether this is primarily a matter of love for God (as in Deut. 10:12–13) or terror. Commentators come to different conclusions in the light of their overall understanding of Qoheleth's view of God.

GOD'S RELATIONSHIP TO HUMANS

Qoheleth's emphasis on the transcendence of God might seem to imply that God does not relate to humans in any direct way. However, he does sometimes speak of God relating to humans, and the most frequent way in which he does so is by speaking of what God 'gives' to humans. God gives to them the gift of life (5:18; 8:15; 9:9), though he eventually takes it back again (12:7). He gives those who please him wisdom, knowledge and joy, while giving sinners 'the work of gathering and heaping, only to give to one who pleases God' (2:26). To some he gives wealth and possessions and the power to enjoy them (5:19), but others are given wealth, possessions and honour, but are not enabled to enjoy them (6:2). He has put the mysterious '*olam* ('eternity', 'sense of past and future', 'the unknown') into human minds so that they remain in ignorance of God's purposes (3:11). The meaning of 1:13 is unclear. Commentators differ over whether the 'unhappy business that God has given to human beings to be busy with' is life in this world, or refers only to the task set out in the first half of the verse, namely 'to search out by wisdom all that is done under heaven'.

The references to God as the giver of these gifts certainly emphasize his sovereignty and human dependence on God. However, it may be significant that the majority of the references to God as giver are in those passages in which there is an admonition to enjoy life. This may indicate that Qoheleth understood God to have a personal, and positive, interest in human welfare.

WISDOM

According to Qoheleth, one of God's gifts to humans is wisdom (2:26). Yet in Qoheleth's view God has deliberately kept humans in ignorance of what they need to know in order to live a successful life (3:11; 8:16–17). The limitations of human wisdom are recognized in the book of Proverbs (20:24; 21:30; 27:1). However, there wisdom is still seen as the key to a successful life, even being compared to the Tree of Life (Prov. 3:18). In ancient Near Eastern wisdom a major key to successful living is knowing the right time to do things. Proverbs speaks of the value of knowing when to speak and when to remain silent (13:3; 15:23), and knowing when to act and when not to (13:15; 14:17). It is just this knowledge, says Qoheleth, that God has kept hidden from humans (Eccl. 3:1–11). Yet, despite its limitations, Qoheleth does see human wisdom as having some practical value (2:13–14; 7:11–12; 9:16–18; 10:12). He regards wisdom as preferable to folly (2:13; 7:5–7; 10:1–3).

Qoheleth's emphasis on God's transcendence and sovereignty leads to a quite deterministic view of life.

I know that whatever God does endures for ever; nothing can be added to it, nor anything taken from it; God has done this, so that all should stand in awe before him. That which is, already has been; that which is to be, already is. (3:14–15)

In the light of this it is somewhat surprising that the book does contain admonitions, which imply that it is possible for humans to change the course of events by the way they behave. Apparently they can even have an effect on God (5:1–6; 7:16–17)! This inconsistency suggests that Qoheleth was grappling with the age-old tension between determinism and free will. Other passages in the Hebrew Bible also grapple with this tension. If Qoheleth seems at variance with them, it is because he leans more towards determinism.

DEATH

A major factor in Qoheleth's conclusion that 'all is vanity' is his preoccupation with human mortality. In the 'royal testament' it is this which leads him to conclude that pleasure, possessions, fame, wisdom and wealth do not, either together or singly, provide the source of meaning for life.

The inevitability of death means that,

> It is better to go to the house of mourning than to go to the house of feasting;
> for this is the end of everyone, and the living will lay it to heart. (7:2)

The difference between the wise and the foolish disappears in the face of death,

> The wise have eyes in their head, but fools walk in darkness.
> Yet I perceived that the same fate befalls all of them. (2:14)

You cannot take your possessions with you when you die. These, and your wealth, will be left to others who may well squander them (2:18–19). After death, fame will fade away with time (2:16).

There are two particular factors that colour Qoheleth's evaluation of the significance of death. The first is his understanding of death as the end of the story (9:4–6, 10). The second is that he thinks only in terms of the advantage (or lack of it) to the individual. For example, he never considers the possible advantage to the community of the sage's wisdom which might be passed on to future generations in some form, such as the book of Ecclesiastes.

Qoheleth does not rage against death, nor does his conclusion about the 'vanity' of life lead him to advocate suicide. Instead it leads him to value life while it lasts. The reasons for this are stated in 9:4–6: the dead have no hope, they know nothing, and do not have any 'share in all that happens under the sun'. While the living have these things they should value them. It is better to be alive than dead. There are two passages that take the opposite view (4:1–3; 6:1–6). However, they refer to exceptional cases. Both refer to situations where people have lost all hope: workers who suffer lifelong oppression (4:1–3) and those who (for whatever reason) cannot enjoy God's gifts. Their situation is in effect a living death, so for them actual death is preferable to life. These exceptions do not prevent Qoheleth coming to the overall conclusion that,

> Light is sweet, and it is pleasant for the eyes to see the sun.
> Even those who live many years should rejoice in them all. (11:7–8)

ECCLESIASTES AND THE CANON OF SCRIPTURE

Some of the early rabbis expressed doubts about the inclusion of Ecclesiastes in the canon of Scripture. It is important to note that the debate was not so much about *whether* or not it should be included, but about *why* it was included. In other words, it began with the fact that it was a canonical book.

The problems were of three main types. First, there were its internal contradictions, which have already been noted and discussed. Second, there were apparent contradictions with other scriptural books, especially the Torah. An example is the exhortation, 'Follow the inclination of your heart and the desire of your eyes' (11:9). This seems to contradict Numbers 15:39 in which the Israelites are told to remember the commandments of the Lord not to 'follow the lust of your own heart and your own eyes'. Finally, the book's stress on the vanity of everything was seen by some as demeaning what God had created. Also, the emphasis on eating and drinking and transitory pleasures (e.g. Eccl. 9:7–10) was considered by some to be closer to Greek Epicureanism than Jewish thought. What seems to have helped overcome these objections were the attribution of the book to Solomon and its orthodox conclusion (12:13–14). Also, as the Targum shows, there are enough orthodox sentiments in the book for it to be interpreted in a way that agreed with Jewish orthodoxy.

In the Hebrew Bible, Ecclesiastes is included in the five Megilloth. These are discussed briefly in Chapter 7 when considering the place of the Song of Songs in the Hebrew canon of Scripture.

The book of Ecclesiastes raises in a particularly sharp way the issue of the 'canonical interpretation' of biblical books advocated by Brevard Childs. Childs has argued that for those Jews and Christians who accept the Bible as their Scripture it is the final canonical form of biblical books that is to be regarded as authoritative. In the case of Ecclesiastes this means that

Think about
ECCLESIASTES AND CANONICITY

It is often asserted (though complete proof is lacking) that Ecclesiastes was accepted as part of the Hebrew canon of Scripture because of the belief that Solomon was its author. As we have seen, most scholars now do not think that Solomon wrote it. What does this imply regarding its canonicity? In thinking about this you might consider the following points.

1. The authorship of several books in the Hebrew Bible is unknown, so authorship is not a necessary 'qualification' for canonicity.
2. Solomonic authorship is not explicitly claimed in the book, but has traditionally been inferred from 1:1. Modern scholars argue that the inference arose from a misunderstanding of the author's use of a literary device.
3. The attribution to Solomon was not totally misguided. It includes a recognition that the book stands in the 'Solomonic' tradition of Israelite wisdom literature.
4. Recognition of the canonicity of certain books is the faith-response of the believing community to those books which it has found nurture the faith of the community.

ultimately the message of the book must be understood in the light of the editorial framework that encloses the words of Qoheleth the sage.

Childs argues that the acceptance of the book into the Hebrew canon, with the literary device of 'Solomon's Testament', has the 'hermeneutical implication' that Qoheleth's views are to be accepted as playing a critical role within Israel's corpus of wisdom literature. However, the framework it is given, especially the epilogue, means that the message of Qoheleth is to be heard and interpreted from a 'rule of faith' that is wider even than the wisdom corpus: the 'fear of God' as understood in the Hebrew Bible as a whole (12:13). Also, by setting it in the context of eschatological judgement (12:14) the message of Qoheleth, who lacks this perspective, is seen to be limited and in need of fresh interpretation in the light of a new and fuller understanding of divine wisdom.

Longman provides another example of such a 'canonical' reading of the book in the light of the epilogue. He regards 12:8 as the editor's summary of Qoheleth's message. 12:9–10 then acknowledge the competence and honesty of Qoheleth's efforts. The following verses (12:11–12) are read by him as a warning against following Qoheleth's conclusions because they will have a destructive effect. Here Longman, following Fox but contrary to most commentators, reads 12:11 in a negative sense. The 'shepherd' is taken to be the wisdom teacher. Longman argues that 'goads' and 'nails' are painful, even dangerous, instruments. If the editor had wanted to speak of Qoheleth's teaching in a positive sense he would have referred to

the shepherd's 'rod' and 'staff'. Hence he is warning of the dangerous nature of Qoheleth's sceptical and pessimistic approach. The editor then counsels the student to follow orthodox teaching and to 'fear God, and keep his commandments' because, contrary to Qoheleth's doubts, 'God will bring every deed into judgment' (12:13–14). As a result, Longman sees the role of Ecclesiastes in the canon as providing an example of the dangers of speculative, doubting wisdom. He draws a parallel with the speeches of Job's friends, which we are told in Job 42:7 provide a misleading picture of God.

> **Think about**
> **'CANONICAL INTERPRETATION' OF ECCLESIASTES**
>
> Is it necessary to choose between the different 'canonical interpretations' of Childs and Longman, or can they be seen as complementary?

FURTHER READING

Items marked * are considered suitable as first ports of call, while others are more complex, or relate to specific issues.

COMMENTARIES

Crenshaw sees the book as the work of a sceptic and pessimist, whereas Whybray sees Qoheleth as a realist who, despite recognizing the problems of life, believes God wants his creatures to enjoy life. Eaton, writing from a more conservative perspective, also sees Qoheleth as a 'preacher of joy'. Gordis' book is a classic.

Although the commentary part of it assumes a knowledge of Hebrew, the introductory articles provide valuable summaries of scholarship up to the time the book was originally published, 1951.

G. A. Barton *The Book of Ecclesiastes*. ICC. Edinburgh: T. & T. Clark, 1908.

W. P. Brown *Ecclesiastes*. Interpretation. Louisville, KY: John Knox Press, 2000.

* J. L. Crenshaw *Ecclesiastes*. OTL. London: SCM, 1988.

R. Davidson *Ecclesiastes and Song of Solomon*. DSB. Edinburgh: St Andrews Press, 1986.

* M. A. Eaton *Ecclesiastes*. TOTC. Leicester: IVP, 1983.

M. V. Fox *A Time to Tear Down and A Time to Build Up*. Grand Rapids, MI: Eerdmans, 1999.

* R. Gordis *Koheleth: The Man and His World*. New York, NY: Schocken Books, 1968.

H. W. Hertzberg *Der Prediger*. Gütersloh: Gerd Mohn, 1963.

J. A. Loader *Ecclesiastes: A Practical Commentary*. Grand Rapids, MI: Eerdmans, 1986.

T. Longman III *The Book of Ecclesiastes*. NICOT. Grand Rapids, MI: Eerdmans, 1998.

R. E. Murphy *Ecclesiastes*. WBC. Dallas, TX: Word, 1992.

G. Ogden *Ecclesiastes*. Sheffield: JSOT Press, 1987.

C. L. Seow *Ecclesiastes*. AB. New York, NY: Doubleday, 1997.

* R. N. Whybray *Ecclesiastes*. NCB. London: Marshall, Morgan & Scott, 1989.

OTHER BOOKS AND ARTICLES

E. F. F. Bishop 'A Pessimist in Palestine', *PEQ* 100 (1968), 33–41.

B. S. Childs *Introduction to the Old Testament as Scripture*. London: SCM, 1979.

* J. L. Crenshaw *Old Testament Wisdom: An Introduction*. Louisville, KY: Westminster John Knox Press, 1998 (rev. edn).

M. J. Dahood 'Canaanite-Phoenician Influence in Qoheleth', *Biblica* 33 (1952), 30–52, 191–221.

S. Dalley *Myths from Mesopotamia: Creation, the Flood, Gilgamesh, and Others*. Oxford: OUP, 1991.

J. Day, R. P. Gordon and H. G. M. Williamson *Wisdom in Ancient Israel*. Cambridge: CUP, 1995.

S. Fischer 'Qohelet and "Heretic" Harpers' Songs', *JSOT* 98 (2002), 105–121.

M. V. Fox 'Aging and Death in Qohelet 12', *JSOT* 42 (1998), 55–77.

M. V. Fox *Qohelet and His Contradictions*. Sheffield: Almond Press, 1989.

D. C. Fredericks *Qoheleth's Language: Re-evaluating its Nature and Date*. Lewiston, NY: Edwin Mellen, 1988.

H. L. Ginsberg *Studies in Koheleth*. New York, NY: Jewish Theological Seminary of America, 1950.

H. L. Ginsberg 'The Structure and Contents of the Book of Koheleth', VTSup 3, 1955, 138–149.

R. Gordis 'The Original Language of Qohelet', *JQR* 37 (1946/7), 67–84.

R. Gordis 'Koheleth – Hebrew or Aramaic?', *JBL* 71 (1952), 93–109.

R. Gordis 'Was Koheleth a Phoenician?', *JBL* 74 (1955), 103–114.

W. W. Hallo and K. L. Younger Jnr *The*

Context of Scripture, vol. 1. Leiden: Brill, 1997.

W. G. Lambert 'Some New Babylonian Wisdom Literature', in J. Day, R. P. Gordon and H. G. M. Williamson *Wisdom in Ancient Israel*. Cambridge: CUP, 1995; pp. 30–42.

J. Loader *Polar Structures in the Book of Qohelet*. BZAW 152. Berlin: W. de Gruyter, 1979.

R. E. Murphy *Wisdom Literature*. FOTL 13. Grand Rapids, MI: Eerdmans, 1981.

* R. E. Murphy *The Tree of Life*. Grand Rapids, MI: Eerdmanns, 1996 (2nd edn).

* L. G. Perdue *Wisdom and Creation: The Theology of Wisdom Literature*. Nashville, TN: Abingdon, 1994.

F. Rousseau 'Structure de Qohélet i–4–11 et plan du livre', *VT* 31 (1981), 200–217.

J. F. A. Sawyer 'The Ruined House in Ecclesiastes 12: A Reconstruction of the Original Parable', *JBL* 94 (1974), 519–531.

A. Schoors *The Preacher Sought to Find Pleasing Words*, part 1. Leuven: Department Orientalistiek/Uitgeverij Peeters, 1992.

C. C. Torrey 'The Question of the Original Language of Qoheleth', *JQR* 39 (1948/9), 151–160.

C. F. Whitley *Koheleth: His Language and Thought*. BZAW 148. Berlin: W. de Gruyter, 1979.

R. N. Whybray 'The Identification and Use of Quotations in Ecclesiastes', VTSup 32 (1981), 435–451.

R. N. Whybray 'Qoheleth, Preacher of Joy', *JSOT* 23 (1982), 87–98.

* R. N. Whybray *Ecclesiastes*. OT Guides. Sheffield: JSOT Press, 1989.

A. D. G. Wright 'The Riddle of the Sphinx: The Structure of the Book of Qoheleth', *CBQ* 30 (1968), 313–314.

A. D. G. Wright 'The Riddle of the Sphinx Revisited: Numerical Patterns in the Book of Qoheleth', *CBQ* 42 (1980), 35–51.

A. D. G. Wright 'Additional Numerical Patterns in Qoheleth', *CBQ* 45 (1983), 32–43.

Chapter 7

SONG OF SONGS

AUTHORSHIP

The opening verse of the Song of Songs, which is clearly a kind of 'title', raises some of the general issues which the book itself provokes. A literal translation of the title is: 'The song of songs which is of Solomon'. The construction 'the song of songs' is the Hebrew way of expressing a superlative sense. Just as 'the holy of holies' means 'the most holy place', so 'the song of songs' means 'the best song'. But could there be an additional meaning? Might it indicate that it is a song made up of several songs? As we shall see, scholars are divided over whether the book is a single song, or an anthology of several, originally independent, songs.

The word 'of' in the literal translation represents the Hebrew preposition l^e, which can be understood in more than one way, depending on the context. It can indicate:

- authorship: *by Solomon*;
- dedication: *to Solomon, for Solomon*;
- subject matter: *concerning Solomon*;
- affinity: *in the Solomonic literary tradition*.

Traditionally it has been understood in the first sense, and so as attributing the book to Solomon as author. This is one reason why, in the LXX (Greek) translation of the Hebrew Bible the Song of Songs is grouped with Proverbs and Ecclesiastes (Qoheleth), the two other books linked with Solomon, the order that is found in the English Old Testament. In the Hebrew Bible it comes in the third section, the Writings, after Psalms, Proverbs and Job. It is the first of the Five Scrolls. These are five short books, each of which came to be linked with a major Jewish festival. The order of the books follows the chronological order of the festivals. They are:

- *Song of Songs*, read at Passover because of references to springtime in the poetry;
- *Ruth*, read at the Feast of Weeks (Pentecost) because of the harvest setting of the story;
- *Lamentations*, read on the ninth day of Ab, the mourning for the destruction of the temple;
- *Ecclesiastes*, read at the Feast of Tabernacles, which commemorates the wilderness experience;
- *Esther*, read at the Feast of Purim, the origin of which is recorded in the story.

The association of the Song of Songs with Passover is first attested in the eighth century AD. Earlier references in the Talmud place it with Proverbs and Ecclesiastes, as do a few later manuscripts of the Hebrew Bible.

Rabbinic sources give evidence of discussion about the place of the Song of Songs in the Hebrew canon of Scripture during the discussions at Jamnia (Yabneh) in the later part of the first century AD. The issue seems to have been the appropriateness of retaining it in the canon, not whether it should be added. Some rabbis were concerned that verses from the book were being sung in the banqueting houses (taverns?). The tradition of Solomonic authorship, together with an allegorical interpretation of the book (to be discussed later) probably helped the argument for retaining it in the canon.

Acceptance of the Solomonic authorship of the book can be supported by appeal to the account of Solomon's wisdom in 1 Kings 4:29–34, part of which says,

> Solomon's wisdom surpassed the wisdom of all the people of the east, and all the wisdom of Egypt . . . He composed three thousand proverbs, and his songs numbered a thousand and five. (1 Kgs 4:30, 32)

Song writing could be considered a 'wisdom' activity on at least two grounds. The first would be the content of the songs, whether they dealt with issues of 'coping with life'. Arguably, love songs, like the Song of Songs, do so. Murphy points out that the Song of Songs concerns one of the four things that the sage of Proverbs 30:18–19 says are 'too wonderful' for him – 'the way of a man with a girl'. Second, a skilled songwriter might be considered 'wise', like the skilled craft workers who worked on the Tabernacle (Exod. 35:30–35; see Jer. 9:17; the word translated as 'skill' in the NRSV is the Hebrew word for 'wisdom'). Since Solomon was renowned for his love of women, he might be expected to write love songs among his multitude of songs. It is also worth noting that there is an element of instruction in the woman's exchanges with the 'daughters of Jerusalem' (Song 2:7; 3:5; 8:4). Munro comments that whereas Proverbs 1—9 contains warnings to young men against the lure of the foreign woman, the Song of Songs implicitly warns young women to take care in their response to the attractions of young men.

Think about
COPING WITH LIFE

Read the 'instruction' given to young men in Proverbs 5 and 7 concerning sexual behaviour and compare it with the Song of Songs read as 'instruction' to young women in sexual matters. Taking into account the difference in the forms of the two books, do you agree with Munro's view (referred to in the main text) that the Song of Songs *can* legitimately be read as 'implicit' instruction to young women concerning their response to the attractions of young men?

WAS SOLOMON THE AUTHOR?

Besides the ambiguity of the meaning of the preposition *l^e*, modern scholars see other reasons in the title and the body of the book for questioning whether Solomon was the author. One reason is that the Hebrew word for 'which' in the title is *ᵃsher*, whereas in the rest of the book the prefix *she-* is always used. This, it is argued, is evidence that the title is a later addition to the book by someone who may have ascribed the authorship of the book to him, or have used the preposition *lᵉ* in one of its other senses. Another reason for questioning Solomonic authorship is the minimal role that he plays in the book. Only three passages mention Solomon explicitly, and in all of them he is clearly the object of the poem, not its author.

- 1:5 uses 'the curtains of Solomon' as an example of something that is black. Some scholars argue that the Hebrew text here does not refer to Solomon but to a south Arabian tribe, the Shalmah (as in the NEB), because this gives a better parallel with the mention of 'the tents of Kedar', a north Arabian tribe.
- 3:6–11 speaks of the glory of Solomon's wedding because of the reflected glory it brings to the institution of marriage. The passage does not say that Solomon married the woman of the Song of Songs.
- 8:11–12 ridicules Solomon for trying to buy the woman's love. It is unlikely that Solomon would have written about himself in this way.

The woman's references to her lover as 'the king' (1:4, 12) need not be taken any more literally than her picture of him as a shepherd (1:7). Similarly 7:5 says no more than that the woman is beautiful enough to entrance a king.

The great majority of modern scholars think that the evidence for the traditional attribution of the book to Solomon is weak and that other evidence stands against it, such as its language and structure (see p. 178). If Solomon was not the author, we do not know who was. One school of thought suggests that the author was a woman. These scholars point out that the woman's voice dominates the book. Brenner notes that of the 117 verses in the book, the woman speaks in 61.5 of them. Moreover, there is a predominance of female characters in the book because of the female 'chorus'. Of course it is not quantity that matters most, but content. There is the fact that the woman often takes the initiative in the relationship and has considerable social freedom. Also, there is no hint of discrimination against women on purely sexual grounds. Interestingly, mothers are mentioned (3:4, 11; 6:9; 8:1) but not fathers. Bekkenkamp and Van Dijk argue that the Song of Songs is part of an extensive tradition of songs sung by women in ancient Israel (see Judg. 5; 1 Sam. 18:6–7; 2 Sam 1:20, 24; Jer. 9:17, 20; Ezek. 32:16).

Digging deeper:
THE AUTHORSHIP OF THE SONG OF SONGS

Summarize the points made about the possible authorship of the Song of Songs in the section on 'Authorship'. You can fill this out by consulting the introduction section of some commentaries or books of introduction to the Old Testament. What conclusion do you come to in the light of the evidence and arguments put forward?

TEXT AND LANGUAGE

TEXT

The Hebrew text of the Song of Songs has been well preserved. Four manuscripts of the book have been found at Qumran (4QCant[a,b,c], 6QCant), all dating from between 30 BC and AD 70. Of these 4QCant[a] and 4QCant[b] contain a considerable portion of the text. In general they support what is now the traditional Hebrew text, the Massoretic Text (MT). The LXX is quite a literal rendering of a Hebrew text close to the MT, completed around 100 BC. The Vulgate (Latin) and the Peshitta (Syriac) translations only occasionally differ from the MT. The Aramaic Targum is not so much a translation as a homiletic interpretation of the book.

VOCABULARY

One of the major problems in translating the Song of Songs is the fact that in its 117 verses there are 47 words (some of them occurring only once) that do not appear elsewhere in the Hebrew Bible. This makes discerning their meaning difficult. Sometimes the early translations or data from cognate Semitic languages provide useful clues to the meaning of these words. There are another 51 words that occur five times or less in the whole Hebrew Bible.

THE LANGUAGE AND THE DATE OF THE SONG OF SONGS

The language of the Song of Songs has a number of peculiar features, which have been appealed to in attempts to date the book. The use of the prefix *she-* has been seen as evidence of a late date for the book, since it is found in Late Biblical Hebrew and Mishnaic Hebrew. However, it occurs in the 'Song of Deborah' (Judg. 5), which is generally seen as an early Hebrew poem. On the basis of Ugaritic evidence, it has been argued that the use of *she-* is evidence of a pre-exilic north Israelite dialect, influenced by Phoenician, rather than post-exilic Hebrew. There is some support for this suggestion from the fact that there are passages in the book that show a good knowledge of northern Israelite territory. The unusual spelling of some words is often seen as evidence of Aramaic influence, and so a relatively late date for the book. On the other hand there are some rare words whose meaning has been elucidated by their occurrence in Ugaritic, which would suggest an early date. The Aramaisms might then once again be explained as the result of the influence of Aramaic on a pre-exilic northern Israelite dialect. Two apparent foreign loan-words are often presented as evidence of a late date. It is claimed that *'appiryon* (3:9, 'carriage'; NRSV has 'palanquin') is a loan word from Greek, and so points to a third century BC date. However, Murphy thinks it could be a loan from Persian or Sanskrit. The other word, *pardes* (4:13, 'park'; NRSV has 'channel'), a likely loan-word from Persian also occurs in Nehemiah 2:9 (which is clearly post-exilic) and Ecclesiastes 2:5 (generally considered post-exilic).

Faced with the mixture of indications of early and late features in the language of the Song of Songs, scholars come to opposite conclusions. Brenner argues that poetry is often archaistic in its language and that late features in the language should be given more weight as indicators of date, especially if fairly widespread, as she thinks the Aramaisms are. She does recognize that the possibility of the book using a northern Israelite dialect is a complicating factor in using the language for dating. However, she still dates the book to the fifth to third centuries BC. On the other hand, Gordis argues that songs that are performed regularly are likely to have their language updated so that later words and expressions replace earlier ones as they become too outdated. He thinks that in its present form the book dates from the fifth century BC, but contains material going back to the tenth century.

DATING THE SONG OF SONGS

As we have seen, appeal to the language of the book as the major basis on which to date it leads to quite divergent conclusions. Some scholars have therefore turned to other evidence in their attempts to date the book.

Segal argued for a date in the time of Solomon, though not arguing for Solomon himself as the author. In his view the book reflects a time of luxury, as seen in the references to the woman's clothing, perfumes and jewellery. He also points to the mention of David's Tower with its many shields (Song 4:4), which he relates to the golden shields made by Solomon (1 Kgs 10:16–17) and later looted by Sishak (1 Kgs 14:26). Since Solomon married an Egyptian princess, he argues that the mention of Pharaoh's horses and chariots (Song 1:9) fits best in Solomon's reign. He suggests that the fact that the Song of Songs mentions places ranging from Lebanon in the north to En Gedi in the south is also a pointer to the period before the break-up of David's empire after Solomon's death. A weakness in Segal's approach is that it is based on a very literalistic interpretation of the poetry. For instance, he takes 1:16–17 to mean that the

woman lived in an expensive house built of cedar wood. However, most commentators see here a reference to a grassy dell in a cedar wood. Similarly, the references to spices and perfumes may often be metaphorical (e.g. 1:12–14). The fact that the woman wears jewellery does not mean that it is necessarily expensive.

Rabin has argued that the Song of Songs and Tamil love poetry have features in common, which suggest some connection between the two. He argues that cultural contact between India and Israel was most likely during Solomon's reign, when Israel was involved in the spice trade with South Arabia, and through South Arabia with India. He finds a clue to this link in the list of rare and expensive spices in 4:12–14, which he thinks reads like the list of goods carried by a South Arabian caravan merchant. There are other places in the Song of Songs where he sees reference to spice caravans. The 'column of smoke' in 3:6, he suggests, is the dust thrown up by a caravan. Although most commentators think 1:7–8 refers to a pastoral idyll, Rabin thinks it refers to a camel caravan. These supposed references to spice caravans seem forced. Rabin may be right in seeing cultural links between the Song of Songs and Tamil poetry (this is discussed further on p. 184) but, as Brenner points out, there were times other than Solomon's reign when contact between India and Palestine was possible, such as the neo-Babylonian and Persian periods.

Gordis regards the book as a collection of separate poems, most of which are undatable because of the lack of historical allusions. However, the fact that most of the place names are from the north and east of Palestine suggests to him that several of the poems date back to before the destruction of the northern Kingdom of Israel by the Assyrians in 722 BC. He also argues that the reference to Tirzah (6:4) means that the poem which contains it must be dated to the time when this city was the capital of the Kingdom of Israel before Omri moved the capital to Samaria around about 876 BC. In his view the use of the Persian loan-word *pardes* (4:13) means that the poem containing it cannot be dated earlier than the sixth century BC.

This brief survey shows that, just as little can be said with confidence about the authorship of the book, so little can be said with confidence about its date. Moreover, what is meant by 'its date' depends on whether the book is seen as a unified composition by a single author or an anthology of poems brought together by an editor. In the latter case, individual poems may come from very different dates.

Digging deeper:
THE DATE OF THE SONG OF SONGS

Summarize the points made regarding the possible date of the Song in the sections on 'Text and Language' and 'Dating the Song of Songs'. You can fill this out by consulting the introduction section of some commentaries or books of introduction to the Old Testament. What conclusion do you come to in the light of the evidence and arguments put forward?

THE SONG OF SONGS AS LOVE POETRY

Since love is a universal human emotion and experience, it is not surprising that scholars have noted similarities between the Song of Songs and love poetry from other cultures. Where there are similarities in the themes dealt with in the poetry, such as the appearance of the loved one, yearning to be with the beloved, the overcoming of obstacles to be together, this can be accounted for by the universality of the human experience being expressed. Poetic imagery is often drawn from the poet's culture and physical environment. It is therefore only to be expected that the closest parallels to the Song of Songs in this respect are found in the love poetry of other Near Eastern cultures – Egypt, Ugarit and Mesopotamia. Similarities in theme and imagery do not, therefore, necessarily indicate that the Hebrew poet has been influenced by the love poetry of other cultures. Nevertheless they can be helpful in aiding our understanding of the Song of Songs. External influence is more likely to be at work when it is possible to demonstrate similarity in literary techniques and literary forms. As we shall see, there are a few interesting examples of this.

SUMERIAN LOVE POETRY

Westenholz divides Sumerian love poetry into three basic groups:

- poems in which deities assume the role of lovers.
- poems in which individual Sumerian kings are praised as they unite with their consorts or with the goddess Inanna.
- poems in which the lovers are neither deities nor kings.

Among these poems there is nothing quite like the Song of Songs, though there are similar themes and imagery. One text describes Inanna's preparation for her marriage to Dumuzi.

**Think about
LOVE POETRY**

Find and read some love poetry from your own culture. Here are two classic love poems from British culture, one Scots and the other English.

O my Luve's like a red, red rose
   That's newly sprung in June!
O my Luve's like the melodie
   That's sweetly play'd in tune!

As fair art thou, my bonnie lass,
   So deep in luve am I;
And I will luve thee still, my dear,
   Till a' the seas gang dry –

Till a' the seas gang dry, my dear,
   and the rocks melt wi' the sun;
I will luve thee still, my dear,
   While the sands o' life shall run.

And fare thee weel, my only Luve!
   And fare thee weel awhile!
And I will come again, my Luve,
   Tho' it were ten thousand mile.

       Robert Burns (1759–1796)

Shall I compare thee to a summer's day?
Thou art more lovely and more temperate:
Rough winds do shake the darling buds of May,
And summer's lease hath all too short a date:
Sometime too hot the eye of heaven shines,
And often is his gold complexion dimm'd;
And every fair from fair some time declines,
By chance, or nature's changing course, untrimm'd.
But thy eternal summer shall not fade,
Nor lose possession of that fair thou ow'st;
Nor shall Death brag thou wand'rest in his shade,
When in eternal lines to time thou grow'st.
So long as men can breathe, or eyes can see,
So long lives this, and this gives life to thee.

       William Shakespeare (1564–1616)

Inanna, at her mother's command,
Bathed herself, anointed herself with
   goodly oil,
Covered her body with the noble *pala*-
   garment,
Took along the . . . her dowry,
Arranged the lapis lazuli about her neck,
Grasped the seal in her hand.
The Lordly Queen waited expectantly,
Dumuzi pressed open the door,
Came forth into the house like the
   moonlight,
Gazed at her joyously,
Embraced her, kissed her.

    Translation from S. N. Kramer
             (1969, p. 77)

This may throw some light on Song of Songs 5:2–8, where the woman is found unready when her lover comes. It may depict the frustration of the lovers' desire to be married. Possibly the closest parallel to the Song of Songs is a text that is not in fact a love poem. It is the so-called *Message of Ludingirra to his Mother* (known from a copy dating from *c.* 1800–1600 BC). It contains a description of the mother, which is intended to enable the messenger to recognize her.

   My mother is brilliant in the heavens, a
     doe in the mountains,
   A morning star abroad at noon,

Precious carnelian, a topaz from
Marhasi,
A prize for the king's daughter, full of
charm,
A *nir*-stone seal, an ornament like the
sun,
A bracelet of tin, a ring of *antasura*,
A shining piece of silver,
....
An alabaster statuette set on a lapis
pedestal,
A living rod of ivory, whose limbs are
filled with charm.

> Translation from J. S. Cooper
> (1971, p. 160)

There are similarities here to the
description of the man in Song of Songs
5:10–16. In both cases the people are
described as if they were a statue adorned
with jewels.

AKKADIAN LOVE POETRY

Very little Akkadian (Babylonian or
Assyrian) love poetry has come to light,
and similarities to the Song of Songs are
very limited.

UGARITIC LOVE POETRY

None of the texts from Ugarit contain
what can strictly be called love poetry,
even though they do describe the sexual
exploits of some characters. One text,
about King Kirtu, contains a passage in
which the king describes Princess Hurriya
to her father in terms that are reminiscent
of the Song of Songs.

> The best girl of your firstborn offspring;
> Whose goodness is like that of 'Anatu,
>   whose beauty is like that of 'Athiratu;
> The pupils (of whose eyes) are of pure
>   lapis lazuli,

whose eyes are like alabaster bowls,
who is girded with ruby . . .

> Translation from D. Pardee in Hallo
> and Younger (1997, p. 335)

EGYPTIAN LOVE POETRY

Since the late 1920s it has been realized
that the closest parallels to the Song of
Songs are to be found in Egyptian love
songs that date from *c.* 1300–1150 BC.
There are four different collections of these
songs: Chester Beatty Papyrus 1, Papyrus
Harris 500, the Turin Papyrus, and the
Cairo Love Songs. Although there are
occasional references to deities in these
songs, there is nothing in them to suggest
that they were intended for anything other
than secular entertainment. There are a
number of notable similarities between the
Egyptian love songs and the Song of Songs
(see the box 'Egyptian Love Songs' on
page 184).

- In both the woman is referred to as
  the 'sister' of her lover. In the
  Egyptian songs, but not the Song of
  Songs, the male lover is referred to as
  'brother'.
- In the Egyptian songs the lovers are
  presented, or present themselves, in
  'fictional roles' as royalty, servant,
  shepherd. In the Song of Songs they take
  on the roles of royalty, shepherd,
  gardener.
- Similar extravagant compliments
  appear in the Egyptian and Hebrew
  songs: 'most beautiful youth'/ 'fairest
  among women' (Song 1:8); 'more perfect
  than the world'/ 'my perfect one' (5:2);
  'like Sothis [Venus] rising at the
  beginning of a good year'/ '[she comes]
  forth like the dawn, fair as the moon,
  bright as the sun' (6:10).
- The descriptions of the beloved in the

Egyptian and Hebrew songs use similar comparisons: 'her arms surpass gold'/ 'his head is the finest gold' (Song 5:11); 'the mouth of my girl is a lotus bud'/ 'his lips are lilies, distilling liquid myrrh' (5:13); 'her breasts are mandrake apples'/ 'your two breasts are like two fawns' (7:3).

A striking difference between the Egyptian songs and the Song of Songs is that whereas there is a genuine dialogue between the lovers in the Song of Songs, the Egyptian songs are soliloquies in which speakers address their own hearts. Even when there is alternation between male and female voices in the Egyptian

---

EGYPTIAN LOVE SONGS

> I am yours like the field
> planted with flowers
> and with all sorts of fragrant plants.
> Pleasant is the canal within it,
> which your hand scooped out,
> while we cooled ourselves in the north wind:
> A lovely place for strolling about,
> with your hand upon mine!
> My body is satisfied,
> and my heart rejoices
> in our walking about together.
> To hear your voice is pomegranate wine [to me]:
> I draw life from hearing it.
> Could I see you with every glance,
> it would be better for me
> than to eat or drink.

No. 18 in Papyrus Harris 500

One alone is my sister, having no peer: more gracious than all other women.
Behold her like Sothis rising at the beginning of a good year:
Shining, precious, white of skin, lovely of eyes when gazing.
Sweet her lips when speaking: she has no excess of words.
Long of neck, white of breast, her hair true lapis lazuli.
Her arms surpass gold, her fingers are like lotuses,
Full [?] her derriere, narrow [?] her waist, her thighs carry on her beauties.
Lovely of walk when she strides the ground, she has captured my heart in her embrace.
She makes the heads of men turn about when seeing her.
Fortunate is whoever embraces her – he is like the foremost of lovers.
Her coming forth appears like [that of] the yonder one – the Unique One.

No. 31 in Chester Beatty Papyrus I

Translations by M. V. Fox, in Hallo and Younger (1997, pp. 125–130)

songs the speakers are not addressing each other, but only themselves. The man always speaks of the woman as 'she'. Although the woman sometimes speaks of the man as 'you', there is never any indication that he is physically present, and there is never any direct response from him.

The similarities between the Song of Songs and the Egyptian love songs are probably to be explained by Egyptian political and cultural influence in Syria and Palestine, which was especially strong during the Late Bronze Age. As a result of this the author(s) of the Song of Songs would probably have been acquainted with the Egyptian tradition of love songs.

TAMIL LOVE POETRY

Rabin identifies similarities between Tamil love poetry and the Song of Songs, which suggest to him that the Hebrew poet was influenced by the Indian poetry. He points to three main areas of similarity.

- The woman is the chief character and speaker in the Song of Songs.
- The role of nature in the poetic similes and reference to the phenomena of growth and renewal as a background to the lovers' relationship.
- The dominant note of the woman's speeches is longing rather than desire.

He argues that these features distinguish the Song of Songs from other Near Eastern love poetry, and the fact that they are shared with Tamil poetry makes influence from it plausible. He seeks to strengthen his case by arguing that six of the names of aromatic plants that are found in the Song of Songs probably have an Indian origin. Brenner, however, has argued that at least some of these names came into Hebrew from either Akkadian or Persian. If Rabin's case is accepted, it at most explains a few characteristics of the poetry of the Song of Songs that give it 'flavour' that differs somewhat from other ancient Near Eastern love poetry. The closest links are still those with the Egyptian love poetry.

LITERARY FORMS AND IMAGERY

In a form-critical study of the Song of Songs, Horst (whose work is helpfully summarized by Pope) distinguished eight different poetic forms.

1. The Song of Admiration, e.g. 1:9–11; 4:9–11; 7:6–9.
2. Comparisons and Allegories, e.g. 1:13–14; 4:12–15; 6:2–3.
3. The Descriptive Song, e.g. 4:1–7; 5:10–16; 7:1–6.
4. Self-Description, 1:5–6; 8:8–10.
5. The Vaunt Song, 6:8–9; 8:11–12.
6. The Jest, 1:7–8.
7. The Description of an Experience, 3:1–4; 5:2–7; 6:11–12.
8. Songs of Desire, e.g. 1:2–4; 2:14.

Some commentators (e.g. Longman, Murphy) have been happy to accept Horst's identification of these forms, though usually with some modifications.

Particularly striking among the forms identified by Horst is the Descriptive Song. It is often referred to as the *wasf* (an Arabic term meaning 'description') form, because it was initially recognized in the study of Arabic poetry. This type of poem describes the lover's body using a series of extravagant and sensuous images. The description normally proceeds from the head to the feet, as in 4:1–7 (describing the woman) and 5:1–16 (describing the man). The description in 6:13—7:6 is unusual in working from feet to head. This may be because the woman is depicted as dancing, and so her feet call for attention first.

Working on a different basis from Horst, Falk identifies six types of 'lyrics' in the Song of Songs.

1. The 'love monologue', which is spoken in the first person to and/or about a

---

Think about
AN ENGLISH *WASF*?

The following poem by Thomas Lodge (1556–1625) seems to be a *wasf*.

Like to the clear in highest sphere
Where all imperial glory shines,
Of selfsame colour is her hair
Whether unfolded, or in twines:
Heigh-ho, fair Rosaline!
Her eyes are sapphires set in snow,
Resembling heaven by every wink;
The Gods do fear whenas they glow,
And I do tremble when I think
Heigh-ho, would she were mine!

Her cheeks are like the blushing cloud
That beautifies Aurora's face,
Or like the silver crimson shroud
That Phoebus' smiling looks doth grace;
Heigh-ho, fair Rosaline!
Her lips are like two budded roses
Whom ranks of lilies neighbour nigh,
Within which bounds she balm encloses
Apt to entice a deity:
Heigh-ho, would she were mine!

Her neck is like a stately tower
Where Love himself imprison'd lies,
To watch for glances every hour
From her divine and sacred eyes:
Heigh-ho, fair Rosaline!
Her paps are centres of delight,
Her breasts are orbs of heavenly frame,

Where Nature moulds the dew of light
To feed perfection with the same:
Heigh-ho, would she were mine!

With orient pearl, with ruby red,
With marble white, with sapphires blue
Her body every way is fed,
Yet soft in touch and sweet in view:
Heigh-ho, fair Rosaline!
Nature herself her shape admires;
The Gods are wounded in her sight;
And Love forsakes his heavenly fires
And at her eyes his brand doth light:
Heigh-ho, would she were mine!

Then muse not, Nymphs, though I bemoan
The absence of fair Rosaline,
Since for a fair there's fairer none,
Nor for her virtues so divine:
Heigh-ho, fair Rosaline;
Heigh-ho, my heart! would God that she
    were mine!

Do you think that in the form and imagery he used the poet might have been consciously dependent on the Song of Songs? If so, how has he adapted it to his own culture? You could try writing your own *wasf*!

beloved, who is the implicit or explicit audience, e.g. 1:9–11; 2:4–7; 4:1–7.

2. The 'love dialogue', which is a conversation between the two lovers, e.g. 1:15–17; 4:12—5:1; 8:13–14.

3. A monologue spoken in the first person by one of the lovers to an audience other than the beloved, 1:5–6; 8:11–12.

4. A monologue spoken by an unidentifiable speaker to an unspecified audience, 2:15; 3:6–11; 8:5a.

5. A dialogue between someone speaking in the first person and a group of speakers, 7:1–6; 8:8–10.

6. A composite poem, 5:2—6:3.

The Song of Songs is full of evocative imagery. The predominant images are those drawn from the world of nature. In her study of the imagery used in the book, Munro finds four main groups of imagery: imagery drawn from the royal court, imagery of family life, nature imagery and images of space (indicating the nearness/distance of the lovers) and time (mention of the seasons, day and night). Longman suggests that there is another significant group of images that she has overlooked: military images. The images often have sensual and erotic associations, but since these are only implicit it is not surprising that commentators frequently disagree over the exact import of the imagery. This is especially so when the imagery may be a euphemistic way of referring to the male or female sexual organs. For example:

- does 5:14b refer to the whole of the man's torso between his arms and his legs, or specifically to his sexual organs?
- is the 'navel' of 7:2 intended as a euphemism for the female sexual organs?
- is 2:17b an invitation to the lover to fondle the woman's breasts or to sexual intercourse, or what else might it mean?

It is part of the nature of poetry to present the readers with such allusive imagery, which invites their imaginative appreciation and interpretation.

> **Digging deeper:**
> **THE IMAGERY OF THE SONG OF SONGS**
>
> Consult a number of commentaries to see how they understand the imagery of Song of Songs 2:17b; 5;14b; and 7:2. Which understanding of each of these verses do you find most convincing?

THE STRUCTURE OF THE SONG OF SONGS

There is a wide divergence of opinion concerning the structure of the Song of Songs. One major reason for this is the division of opinion about the nature of the book and its interpretation. Those who see the book as a unified composition that is a 'narrative poem' telling some kind of story tend to structure it according to their understanding of the 'storyline' and the characters involved. The division into subunits is then based on identifying the 'speeches' of the characters. There is a major disagreement between those who see two main characters (the lovers) and a few minor voices, and those who see three main characters (the woman and two rival male lovers) and a few minor voices. We will discuss these approaches further when discussing the interpretations of the Song of Songs. One practical problem with these approaches is that although Hebrew has different gender forms for second and third person pronouns and verb forms, which usually enables differentiation between male and female speakers, there are passages in the book where it is not clear who is speaking, e.g. 1:2–4 (with its apparent abrupt changes of speakers); 3:6–11; 6:13—7:5; 8:5.

Because of the problems with the 'dialogue analysis' approach, and the lack of agreement among the scholars who have used it, other scholars have taken a 'literary analysis' approach. They look for literary devices, which might mark out different poems or sections of poems, such as: change of speaker (indicated by change of gender or person in pronouns and verbs), repeated refrains, *inclusios* (the same or similar phrases used to mark the beginning and end of a section), the appearance of the 'chorus', parallels

---

THE STRUCTURE OF THE SONG OF SONGS

Exum's analysis

I (Frame)	1:2—2:6	Forms an *inclusio* with VI
II (A)	2:7—3:5	Parallels IV in phrases, images and content
III (B)	3:6—5:1	Parallels V in phrases and content
IV (A')	5:2—6:3	
V (B')	6:4—8:3	
VI (Frame)	8:4–14	NB 'vineyard', 'keeper(s)' in 1:6; 8:11–12

Shea's analysis

A	1:2—2:2	parallels	A'	5:1—7:9 (5:1—7:10 in Hebrew)
B	2:3–17	parallels	B'	7:10—8:5 (7:11—8:5 in Hebrew)
C	3:1—4:16	parallels	C'	8:6–14

Goulder's analysis

1. The Arrival	1:1–8	1:7–8	
2. The Audience	1:9—2:7	2:7	
3. The Courtship	2:8–17		
4. In the Night	3:1–5	3:5	
5. The Procession	3:6–11	3:6–11	
6. The Wedding	4:1–7		
7. The Consummation	4:8—5:1	5:1	
8. A Knock at the Door	5:2–9	5:8–9	
9. A Lover Lost and Found	5:10—6:3	6:1	
10. The One and Only	6:4–12		
11. The Dance	6:13—7:9	6:13	(7:1–10, 7:1 in the Hebrew Bible)
12. A Night in the Country	7:10—8:4	8:4	(7:11—8:4, 8:4 in the Hebrew Bible)
13. Love's Demand	8:5–10	8:5	
14. The Queen	8:11–14	8:11	

The second column gives references to mentions of, or words of, the 'chorus', which Goulder uses as the major marker of the beginning or end of a poem.

between sections. In theory this ought to be a more 'objective' approach. However, it has not led to agreement on the structure. Perhaps this is because literary analysis involves making aesthetic judgements that are never purely objective. The range of disagreement is considerable, indicating the difficulty of deciding on the limits of the 'basic units' of the Song of Songs. Some examples are: 31 poems (Falk), 30 (Murphy), 29 (Gordis), 23 (Longman), 14 (Goulder), 6 (Exum), 6 (Shea, but not the same as Exum!). See the box 'The Structure of the Song of Songs' on p. 187 for more detail on some of the examples.

Scholars who use the literary analysis approach also differ widely in their conclusions concerning the nature of the book. Both Falk and Gordis see it as simply an anthology of love lyrics written by different authors over a considerable period of time. What unity there is of theme, style and imagery is due to the conventions of Hebrew poetry. Because of the structural unity she sees in the Song of Songs, and its poetic sophistication, Exum concludes that it is the work of a single author. Goulder also thinks that it has a single author, but this is because he thinks it tells a unified story, from the arrival of a princess at Solomon's court to her establishment as his beloved queen. He suggests that the poem was written as a tract against the post-exilic Jewish policy of banning marriages to foreign women, since in it Solomon is depicted as marrying a 'black', and so foreign, woman who is of outstanding beauty and shows him great affection. This seems to be forcing an interpretation on the text.

A BRIEF OVERVIEW

This overview assumes that the Song of Songs is an anthology of independent pieces. The section divisions are similar to those argued for by Longman, but with some modification.

SONG OF SONGS 1:1
This superscription has already been discussed at some length.

SONG OF SONGS 1:2–4
The first words of the Song are the woman's expression of yearning for her lover. A characteristic of the Song appears here at the start, the woman takes the initiative.

SONG OF SONGS 1:5–6
This is a short poem in which the woman describes herself, with some diffidence, to the daughters of Jerusalem. She is sensitive about her dark colouring. The meaning of v. 6b is unclear but, given the context, it may be that her lack of care for her appearance has angered her brothers – it would make her less eligible for marriage.

SONG OF SONGS 1:7–8
The woman addresses the man as a shepherd, seeking to arrange a tryst.

SONG OF SONGS 1:9–11
The man speaks of the woman's beauty, likening her to a beautiful mare. Because of the shift to the plural, v. 11 is sometimes attributed to the 'chorus' of friends, but it could be spoken by the man.

SONG OF SONGS 1:12–14
This speech by the woman centres on the theme of sweet fragrances. The woman's response to the presence of her lover,

spoken of as a king, is expressed in terms of a fragrance. He is then compared to the fragrance of myrrh and henna blossom.

SONG OF SONGS 1:15—2:3

The extent of this poem is unclear. Some would take 2:1–3 with what follows, or treat them, or 2:1–2, as a separate unit. If taken as a unit, 1:15—2:3 can be seen as a piece of lovers' banter. The changes of gender are clear in the Hebrew. The sequence is man (1:15), woman (1:16–17), woman (2:1), man (2:2), woman (2:3). The connecting theme is the nature imagery, mainly to do with plants.

SONG OF SONGS 2:4–7

The mention of apples (v. 5) may provide a catchword link with v. 3. In this poem the woman describes the man taking her to a 'wine house' (tavern?) where they embrace. The verb used (hvq) does not necessarily indicate sexual intercourse. Both vv. 6 and 7 are repeated later in the book.

SONG OF SONGS 2:8–17

The imagery of vv. 8–9a is repeated in v. 17b, suggesting that this is a distinct unit. The poem begins with the woman excitedly announcing her lover's arrival, like that of a gazelle or stag bounding over the mountains. On arrival at her house he looks over the wall, trying to catch sight of her through the windows. She describes how he calls to her, inviting her to a tryst, expressing his desire both to see her and to hear her voice. Her response in v. 15 is puzzling, but may refer to obstacles in the way of their meeting. The poem ends with her expression of desire for him.

SONG OF SONGS 3:1–5

The mood of this poem is very different from what has gone before. Its content is rather surreal, suggesting that it is some kind of dream or fantasy produced by the woman's yearning for her lover. It begins with the woman in bed at night. She seeks intently for her lover. Unable to find him, she goes out to scour the streets, meeting the watchmen and asking them whether they have seen him. Immediately after that encounter she finds him and takes him back to her mother's bedroom. The poem ends by repeating advice given to the daughters of Jerusalem in 2:7 not to awaken love until it is ready.

SONG OF SONGS 3:6–11

There is general agreement that this is a distinct unit and that it describes a wedding procession. There is divergence over whether it describes an actual event, a wedding procession associated with Solomon, or is simply a poetic creation that celebrates love and marriage using imagery drawn from the tradition of the opulence of Solomon's lifestyle.

SONG OF SONGS 4:1–7

This *wasf* is marked out by the *inclusio* of vv. 1a and 7. It describes the woman's head and breasts, followed by a statement of the man's desire for her (v. 6).

SONG OF SONGS 4:8–15

The references to Lebanon in vv. 8 and 15 probably justify taking this as a distinct section. The man invites the woman to come to him (v. 8) and expresses his admiration of and desire for her (v. 9). He then describes her beauty in terms of the metaphor of a lovely garden.

SONG OF SONGS 4:16—5:1

This short piece may be an independent poem, or the climax of the previous one. It is linked to it by the garden imagery. The invoking of the winds to spread the fragrance of the garden is a way of saying that it is going to be made available, at least to the man, who is then explicitly invited to enter and enjoy its fruits. This is probably an invitation to sexual union. Understandably, the man responds positively. He enters the garden and eats its fruit. The 'chorus' then expresses its approbation of the union. It may be significant that this short section comes at the middle of the Hebrew text, based on a count of the number of lines of text (there are 111 lines both before and after it).

SONG OF SONGS 5:2—6:3

This section seems to form a coherent narrative unity. There are distinct subsections within it. In the first unit (vv. 2–8) the man comes to the woman's door, but she is reluctant to open it (in this there may be a double entendre, a description of the man asking the woman to be open to sexual intercourse). By the time she has changed her mind, he has gone. She sets out in search of him but fails to find him. Instead she meets the city sentinels, who beat her. She calls on the daughters of Jerusalem to help her find her lover.

When the other women ask for a description of her beloved (v. 9) she responds with a *wasf* (vv. 10–16) extolling his physical beauty. This is the only *wasf* in the Song where the woman describes the man. The description moves from his head to feet. It ends with a reference to the sweetness of his 'palate'. This may refer to his 'speech' (so the NRSV), or to the pleasure of kissing (as in 7:9, NRSV). Finally the woman, in response to their request (6:1), tells the daughters of Jerusalem where to find her lover – in his garden (6:2). She ends with an expression of their mutual love and commitment (6:3).

SONG OF SONGS 6:4–10

This poem opens and closes with the *inclusio* 'terrible as an army with banners'. It is another *wasf* in which the man describes the beauty of the woman, and there is some repetition of the imagery used in 4:1–7. The woman is more beautiful than any other (vv. 8–9), her beauty overwhelms the man (v. 5), like fear at the sight of a great army ready for battle.

SONG OF SONGS 6:11–12

This seems to be a short, independent unit. Unfortunately its meaning is unclear because the text of v. 12 is very difficult to understand. It seems to express the woman's excitement or passion when meeting her lover.

> **Digging deeper:**
> **SONG OF SONGS 6:12**
>
> Consult several commentaries in order to get a grasp of the difficulties in this verse, and how it may be interpreted.

SONG OF SONGS 6:13—7:10

The exact extent of this section is open to debate. Some prefer to take 6:13 and 7:10 as separate verses. However, 6:13 does provide a possible introduction to the following *wasf*. The 'chorus' calls on the Shulammite to let them look at her. When she asks why they want to do this, the man replies with a description of her beauty. As already noted, the description is unusual in that it works upward from the feet to the head, but this is because the woman is apparently dancing (6:13b). As a result it is her feet that initially catch the attention. The *wasf* ends at 7:5. In 7:6–9 the man continues to extol the woman's beauty, using the imagery of a palm tree. The section ends with a statement by the women of their mutual desire for each other.

SONG OF SONGS 7:11–13

In this poem the woman invites the man to go into the vineyard with her in springtime to see the awaking of new life in nature. She makes clear her desire to give him her love.

SONG OF SONGS 8:1–4

This poem expresses the woman's yearning for her lover and his embrace. The implication of 8:1 is that in her culture brother and sister could make public display of affection, but lovers could not. Verse 4 repeats the caution about premature arousal of love (2:7; 3:5).

SONG OF SONGS 8:5–7

The 'chorus' opens this section with a question (v. 5a), presumably as they see the woman and her lover approaching in the distance. This seems to be a rhetorical 'scene-setting' question. When the woman responds she addresses the man. She declares that she aroused him under the apple tree (v. 5b), and then asks him to commit himself to her alone (v. 6a) and goes on to speak of the power of love (vv. 6b–7). This poem is one of the most powerful in the book. It makes a major contribution to its message despite its brevity.

SONG OF SONGS 8:8–10

This poem is a dialogue between the woman and her brothers. It makes

something of an *inclusio* with the mention of the brothers in 1:5–6. The brothers see themselves as responsible for the protection of their sister until she is married. Their attitude implicitly questions her maturity. She replies indignantly asserting both her maturity and chastity, as a result of which she will bring 'peace' ('contentment, wholeness') to her husband.

SONG OF SONGS 8:11–12

This is an enigmatic poem. It is not clear who is the speaker. Perhaps the best solution is to take it as a speech of the woman in which she asserts her independence from oppressive men like Solomon who think they have the right and power to own women.

SONG OF SONGS 8:13–14

The final short poem is a dialogue between the man and the woman expressing their yearning for union. It seems strange to end the book on this note rather than on one of love consummated. It harks back to 2:9, 14, 17, and so, with 8:8–10, 11–12, may be intended to end the book with a reprise of earlier motifs.

THE INTERPRETATION OF THE SONG OF SONGS

The Song of Songs has been one of the most widely written about biblical books. In his survey of the interpretation of the book Murphy says that during the later patristic period and the Middle Ages Christian interpreters wrote more books on the Song of Songs than on any other book of the Old Testament. In his commentary Pope provides a detailed survey of the history of both Jewish and Christian interpretation of the book. Here we can provide only a brief outline of it. Fortunately there are a limited number of major types of interpretation that have been popular, which makes a general survey possible.

ALLEGORICAL INTERPRETATIONS

The recorded comments of the early rabbinical discussions of the book, especially those of Rabbi Aqiba, suggest that *c*. AD 100 the rabbis were favouring an allegorical interpretation of the book. Rabbi Aqiba objected strongly to poems from the Song of Songs being sung for entertainment at secular gatherings (indicating that some Jews were taking it literally as a collection of love songs). His few surviving references to verses from the Song of Songs imply that he interpreted it allegorically of God's love for Israel.

An allegory is a piece of writing in which the author intends readers to take the surface meaning as symbolic of another level of meaning. Probably the best-known allegory in English literature is John Bunyan's *Pilgrim's Progress*. This tells the story of Christian's journey to the Celestial City, and of obstacles he meets on the way, such as the Slough of Despond, and friends who help him, such as Mr Faithful. It is clearly meant to be an allegory of the Christian life. There are allegories in the Hebrew Bible (e.g. Judg. 9:7–21; Ezek. 17:1–21). These are clearly intended as allegories, and their meaning is indicated. There is nothing to indicate that the Song of Songs was intentionally written as an allegory. However, 'allegorizing' can be adopted as a means of interpretation in which the reader looks for a level of meaning other than the surface meaning of the text, quite irrespective of what the author may have intended. Greek

philosophers began to use allegorical interpretation *c*. 500 BC as a means of re-interpreting the classic myths about the Greek gods and heroes so as to make them more acceptable to the enlightened thinkers of their own day. They gave symbolic meanings to the various gods and their often capricious actions. The method was taken up by both Jewish (e.g. Philo of Alexandria, 20 BC – AD 54) and Christian (e.g. Origen, AD 185–254) scholars.

The Targum of the Song of Songs (*c*. AD 800) interprets it as an allegorical account of God's relationship with Israel from the time of the exodus to the destruction of the second temple and then the coming of the Messiah. The treatment of the opening verses gives a flavour of the method. The woman (Israel) begs the man (God) to kiss her, showing her desire for a relationship with him (the kissing is the giving of the Torah). She asks him to take her into his private room (the Promised Land). Another, but less common, approach by the rabbinic scholars, saw the book as an allegory of God's relationship with the individual soul. There were many variant forms of these two basic allegorizing approaches developed by Jewish scholars down to the nineteenth century.

The Christian Church grew out of the Jewish community, so it is not surprising to find Christian scholars following the same basic approaches to the Song of Songs as the rabbis. However, they naturally transferred the meaning from the relationship between God and Israel to that between Christ and the Church, or Christ and the individual soul. Origen's treatment of the book was very influential. He wrote a ten-volume commentary on it as well as several homilies. He did not ignore the surface meaning of the book. In his view it was a 'marriage song' written by Solomon for one of his wives, and he gives his interpretation of it on that level. However, his primary interest is in interpreting it as an allegory of Christ's relationship with the Church. He also occasionally interprets it with reference to Christ's relationship with the individual soul. Down through the Middle Ages Christian interpretations of the Song of Songs were largely variations on what Origen had done. A few commentators identified the woman in the song with the Virgin Mary, sometimes seeing her at the same time as a representation of the Church, and so also maintaining the allegory of the Christ–Church relationship.

It may well be, as many scholars have suggested, that the popularity of allegorical interpretation of the Song of Songs among both Jewish and Christian scholars was due to a considerable extent to the influence of Platonic philosophy. This made a sharp distinction between the material and non-material worlds, and regarded the body as the 'prison house' of the soul. As a result, it tended to encourage an asceticism which denigrated physical desires, and sex in particular. Allegorizing provided a way of going beyond, and marginalizing, the obvious sexual meaning of the Song of Songs. However, one should not discount the simple desire to find a 'spiritual' meaning in a book where such a meaning was not obvious. The allegorical method was also applied by Christians to other biblical texts, such as the historical narratives and legal codes, that also lacked a clear 'spiritual' meaning.

The obvious problem with the allegorical approach is that it allows the readers to see almost any meaning they like in the text. Take, for example, some interpretations of 1:13, 'My beloved is to me a bag of myrrh that lies between my breasts.'

- Some Jewish commentators saw in this a reference to the Shekinah glory between the two cherubim that stood over the Ark of the Covenant.
- Christian interpreters often took it to refer to the Old and New Testaments, between which stands Christ.
- Other Christian interpreters understood it to refer to the believer keeping the remembrance of the crucifixion of Christ in the heart (i.e. 'between my breasts').

The subjectivity of the allegorical method led the Protestant Reformers to reject it as a general method for interpreting Scripture. They emphasized the importance of the 'natural' or 'literal' sense of the text. How far they applied this to the Song of Songs is debatable. Luther rejected Origen's allegorical interpretation of the Song of Songs. He argued that Solomon is talking in poetic language about his intimate relationship with God and God's relationship with Israel through his reign. Arguably, he turned it into a political allegory. Calvin objected strongly to Castellio's view that the book was simply a love poem and should have no place in the canon. There is debate over whether he objected only to the suggestion that it should not be in the canon, or also to the literal interpretation of it.

NATURAL/LITERAL INTERPRETATIONS

Dissatisfaction with allegorical interpretation of the Song of Songs grew among scholars during the eighteenth century. In part this was probably due to the cultural change of the Enlightenment. The conviction grew that the interpretation of a text should be established by reasonable arguments, not the imagination of the interpreter or the authority of tradition. Lowth, who did pioneering work on the nature of Hebrew poetry, regarded the Song of Songs as a celebration of Solomon's marriage to the daughter of Pharaoh, but did allow an allegorical interpretation, though urging caution in this respect. However, the real turning point came in the nineteenth century. An important factor was the growth in knowledge about the ancient Near East as a result of archaeological discoveries. As the ancient languages were deciphered and texts from the biblical period and earlier came to light, they provided a context in which the 'natural' or 'literal' sense of the Song of Songs seemed more and more convincing over against allegorical readings. Another factor was growing acquaintance with modern Middle Eastern customs. An important instance of this with regard to the Song of Songs was the observation of J. G. Wetzstein, the German Consul in Syria, of Arab wedding customs. He saw similarities between the songs sung at the weddings, especially the *wasf*, and the Song of Songs. Also, the bride and groom were crowned as king and queen, and the bride performed a kind of 'sword dance', which reminded Wetzstein of the dancing woman in the Song of Songs. He published his observations in 1873, and they were included as an appendix in Delitzsch's commentary in 1885.

In the nineteenth century a 'natural' interpretation of the Song of Songs as a dramatic love poem gained popularity.

The two most common interpretations were as either a two- or a three-character drama. Delitzsch was a supporter of the two-character dramatic interpretation. For him the main characters were Solomon and the Shulammite. In his view the Shulammite was an actual historical person, a humble country girl whose beauty and charm captivated Solomon and drew him away from 'the wantonness of polygamy'. He divided the Song of Songs into six acts, with two scenes in each. Others – for example, Ewald – found three principal characters in the drama: Solomon, the Shulammite and her rustic lover. In this version of the story, the woman resists the king's advances and, though she is carried off to his palace, she remains true to her original lover and the king eventually allows her to return home to him. Driver, who favours Ewald's version, provides a useful synopsis of both forms of the drama. Critics of the dramatic interpretations point out that they require the whole plot to be read into the book when it is not obviously there. This reading sometimes strains credulity, as when, in the three-character version, 1:15—2:3 is seen as a dialogue between Solomon and the woman, but all the woman's comments need to be taken as asides (1:16; 2:1; 2:3) addressed to her absent rustic lover. Moreover, the assigning of the shepherd imagery to the rustic lover and the king imagery to Solomon in the three-character drama seems forced. Then there is the problem of 'dialogue analysis' that we have already discussed. Also, as we've seen when considering the authorship of the book, the distribution of the name 'Solomon' in it does not fit well with him as the author or main character. Because of the force of these kinds of criticisms the dramatic

Digging deeper:
DRAMATIC INTERPRETATIONS OF THE SONG OF SONGS

Delitzsch's two-character, six-act drama is summarized below.

1. Act 1: 1:2—2:7. The mutual affection between Solomon and the Shulammite, concluding with, 'I adjure you, O daughters of Jerusalem.'
2. Act 2: 2:8—3:5. The mutual seeking and finding of the lovers, with the conclusion, 'I adjure you, O daughters of Jerusalem.'
3. Act 3: 3:6—5:1. The fetching of the bride and the marriage. This begins with, 'What is that...?' and ends with, 'Drink and be drunk with love.'
4. Act 4: 5:2—6:9. Love is scorned but won again.
5. Act 5: 6:10—8:4. The Shulammite, the attractively fair but humble princess. This begins with, 'Who is this ...?' and ends with, 'I adjure you, O daughters of Jerusalem.'
6. Act 6: 8:5–14. The covenant love between Solomon and his bride is ratified in the Shulammite's home. This begins with, 'Who is that...?'

Compare this with Provan's three-character drama.

1. Chs 1—2. The woman, already a member of the king's harem, expresses her continu- ing love for the lover she has been taken away from, and he reciprocates.
2. Ch. 3. The woman expresses her determin- ation to overcome threats to the relation- ship with the man she really loves and her negative view of the royal bed and its owner.
3. Chs 4—5. The depth of, and threats to, her love relationship become clearer. The language and imagery speak of a committed, marriage-like relationship.
4. Chs 6—7. The nature of the relationship is described in further graphic detail. In particular, the man's views are expressed.
5. Ch. 8. This gives a strong closing statement of the woman's passion for the man she loves and her resistance to those other males who claim possession of her, whether her brothers or the king.

Overall, Provan sees it as a story of faithfulness to a first love in the face of royal power and coercion and the temptations of the court. It expresses the superiority of a true love relationship over a purely legal relationship.

How convincing do you find these attempts to see a drama in the Song?

---

interpretations lost scholarly support in the course of the twentieth century, though Provan is an exception to this trend.

CULTIC INTERPRETATIONS
The rediscovery of ancient Near Eastern literature in the nineteenth century also prompted 'cultic' interpretations of the Song of Songs. Sumerian texts tell of a sacred marriage between the deities Dumuzi and Inanna, which ensured fertility for the coming year. In Akkadian texts this becomes a marriage between Tammuz and Ishtar. In Canaan the

marriage of Baal and Astarte may have had the same significance. It seems that this marriage was 'acted out' in the cult by the king and queen, or the king and a priestess of the goddess. The cult of Tammuz is mentioned (negatively) in the Hebrew Bible (explicitly in Ezek. 8:14 and, probably, implicitly in Isa. 17:10–11 and Zech. 12:11), so was known to the Hebrews. Meek popularized the idea that the Song of Songs originated as a liturgy of the Tammuz cult. However, there is nothing in the Song of Songs itself to suggest that it is part of a Hebrew sacred marriage ritual, nor is there any hint of such a ritual elsewhere in the Hebrew Bible. The Song of Songs seems to be very much about love between humans, not deities. There is evidence, namely the prophetic condemnations of it, that some Israelites were involved in the Tammuz cult, or something akin to it. However, it would be very strange if the mainstream worshippers of Yahweh accepted into their sacred literature a pagan liturgy of a cult they condemned. After a period of some popularity, support for Meek's thesis has faded away.

More recently Pope has suggested that the original setting of the Song of Songs was the ancient Near Eastern *marzeah* festival. This was a meal that asserted the force of life, with which Pope associates sex, over against death. It involved eating, heavy drinking, singing and sexual activity in the context of a funerary cult. Pope's main support for this suggestion is found in 8:6b, 'for love is strong as death, passion fierce as the grave', which he sees as the climax of the Song. This festival may be mentioned in Jeremiah 16:5 and Amos 6:7 but, if so, these are condemnations of it, and the same argument applies as does to the idea

that the Song of Songs is a liturgy from the Tammuz cult. Also, Pope seems to hang a lot on one couplet in the Song, even if it is the climax, a view with which many would not agree. It is more likely that the Song of Songs and the *marzeah* festival contain independent recognitions of the power of love over death.

The discovery of the Egyptian love songs, and then other ancient Near Eastern love songs, encouraged the view that the Song of Songs is a collection of love poems, whether they are by one author or an anthology drawing on the work of several poets. This is now by far the majority view, and we have discussed some examples of it when considering the structure of the Song of Songs.

FEMINIST INTERPRETATIONS

In 1857 Ginsburg published a commentary on the Song of Songs. A section in the introduction entitled 'The Importance of the Book' argued strongly that the book is a liberating text for women. He took up several issues that are now central concerns of feminists: the moral and intellectual equality of women and men, the cultural repression of women in both biblical and modern times, the restoration of the female image in the Song of Songs, and links between the book and the Garden of Eden story in Genesis 2—3.

In discussing the authorship of the book we have already noted the features of the Song of Songs that feminist scholars, and others, have emphasized: the absence of sexist attitudes; the equality of the sexes in the love relationship depicted, with the women often taking the initiative; the prominence of the role of the mother, with no mention of the father; the possibility of female authorship for some or all of the poems in the book, since much of the poetry seems to be written from a feminine perspective.

Trible has carried out an important intertextual study of the Garden of Eden story in Genesis 2:4b—3:24 and the Song of Songs. She argues that whereas the Garden of Eden story is one of tragic disobedience, which results in the love relationship between man and woman going wrong, the Song of Songs gives a picture of that relationship redeemed. In the Song of Songs the garden imagery, which is used as a metaphor for the enjoyment of erotic pleasure, is reminiscent of the Garden of Eden, and the eating of fruit seems to be a figure of speech for the enjoyment of sexual pleasure (Song 2:3; 4:16; 5:1). A striking connection between the two biblical passages is the word used for desire in Song of Songs 7:10 and Genesis 3:16 (*t^eshuqah*). Its only other occurrence in the Hebrew Bible is in Genesis 4:7. The comparison between Genesis 3:16 and Song of Songs 7:10 is illuminating.

> Your desire shall be for your husband
> and he shall rule over you. (Gen. 3:16b)

> I am my beloved's, and his desire is for
> me. (Song 7:10)

The Genesis statement is part of the 'divine judgement' on the woman. It speaks of the woman's desire in a context of sexual disharmony and male domination. The Song of Songs speaks of the man's desire in a context of sexual mutuality and harmony (cf. Song 2:16a: 'My beloved is mine and I am his'). Also, the disobedience in the Garden of Eden led to death, but the love of the Song of Songs can face death undaunted,

> Love is strong as death, passion fierce as
> the grave.
> Its flashes are the flashes of fire, a raging
> flame. (Song 8:6bc)

The fire imagery may evoke the flaming sword of the cherubim posted to guard the entrance to the Garden and the Tree of Life in Genesis 3:24. So, Trible sees in the Song of Songs evidence that love can be redeemed so that sex can be enjoyed without the shame that was felt after the disobedience in the Garden of Eden (Gen. 3:10) and can result in relationships in which there is no domination of the female by the male, and no stereotyping of either sex.

Digging deeper:
THE SONG OF SONGS AND THE GARDEN OF EDEN STORY

Read Trible's study, 'Love's Lyrics Redeemed', which is summarized in the subsection on 'Feminist Interpretation' for yourself and come to your own assessment of it.

THE MESSAGE OF THE SONG OF SONGS

The Song of Songs is a frank celebration of the joys of human love and sexuality. Although the poetry is often explicitly erotic it never verges on being pornographic. It concentrates on the emotions of love, not the clinical details of lovemaking. The love relationship it portrays is marked by certain characteristics. As we have seen, one that has been particularly emphasized in recent studies is the equality of the relationship. Another is its mutuality, which is summed up in the two phrases: 'My beloved is mine and I am his' (2:16) and 'I am my beloved's and my beloved is mine' (6:3). These statements also imply that it is a deeply committed relationship. What is often not noticed is that they also imply that there is an exclusivity about the relationship. This becomes explicit in 8:6a. The meaning of the imagery used here is brought out clearly in the following translation from the *Good News Bible*.

> Close your heart to every love but mine; hold no one in your arms but me.

There is also what might be called a 'responsible' attitude to love. The fact that it is powerful and precious is asserted strongly in 8:6b–7. It is no doubt in the light of this that we are to take seriously the warning 'not to stir up or awaken love until it is ready', which is repeated three times (2:7; 3:5; 8:4).

In the light of this picture of the love relationship given in the Song of Songs, there seems little basis for saying, as a few scholars have, that it encourages 'free love' or promiscuity. The only grounds for suggesting this is the rare use of the language of marriage in the book (the most obvious references are in 3:11; 4:8, 9–12). This is a problem for some of the interpretations that see the book as telling a story which ends in the marriage union of the woman with her lover (whether Solomon or a rustic shepherd), because there seems to be considerable sexual intimacy, if not intercourse, earlier in the book. This problem is not there if the book is seen as an anthology of love poems without a coherent narrative.

Childs has argued that a 'canonical' reading of the book as part of the Hebrew Bible must take seriously the attribution of it to Solomon, not as a claim to authorship but as identifying the book as wisdom literature. This, he argues, rules out reading it as purely secular literature because it does not mention God. There is often no explicit mention of God in biblical wisdom literature. However, there is the foundational understanding that 'the fear of the LORD is the beginning of wisdom [NRSV has 'knowledge']' (Prov. 1:7). On this basis the Song of Songs' reflection on the nature of love must be taken to assume that the appropriate context for the fulfilment of love is marriage, as Genesis 2:23–24 states was the Creator's purpose.

It is entirely appropriate that the Song of Songs should be in the canon of Scripture since that canon also includes the claim that sex was part of the Creator God's purpose for human beings (Gen. 2:18–25). That story goes on to speak of the disruption of the intended harmonious relationship between man and wife as a result of the alienation of humans from their Creator (Gen. 3:1–21). We have seen how Trible has shown that the Song of Songs holds out the promise of the redemption of the human love relationship.

Although nearly all modern scholars reject the allegorical interpretations of the Song of Songs, there is a recognition that they do point to something important. In the Hebrew Bible the metaphor of marriage is used in a number of places and ways to speak of God's relationship with Israel. In the New Testament the marriage metaphor is used of Christ's relationship to the Church. Therefore it is appropriate to

Think about
JEALOUSY

In modern English the word 'jealousy' is primarily a negative term, expressing a selfish, destructive emotion. The *Oxford English Dictionary* does, however, include among its meanings the 'neutral' one of 'watchfully tenacious'. This is closer to the meaning of the Hebrew root (*qn'*) that the NRSV translates as 'passion' in Song of Songs 8:6 and that is often translated as 'jealousy' when applied to God in the Hebrew Bible. The God of Israel is said to be a 'jealous' God because he is protective of his covenant relationship with Israel (Exod. 20:1–6). This jealousy is expressed negatively in punishment when the relationship is threatened by the Israelites worshipping other gods. It is expressed positively by acts of deliverance when Israel is oppressed by other nations (Zech. 1:14–17). It seems that this 'jealousy' is God's 'watchfully tenacious concern' for the well-being of Israel. That well-being is founded on the covenant with her God, and so that covenant relationship has to be carefully guarded. Can you think of a better English word than 'jealousy' to express this concept? The NRSV uses 'passion' in Song of Songs 8:6 and 'zeal' in Isaiah 9:7. Each seems reasonable in its context, but would they, or some other word, make better sense than 'jealousy' in other contexts, such as Exodus 20:5, Joel 2:18 and Zechariah 1:14?

reflect on the relevance of what the Song of Songs says about the love relationship between humans for understanding our relationship to God. Where the allegories go wrong is that they suppress the human dimension of the Song of Songs and press the details of it in arbitrary ways in the search for a religious meaning. One

striking point that is highlighted in the Hebrew Bible by the application of the marriage metaphor to God's relationship with his people is that there are only two relationships in which 'jealousy' can have a positive and legitimate role: God's covenant relationship with his people, and the human marriage relationship – because they are meant to be relationships that are to be protected from the intrusion of rivals.

FURTHER READING

Items marked * are considered suitable as first ports of call, while others are more complex, or relate to specific issues.

COMMENTARIES
Carr provides a fairly popular exposition of the Song and makes a fair presentation of alternative approaches. Gordis and Snaith also provide good, fairly brief, introductory commentaries on the book, from somewhat different perspectives. Longman's commentary is more detailed and scholarly but still accessible. Like other DSB volumes, Davidson's has a devotional slant. It gives helpful analysis of the book's use of imagery. A special feature of Keel's work is the inclusion of copies of relevant Near Eastern art. It is also good on literary appreciation of the Song. Delitzsch and Provan are examples of nineteenth- and twenty-first-century 'dramatic' interpretations of the Song. Both Murphy and Pope have written major scholarly commentaries. In both cases their 'Introductions' contain a wealth of helpful information.

* G. L. Carr *The Song of Solomon*. TOTC. Leicester: IVP, 1984.

R. Davidson *Ecclesiastes and Song of Solomon.* DSB. Edinburgh: Saint Andrew Press, 1986.

F. Delitzsch *Proverbs, Ecclesiastes, Song of Solomon.* Grand Rapids, MI: Eerdmans, 1975 (translation by M. G. Easton of the 1885 edn).

* R. Gordis *The Song of Songs and Lamentations.* New York, NY: Ktav, 1974 (rev. edn).

O. Keel *The Song of Songs.* Continental Commentary. Minneapolis, MN: Fortress, 1994.

T. Longman III *Song of Songs.* NICOT. Grand Rapids, MI: Eerdmans, 2001.

R. E. Murphy *The Song of Songs.* Hermeneia. Minneapolis, MN: Fortress Press, 1990.

M. H. Pope *Song of Songs.* AB. New York, NY: Doubleday, 1977.

I. Provan *Ecclesiastes and Song of Solomon.* NIVAC. Grand Rapids, MI: Zondervan, 2001.

* J. G. Snaith *Song of Songs.* NCB. London: Marshall Pickering, 1993.

OTHER BOOKS AND ARTICLES

J. Bekkenkamp and F. Van Dijk, 'The Canon of the Old Testament and Women's Cultural Traditions', in A. Brenner (ed.) *A Feminist Companion to the Song of Songs.* Sheffield: Sheffield Academic Press, 1993; pp. 67–85.

A. Brenner 'Aromatics and Perfumes in the Song of Songs', *JSOT* 25 (1983), 75–81.

*A. Brenner *The Song of Songs.* OT Guide. Sheffield: JSOT Press, 1989.

A. Brenner (ed.) *A Feminist Companion to the Song of Songs.* Sheffield: Sheffield Academic Press, 1993.

A. Brenner 'Women Poets and Authors', in

A. Brenner (ed.), *A Feminist Companion to the Song of Songs.* Sheffield: Sheffield Academic Press, 1993; pp. 86–97.

A. Brenner and C. R. Fontaine, *The Song of Songs: A Feminist Companion to the Bible (2nd Series).* Sheffield: Sheffield Academic Press, 2000.

B. S. Childs *Introduction to the Old Testament as Scripture.* Philadelphia, PA: Fortress, 1979.

J. S. Cooper 'New Cuneiform Parallels to the Song of Songs', *JBL* 90 (1971), 157–162.

P. C. Craigie 'Biblical and Tamil Poetry: Some Further Reflections', *SR* 8 (1979), 169–175.

S. R. Driver *An Introduction to the Literature of the Old Testament.* Edinburgh: T. & T. Clark, 1913 (9th edn).

J. C. Exum 'A Literary and Structural Analysis of the Song of Songs', *ZAW* 85 (1973), 47–79.

M. Falk *Love Lyrics from the Bible.* Sheffield: Almond Press, 1982.

M. V. Fox *The Song of Songs and Ancient Egyptian Love Songs.* Madison, WI: University of Wisconsin Press, 1985.

C. D. Ginsburg 'The Importance of the Book', in A. Brenner (ed.), *A Feminist Companion to the Song of Songs.* Sheffield: Sheffield Academic Press, 1993; pp. 47–54.

M. D. Goulder *The Song of Fourteen Songs.* Sheffield: JSOT Press, 1986.

W. W. Hallo and K. L. Younger Jnr (eds.) *The Context of Scripture*, vol. 1. Leiden: Brill, 1997.

S. N. Kramer *The Sacred Marriage Rite.* London: Indiana University Press, 1969.

T. J. Meek 'Babylonian Parallels to

the Song of Songs', *JBL* 43 (1924), 245–252.

J. M. Munro *Spikenard and Saffron.* Sheffield: Sheffield Academic Press, 1995.

R. E. Murphy *Wisdom Literature.* FOTL 13. Grand Rapids, MI: Eerdmans, 1981.

C. Rabin 'The Song of Songs and Tamil Poetry', *SR* 3 (1973), 205–219.

* H. H. Rowley 'The Interpretation of the Song of Songs', in H. H. Rowley *The Servant of the Lord.* Oxford: Blackwell, 1965 (2nd rev. edn), pp. 187–234.

M. Sadgrove 'The Song of Songs as Wisdom Literature', in E. A. Livingstone (ed.) *Studia Biblica 1978*, vol. 1, JSOTSup 11. Sheffield: JSOT Press, 1979; pp. 245–248.

M. H. Segal 'The Song of Songs', *VT* 12 (1962), 470–490.

W. H. Shea 'The Chiastic Structure of the Song of Songs', *ZAW* 92 (1980), 378–396.

*P. Trible 'Love's Lyrics Redeemed', in P. Trible *God and the Rhetoric of Sexuality.* Philadelphia, PA: Fortress Press, 1978; pp. 144–165.

J. G. Westenholz 'Love Lyrics from the Ancient Near East', in J. M. Sasson (ed.) *Civilizations of the Ancient Near East*, vol. 4. New York, NY: Charles Scribner's Sons, 1995; pp. 2471–2482.

J. B. White *A Study of the Language of Love in the Song of Songs and Ancient Egyptian Love Poetry.* Missoula, MT: Scholars Press, 1975.

GLOSSARY

Aristotelianism Aristotle (384–322 BC) founded one of the major schools of Greek philosophy. He was a student of Plato, another great philosopher. In 335 BC, some years after Plato's death, he founded his own school in Athens, the Lyceum. His teaching was wide-ranging, covering metaphysics, logic, ethics, politics, and natural science.

Canonical criticism In this book this is used to refer to the approach to interpreting the Old Testament advocated by Brevard Childs, especially in his *Introduction to the Old Testament as Scripture* (1979). He advocated focusing on the individual biblical books in the form that they have in the canon of Scripture. This puts the emphasis on the theological meaning of the book as it was received by the believing community, rather than meanings that it might have had at different (often largely hypothetical) stages in its composition. A further level of 'canonical meaning' is the understanding of the individual book in the context of the canon of Scripture as a whole.

Chiasm/chiastic A chiasm, or chiasmus, is a literary pattern in which there is a reversal of the order of corresponding items, such as: A, B, C : C', B', A'. It is a fairly common device in the parallel lines of Hebrew poetry, e.g. 'For we are consumed (A)/ by your anger; (B)/ by your wrath (B')/ we are overwhelmed (A') (Ps. 90:7). The pattern can be extended to the structure of a whole narrative, or even a whole book.

Cult/cultic As used in religious studies the term 'cult' refers to a system of religious belief and the way it is expressed in various religious practices.

Epicureanism Epicurus (341–270 BC) founded his philosophical school in Athens in 307 BC. He taught that pleasure is the only worthwhile aim in life. By pleasure he meant the state of being in which natural and necessary desires are satisfied.

Form criticism Form critics seek to discern the different typical forms within a piece of literature. It is often assumed that these forms are related to the function that the form had in its original *sitz im leben* (situation in life).

Hermeneutics The study of the principles, methods and rules involved in the interpretation of written texts.

Hypostasis A distinct individual entity.

Inclusio This Latin term refers to the marking out of a literary unit by using the same, or similar, word or phrase at the beginning and end of it.

Lexeme The basic or root form, or stem, of any set of related words.

Metaphor A figure of speech by which one thing is spoken of as being something else, which it resembles in a limited way, e.g. the string of metaphors used of God in Psalm 18:2, 'my God, my rock in whom I take refuge, my shield, and the horn of my salvation, my stronghold'.

Morphology The study of the form of words.

Narrative criticism The study of the elements by which the meaning of a narrative is communicated, such as plot, characterization, style, changes of scene. More recent narrative criticism also takes into account the role of the reader in making sense of a narrative.

Rhetorical criticism The study of how language is used to persuade the reader to adopt the writer's point of view. See also 'Structural analysis' below.

Semantic Related to meaning, especially the meaning of words.

Stoicism This philosophical school was founded by Zeno of Citium around 300 BC. It derives its name from the *stoa poikile* (painted colonnade), the place in Athens where Zeno taught. He taught that reason is the governing principle of nature, that virtue is based on knowledge, and that the individual should seek to live in harmony with nature.

Structural analysis This can operate at various levels. The study of 'surface structure' looks for the patterns employed in the fashioning of the text and for the various literary devices that are used, such as parallelism, chiasm and *inclusio*. Somewhat confusingly, this kind of structural analysis is sometimes referred to as 'Rhetorical criticism' (see above). The study of 'deep structures' is based on the theory of 'Structuralism'. This assumes that there are underlying conventions that govern the way narratives are put together. At a fundamental level these are common to all narratives.

Syntax This refers to the way that words are ordered into longer units such as sentences.

Vassal In the ancient Near East, a vassal was a ruler who was subordinate to a more powerful ruler, to whom he owed allegiance and paid tribute. The details of the relationship were often set out in a 'vassal treaty'.

INDEX

Note: Topics that can be found readily using the 'Contents' list are not included in this index.